Governing Bodies

POLITICS AND CULTURE
IN MODERN AMERICA

Series Editors:
Margot Canaday, Glenda Gilmore,
Michael Kazin, Stephen Pitti, Thomas J. Sugrue

Volumes in the series narrate and analyze political and social
change in the broadest dimensions from 1865 to the present,
including ideas about the ways people have sought and wielded
power in the public sphere and the language and institutions of
politics at all levels—local, national, and transnational. The series
is motivated by a desire to reverse the fragmentation of modern
U.S. history and to encourage synthetic perspectives on social
movements and the state, on gender, race, and labor, and on
intellectual history and popular culture.

GOVERNING BODIES

American Politics and the Shaping
of the Modern Physique

Rachel Louise Moran

PENN

UNIVERSITY OF PENNSYLVANIA PRESS

PHILADELPHIA

Published by
University of Pennsylvania Press
Philadelphia, Pennsylvania 19104-4112
www.upenn.edu/pennpress

Printed in the United States of America
on acid-free paper
1 3 5 7 9 10 8 6 4 2

Library of Congress Cataloging-in-Publication Data

Names: Moran, Rachel Louise, author.
Title: Governing bodies : American politics and the shaping of the modern physique / Rachel
  Louise Moran.
Other titles: Politics and culture in modern America.
Description: 1st edition. | Philadelphia : University of Pennsylvania Press, [2018] | Series: Politics
  and culture in modern America | Includes bibliographical references and index.
Identifiers: LCCN 2017047727 | ISBN 9780812250190 (hardcover : alk. paper)
Subjects: LCSH: Physical education and training—Political aspects—United
  States—History—20th century. | Human body—Political aspects—United
  States—History—20th century. | Diet—Political aspects—United States—United
  States—History—20th century. | Physical fitness—Political aspects—United
  States—History—20th century. | Health promotion—Political aspects—United
  States—History—20th century.
Classification: LCC GV223 .M67 2018 | DDC 613.7—dc23
LC record available at https://lccn.loc.gov/2017047727

To my parents, Tom and Marilyn

CONTENTS

INTRODUCTION

Weight of the Nation

In 2010 First Lady Michelle Obama announced a national weight loss and fitness initiative called "Let's Move." The public health project encouraged increased nutrition education and labeling as well as changes to school lunches. It emphasized cooperation between schools, corporations, celebrities, and government.[1] Almost immediately, the initiative came under sharp criticism. Fox News correspondent Sean Hannity said the program was "taking the nanny state to a new level." "Michelle Obama," he explained, "is suggesting what you should feed your children."[2] On another television show that night, outspoken conservative Glenn Beck also sounded off on the initiative. Sure, it seemed like it was just a suggestion now, but Beck insisted such a plan would eventually become coercive. When people continued to make bad choices despite federal suggestions, he reasoned, "now you have to start thinking about punishments. Maybe a fine, maybe even jail." The road to the french fry police, he explained, "always starts with a nudge."[3]

Glenn Beck's concern about so-called government nudges was pointed. At the time, Cass Sunstein, President Barack Obama's regulatory czar, was working to make nudging central to administration policy.[4] In 2008 Sunstein had coauthored a book, *Nudge*, in which he argued that most people do a poor job of making their own decisions on everything from health to finances to the environment. Sunstein advocated managing citizens' choices through what he called "libertarian paternalism."[5] This meant nudging people, or changing the way different choices were presented in ways that would encourage citizens to make more desirable choices while still letting them believe they were choosing freely. President Obama appointed Sunstein to head the White House's Office of Information and Regulatory Affairs; Glenn Beck labeled him "the most dangerous man in America."[6]

At the heart of the controversy over "Let's Move" and government nudging was a larger debate about the proper boundaries of state power.[7] The body is often imagined as too intimate or too private a matter for regulation. Indeed, such body projects involving the government are often hotly contested, whether they concern abortion, maternity care, smoking, or disability. American physique and related matters like diet and physical activity fall into this category. Over the course of the twentieth century, policy questions ranging from physical standards to nutrition guidelines have helped make the shape, size, and development of a person's body an object of government regulation. These body projects belie the idea of any clear boundary between the public and private or the personal and political.[8]

This book centers on the physical bodies of citizens and the government efforts meant to reshape those bodies. From federal research on working-class dietary needs to programs for measuring and weighing children in the 1920s, and from physical standards for soldiers during World War II to Cold War school fitness programs, there is a rich history of the political uses of physique. I place these cases of government intervention into a century-long narrative. This is a history of federal governance that infuses political history with cultural and social history, gender and sexuality, and the body itself. In the process, I draw attention to the body as both an instrument and an object of public policy. This allows us to see state power at work in unexpected ways.

Most government projects designed to shape American bodies were part of what I call the advisory state. Advisory state projects are instituted through neither physical force nor legal obligation. I conceptualize the advisory state as both a repertoire of governing tools, such as quantification, advertising, and voluntary programming, and the actual implementation of these tools. The aim is to encourage citizens to engage in behaviors that cannot be explicitly legislated within the American political context. The advisory state is subtle but powerful.[9]

While state interest in weight and physique has been a constant for the last hundred years in the United States, the implementation of such policy has varied over time along a spectrum from the understated nudge to the forceful prod. In the modern context, these advisory state approaches to monitoring citizen physique appeared around World War I. Progressive Era nutrition science and increased attention to low-income Americans' food choices were mobilized around physique when the United States entered the war. The Children's Bureau used the context of anxiety over military unfitness to propel programs that encouraged mothers to weigh and measure their children and use the new height-weight tables to assess the children's health. World War I brought attention to military unfitness, and spurred efforts to improve the bodies of future generations. That goal, alongside the fact that already existing child health projects could be easily adapted, made an advisory approach ideal in this moment.

While this advisory approach worked in the 1910s and 1920s, in the following decades economic depression and another world war changed the landscape for American body projects. During the Great Depression, low-income young men who enlisted in the Civilian Conservation Corps experienced a more intensive state management of weight and physique than previous civilians. Since these men were welfare clients, and since state expansion was somewhat normalized through the New Deal, the agency had a lot of leeway in monitoring these men's bodies without it appearing to be federal overreach. The context of World War II then allowed for an even greater expansion of federal management of physique, this time through the Selective Service. Since the Selective Service was a draft system, both men who did and men who did not want to participate now found that they were part of a federal body project. This World War II moment transcended the gentle arm of the advisory state. The physical examinations had material consequences for the young men on the scale. While there was some discontent with the Selective Service and the draft, for the most part the context of war emergency, and vastly increased federal spending and power, meant that this unusual, aggressive federal body project raised few eyebrows.

After World War II, however, the "hot war" context gave way to an extended Cold War. While the desire for strong men was as intense as ever, the changing political context necessitated a move back to gentler advisory state mechanisms for managing physique. The President's Council on Youth Fitness became an exemplary body project of the early years of the Cold War—years when federal power continued to grow in many arenas while, at the same time, the shadow of the U.S.S.R. convinced Americans to fear a powerful centralized government. As a result, the President's Council on Youth Fitness of the 1950s and 1960s encouraged fitness through a revival of advisory work. Its body projects relied on relatively informal structures and voluntary efforts, with an emphasis on public service announcements, celebrity endorsements, and noncompulsory fitness tests.

As the President's Council for Youth Fitness expanded the role of the advisory state in the lives of middle-class youth in the 1960s, other federal agencies began more aggressive body projects focused on low-income children. It was in this period that the nation rediscovered extreme poverty, and as criticism of government intensified over the course of the 1960s, the image of the emaciated black body came to symbolize the limits of existing social policy. Amid that critique, left-leaning politicians came to embrace an expansion of food aid in the late 1960s. By the 1970s, however, this fueled the political project of increased control over welfare clients' diet and physique. While food aid expansions of the late 1960s offered material aid with limited control, by the early 1970s programs like WIC (the Supplemental Food for Women, Infants, and Children program) suggested the physiques of low-income Americans ought to be addressed through advice. Liberals and conservatives alike argued that low-income Americans, especially mothers, were irrational consumers. Echoing the nutrition science arguments at the turn of the century, the dietary choices poor women made on behalf of their families were once again on trial. Building on previous twentieth-century body projects, WIC adopted advisory state techniques and then added a degree of force and compulsion not found in programs aimed at middle-class Americans. Advisory techniques of governance were applied regularly in modern American politics, and we must recognize their role. At the same time, we must also recognize that, by design, body projects were not applied consistently or equally.

Concern over body image and physique has a long history in the United States. Late nineteenth-century dieting often focused on improving male bodies, alongside improving male financial and social status.[10] In 1863 William Banting published A Letter on Corpulence. The pamphlet advocated limiting bread, sugar, and beer for rapid weight loss (four to five glasses of wine a day, though, was fine).[11] Middle- to upper-class men increasingly fought body fat in the late nineteenth century, associating it with femininity and a lack of self-control. At the same time, plumpness was valued in women of the same socioeconomic class. Victorian women were encouraged to have curvier figures, and the corset reigned supreme.[12] The famous Gibson Girl of the early 1900s offered a thinner but softer bodily aesthetic, although she showed more skin than the Victorian woman.[13] This ideal for women's bodies had shifted by the early 1910s, as women's magazines, advertising, and silent films began adopting a thinner female form. Once the flapper ideal emerged in the 1920s, the growth of off-the-rack (rather than tailored) clothing necessitated size and measurement standards, and ultimately defined some bodies as normal and others as abnormal.[14] It was in this context that a commercial weight loss industry emerged, selling diet advice, cigarettes, and magic bullets.[15] Dieting became a rite of passage for adolescent girls and twenty-something women, an obsession that intensified over the course of the century as diet plans, fads, and foods exploded in popularity. This history of the popular promotion of dieting is critical to understanding American bodies, but the emphasis on it tends to obscure the role of the state in shaping those bodies, too. *Governing Bodies* works from existing cultural and social histories of dieting and weight, but differs from them in its focus on the political and policy dimensions of such body projects.[16]

This is the story of why the federal government cares about weight and muscles and of the mechanisms through which it regulates them. It is the story of which bodies it cares about, which bodies seem in need of regulation at which moments, and which bodies go untouched. Above all, it is a story about redefining what we understand as politics. In this story, federal agencies, voluntary organizations, politicians, and ordinary citizens take center stage in efforts to shape the American physique. Readers should note that this is not the story of all body projects undertaken in the twentieth century. For example, I do not discuss food rationing, pure food and drug laws, water fluoridation, or mandates to enrich foods with vitamins. Nutrition, enrichment, rationing, and public health all certainly have an indirect impact on the shapes and sizes American bodies take. Rationing might whittle away at a citizen's waistline, while milk supplemented with Vitamin D might increase skeletal development in youth.[17] For my purposes, though, I have chosen to focus on those body projects in which physique was a stated and central concern of policy makers. Sometimes the justifications were related to the military, other times to public health and nutrition, and still others to social welfare. The thread I follow across this varied terrain is that of a stated, central concern for physique during policy debates.

The subtlety of state behavior has become a topic of greater interest in political history over the past decade. Historians and political scientists have revealed a hidden state that has influenced everything from security, to transportation, to tax cuts, to trade: all federal interventions critical to American development yet often overlooked.[18] Scholars have looked at the way different levels of government operate, at the voluntary state that has

relied on the unpaid labor of women's clubs, schools, and charities, and at
the public-private and often improvisational organization of the modern
state.[19] Recognizing the hidden, voluntary, and public-private aspects of the
American state expands our understanding of the meaning and means of
federal governance, and the interdependence of state and society.[20] Advice,
standards, and outsourced government must be understood in conversation with one another, and as part of a single conversation about state
development. Ultimately, paying attention to advisory state projects shows
the inadequacy of big government versus small government models of state
capacity and models of state power that assume a simple dichotomy
between choice and coercion.

In chronicling the advisory state, I draw from the literatures on weight
and physique culture, biopolitics, and feminist body history, while insisting
on their connection to policy, politics, and American state development.
Recognizing the connection between the realm of governance and the realm
of culture obliges us to refocus our ideas about how federal policy-making
works. Policies and projects of the advisory state are not peripheral but are
in fact central to modern governance. Sometimes federal body projects
related to weight and physique were subtle or indirect. Sometimes they
were more aggressive. The implementation of such policies varied widely
by era, by agency, and by policy subject. One needs an advisory state during
peacetime to accustom citizens to the more intensive body projects of wartime, for instance. This book considers a range of state interventions into
physique, as those interventions moved along the spectrum between the
subtle and the aggressive, and as citizens maneuvered their physical bodies
through the apparatus of the state.

That apparatus took many forms, but one regular feature of advisory
state body projects was a reliance on the authority of numbers and quantification. Height-weight statistics, physical standards, and scale readings
offered an aura of unassailable truth to political ideas about the body.[21]
Statistics gave the appearance of objectivity, of making knowledge seem
neutral.[22] The use of standards conjured the image of a rational, organized
project. When height-weight standards were invoked to determine whether
or not a body was war-ready or work-ready, the assessment appeared to be
expert, above the fray of opinion and bias.[23] In this regard, I use weight and
related health data as evidence like any other historical evidence, but I do
not accept that there was a single, stable scientific or medical concept of
physique that ever existed (or that exists today) outside of politics. This

distinction is critical in assessing the history of weight and physique for its larger political meaning.

The federal reliance on quantification was especially important when tied to another tool of the advisory state, maternalism. The nurturing roles accepted by most American women in the first half of the twentieth century, whether through motherhood and wifehood or through the caring professions such as teaching and nursing, made women useful allies.[24] Wrapping state body projects in gendered, maternal language made certain advisory projects possible, normalizing everything from scientific meal planning to child measurement. Mothers, wives, nurses, and teachers were called on to monitor bodies and implement health standards, while making American body projects seem apolitical and personal. When agencies asking women to monitor bodies relied on numerical standards for that monitoring, they simultaneously heightened the apparent importance of women's labor by making it more scientific *and* decreased anxieties about shifting health monitoring from expert to lay hands by emphasizing the seeming objectivity of numbers. When lay women engaged with these health projects, their involvement was technically voluntary labor, but it was voluntary within a system of gendered political power undergirded with powerful languages of medical and professional expertise. In such a system, women's so-called voluntary political participation was often closer to obligatory.[25]

Although female actors are at the heart of the maternalist component of this advisory state story, adult female bodies were rarely the ones being measured and monitored. Following decades of feminist scholarship on the body, it may seem strange that a study of weight, shape, and physique in the United States is heavily focused on male bodies. While other aspects of women's bodies, especially anything related to reproduction, have long been monitored and managed by state entities, women's body weight only developed as a serious state concern when participation in the paid workforce became permanent for large numbers of white middle-class women, roughly in the early 1960s.[26] The story of twentieth-century advisory state body projects, perhaps surprisingly, is a story of primarily male bodies. Male bodies were more present in the public gaze and in public roles in the first half of the twentieth century. At the very least, publicly laboring and militarized bodies were imagined as male, even when they were not actually all male. These imagined male citizen bodies became the objects of advisory state body projects with far greater frequency than female bodies did.

The fact that male bodies, usually white male bodies, are so often the object of government interest is evidence of how important both masculinity and heteronormativity have been to the modern state. American masculinity has long been grounded in the ideals of independence, autonomy, and self-reliance.[27] With these ideals, white men differentiated themselves from white women, who were increasingly defined as both selfless and dependent in the early nineteenth century.[28] These ideals also served to reinforce heteronormativity, which has been imagined by some as a building block of society and is embedded in many state policies and institutions, from marriage to breadwinner wages to immigration policy.[29] As a result, for much of the twentieth century, the federal government has maintained its investment in at least the appearance of the heteronormative family unit, which has compounded the state compulsion to manage and monitor sexuality alongside masculinity.[30] With the critical exception of the draft, political interventions designed to repair American manhood—to improve laborers, providers, or soldiers—could not be too aggressive without undermining autonomy, heteronormativity, and independence as central tenets of white masculinity.[31]

The importance of highlighting male autonomy while initiating body projects was not only about masculinity and heteronormativity, but also about emphasizing the value of certain types of bodies to the nation. As historians of disability have found, normative American masculinity is deeply tied to ideals of the male body.[32] While those ideals have changed over time, the notion that a man must be able-bodied to function as a breadwinner has deep roots.[33] That man's status as a useful citizen might also be tied to his earning potential, in ways that favor the able-bodied man as a more competent citizen than a man unable to materially provide for a family.[34] Anxieties about improving the physical body of the breadwinner regularly channeled fears of dependency. Whether dependent on the state or on other family members, whether barred from factory labor, the military, or white-collar work, the man with a physical disability appeared unable to fulfill the obligations of the autonomous breadwinner. As a result, state agencies concerned with these bodies had to intervene to protect or improve male bodies without appearing to threaten men's autonomy and independence.[35]

At the same time, otherwise able-bodied male citizens could also be subjected to the methods of the advisory state—especially when claims of medical objectivity undergirded those methods. From advice about what wives and mothers should feed these men to standards defining the proper male body, the advisory state chose from an arsenal of quiet methods. These techniques often shaped a man's mind before they shaped his body.[36] The result was a male body—and an American masculinity—far more structured by social and political concerns than most histories acknowledge. This is especially critical since the ideal male citizen (imagined as white, able-bodied, and native-born) is so frequently disembodied in histories, particularly political and policy histories, which allows us to miss how critical his own physiological body can be to policy interests.

Considering advisory state projects complicates discussions of both federal interests and techniques of governance. The bullying "french fry police," for instance, are fantasy. Even amid very different political contexts over the span of the twentieth century, the notion of a federal government explicitly and aggressively intervening in most private citizens' physiques remained untenable and, in most cases, undesirable. While economic depression and mobilization for war intensified federal concerns over citizen physique, the techniques of governance that agencies used to address these concerns were never truly policing. That was simply no way to manage the seemingly intimate realm of the citizen body. Moreover, the most aggressive body projects have rarely been meant for those citizens vocalizing a contemporary anxiety about "french fry police." Especially after World War II, when American worries about big government intensified, it was almost exclusively low-income (and typically female and nonwhite) citizens who faced the sharpest interventions of the federal government around body weight and physique. For other citizens in the same period, a subtler advisory approach dominated. State interest and investment in citizens' productive bodies has a long history, but it is a history built on programs often as concerned with producing and maintaining the illusion of citizen autonomy—especially white, male, middle-class autonomy—as they are concerned with citizen reshaping.

CHAPTER 1

The Advisory State World War I Made:
Scientific Nutrition and Scientific Mothering

Dr. Wilbur Olin Atwater was best known for his calorimeter tests—dietary experiments in which he kept graduate students in sealed chambers while they burned up energy performing various tasks. He then measured the energy they exerted with an aim of understanding the physiology of calorie expenditure. Atwater ultimately dispensed dietary advice based loosely on these findings. In an 1888 treatise on nutrition science, this man sometimes described as the "father of American nutrition" expressed a paternalistic concern over women's food-shopping habits. "The good wife and mother does not understand about protein and potential energy," he wrote. Nor did she understand "the connection between the nutritive value of food and the price she pays for it." Atwater believed that improving American diets required his scientific approach. Once this nutrition science spread, once it was available to doctors, public health workers, and settlement house professionals, Atwater argued, it would become the new American way of nutrition.[1] Atwater's research was the vehicle through which concerns over American strength, vigor, and vitality began to receive direct federal research attention and funding. This federal attention, well positioned amid Progressive Era attention to health and better living through science, marked the growth of the modern advisory state.

Economic, racial, and national divisions produced anxiety in late nineteenth-century America, especially for the middle to upper classes. The *Plessy v. Ferguson* case codified racial segregation. European immigrants worked twelve-hour days in dirty, dangerous northern factories.[2] In response to a society that seemed out of control—and poised to erupt at any moment—a number of Americans sought to reorganize the nation in ways that promised to reestablish order.[3] Against big banks and big railroads, against monopolies and trusts, against rampant political corruption, a middle class sought to respond to these end-of-century social problems through expertise and scientific management.[4] Food reformers most famously embraced pure food and drug standards and meat inspections in this era.[5] In fact, reformers interested in dietary management positioned themselves as central to this larger Progressive agenda.[6]

Wilbur Atwater and his Progressive-minded supporters pushed for food reform that went far beyond safer foodstuffs for the middle classes. Instead, they argued that scientific nutrition could help immigrants Americanize, ease the problems of the working poor, and prepare the nation for continued industrial progress. This approach reverberated loudly for Progressives. Nutrition education promised a "sound and economical basis" for human health.[7] Atwater, for instance, referred to dietary plans as the "pecuniary economy" of food.[8] Women—wives, mothers, and household managers— stood at the forefront of everyday American decisions about nutrition. Progressive nutritionists, through the wives and mothers of laborers in particular, held the key to industrial progress by using home economics to literally strengthen the nation's men. Through scientific nutrition, activists like Atwater and his supporters hoped the workingman's wife might improve American physique. In the process, Atwater, home economists, and the later federal agencies who sought to assess these women's progress, all suggested that women had the responsibility of ensuring male labor power through educated consumer choice. The Progressive nutrition agenda included this understanding of familial responsibility for a manageable and malleable human body, alongside the belief that such responsibility required scientific education and training rather than intuition or tradition. Proper discipline would make an ideal citizen inside and out. Less-than-ideal bodies, by extension, must be the product of ignorance or bad choices.

The emphasis on advising women on nutrition, and then expecting their compliance, played a key role in shaping women's Progressive reform work. Then the emerging public health work of middle-class female reformers fueled a 1910s and 1920s effort to improve a new generation of workers by focusing on children's bodies. The Children's Bureau's voluntary networks reshaped the public discourse around child health and physique through height-weight measurements, maternal education, and conferences and other events. These women's adaptations of scientific

nutrition and public health measures offered a subtler approach than con-
temporaneous eugenics efforts. They placed responsibility for children's
health—typically quantified as appropriate weight and height—on mothers
rather than genetic inheritance. The reform projects also avoided most controversy by emphasizing maternal approaches to distinguish themselves
from medical projects, and by relying heavily on the use of quantification
and standards that promised an objective approach to health concerns.

Calorie counts and dietary studies in the 1890s and 1900s, and child
weighing and measuring efforts in the 1910s and 1920s, all offered neatly
scientific, quantified methods of addressing otherwise overwhelming social
problems. Notably, it was at the height of the Great War when American
male strength seemed most embattled, that federal nutrition experts moved
from the laboratory setting into the health clinic setting. World War I
provided an opportunity for reformers to expand federal advisory state
body projects. The advisory state of American physique was built in late
nineteenth-century nutrition research, and then deployed in World War
I–era child health programs. The World War I and post–World War I state
enlisted women's labor and allegiance without apparent federal overreach
to construct a narrative of individual responsibility around food choices
being beneficial to the civic whole.

Wilbur Atwater and Scientific Nutrition

Chemist Wilbur Atwater, inspired by a few years of study abroad, pursued
federal funding for his research on which U.S. agricultural feeds were most
effective.[9] Federal government money for nutrition research was new, but
money for agricultural research dated back to land grant institutions and
the Morrill Acts of 1862, making the transition possible. In the early 1870s,
he helped found the first federally funded Agricultural Experiment Station
in the country in Middletown, Connecticut.[10] Then, in 1877, an opportunity
from the United States Commission of Fisheries pushed the professor's
study from the food composition of animal feed to the food composition
of animals themselves. For the next three years, Atwater and his students
analyzed fish that might be part of a typical American diet. These "human
feed" studies made his name. The study shifted Atwater's interest in the
composition of animal feed toward work on the composition of food eaten

by humans. After determining the amount of crude protein, ash, and carbo-hydrates in each of these fish, Atwater began to direct experiments on a diversity of human-consumed foods. By 1879 he had analyzed the composi-tion of 1,300 foods.[11] Following the influence of human nutrition studies across the Atlantic, Atwater also became absorbed in research on calories. European calorie studies emerged from projects that attempted to under-stand the human body, especially to understand how it compared to other machines. As American and European physiologists of the late nineteenth and early twentieth century began to analogize the human body to a machine, a system of interlocking parts, they also came to understand the body as something improvable. Like other technologies of the moment, a human-machine could be assessed and managed piece by piece.[12] As Ger-man and French chemists tried to rationalize the human body in the late nineteenth century, they conceived of it as a study of labor input and out-put. The laboring body was a machine, and food calories provided an authoritative, quantitative, way of evaluating human physiology. Research in the late 1850s and through the 1860s tried to understand calorie-use in terms of the heat produced by the laboring body, just as well as its energy output, evaluating how the human body stood up to the laws of thermody-namics. American research only caught up to European nutrition research through Atwater, who built the first domestic respiration calorimeter in 1896.[13] The device measured research subjects' intake of food and output of heat. At the core of this research was the project of evaluating the body through laboratory means, assessing input and output, and imagining an ideal management of the human body under carefully calculated rules.[14]

For Atwater, understanding consumption through a unit like the calorie offered a way of making sense of how food composition related to energy and physique. It offered a simplifying language.[15] Atwater contributed the concept of Atwater Units—now usually called macronutrient ratios—to the study of calories. The general idea of Atwater Units was that one gram of fat contained nine calories, one gram of protein contained four calories, and one gram of carbohydrates contained four calories. This idea, still cen-tral to contemporary nutrition, allowed Atwater to use the research subjects and studies available not only to understand laboring men's basic caloric needs, but also how the composition of foods affected laborers' energy and strength. It allowed scientists to "rationalize quality."[16] It was one substan-tial step beyond simply counting calories to decide what foods one should consume for optimal energy.

Atwater's ideas were developed in a moment when the quantification of wellness was the gold standard. He also contributed to that moment. Atwater believed that the working-class "good wife and mother" needed a translated and simplified version of this emerging gospel of scientific nutrition. In the years leading up to the development of the calorimeter, he was primarily concerned about the poorest American families, with a special interest in the families of factory workers and laborers. It was working men who needed the most calories and protein to get through the workday, according to Atwater's research on how the body-as-machine used its fuel. Yet it was, Atwater explained, "the poor man's food that is the worst cooked and served at home."[17] Atwater argued that women's faulty understanding of nutrition was part of the reason American laborers had tight food budgets, and that their reeducation was necessary for progress.

The chemist explained that the poorest women often insisted on purchasing the most expensive groceries, presumably because they believed that a high cost indicated high value. Atwater recounted the complaints of a butcher who observed that working-class women chose expensive tenderloin over cheaper round or sirloin cuts of beef. While the tenderloin was pricier, the butcher insisted that the sirloin would do just as good a job of feeding a family. The butcher complained specifically about one seamstress who indignantly asked, "Do you suppose because I don't come here in my carriage I don't want just as good meat as rich folks have?"[18]

Choosing food based on taste, pride, or misinformation, Atwater thought, was an epidemic in America.[19] He dismissed the complexity and labor involved in navigating the marketplace.[20] Women, especially immigrant women, were widely understood as poor consumers by the new consumer sciences. Progressives often characterized the female consumer as emotional and easy to persuade or trick.[21] Supposedly, the dawn of a new nutrition would replace the irrational behavior of women with rational consumer behavior. Atwater's pecuniary economy of food never considered female labor, and he implicitly calculated working-class women's time and effort as zero cost. Any unwillingness to put in the labor was evidence that these women were poor consumers and homemakers.

Meanwhile, Atwater's food plans mostly ignored women's own nutritional needs. Atwater used "a man at moderate muscular work" as a physiological norm, the basis of his nutrition math.[22] Then Atwater determined the nutritional needs of that laboring man's family through rough estimates. A thirteen-year-old boy counted as 80 percent of "a man at moderate muscular work." A twelve-year-old girl was considered 60 percent of "a man at moderate muscular work."[23] This data on caloric needs and macronutrient needs (how much protein, fat, and carbohydrate each man needed) became the basis of new food plans designed for the poor and working class. Atwater and the emerging field of home economics calculated the entire family's nutritional needs based on their fractional relationship to an employed and ablebodied patriarch.

Ellen Swallow Richards, the "mother of American home economics," and Democratic politician Edward Atkinson had no qualms about these calculations. Instead, they extensively promoted the practical application of Atwater's research, especially the development of family food plans.[24] Atwater himself lost interest in research applications over time, but Progressive reformers continued to make use of his work.[25] Scientific nutrition offered the pleasing promise of rational actors and utopian results: if precise amounts of calories and nutrients might be cheaply and efficiently parceled out, everyone could be well-fed, everyone could work hard, and there would be no waste in the process. It was a Progressive Era reformer's dream. Atkinson imagined that this approach to nutrition would teach working-class Americans to embrace cheaper meats, soups, stews, and flours, which they supposedly avoided out of "false pride of show."[26] Scientific nutrition seemed an essential tool for social management. Richards wrote that "it is . . . not too much to say that women are the stumbling blocks in the way of higher industrial, social, and ethical progress."[27] She believed guidance on calories and macronutrients would help them toward that progress. Atwater's nutrition science had the potential to help women take the so-called rational costs of food to heart, to transform the supposedly superstitious immigrant into the imagined rational American consumer. It also had the potential to hold workers and their families responsible for their own poverty at an intimate, even biological level.

Atwater's first major Department of Agriculture publication, the 1894 booklet called *Foods: Nutritive Value and Cost*, was critical in developing a quantification of nutrition useful to practitioners and laboratory researchers. The body was like a steam engine, Atwater wrote, except the body's fuel was food.[28] There were many ways to adequately fuel the human body, then, and with careful management that body could be fueled on the cheap. In the 1902 revision, Atwater explicitly took women to task for not managing food budgets appropriately. Too often women obtain food by overpaying at the market, he wrote, "rather than by skillful cooking and tasteful serving at home."[29] Around this time, Atwater also released tables on the chemical composition of foods, which remained the primary government publication on food composition for decades after his death.[30] In the subsequent years, the Department of Agriculture received requests for food composition charts from sources as diverse as U.S. senators, Better Baby Contests, the U.S. Army, and *Cosmopolitan Magazine*.[31] These were the first federal publications on human nutrition designed for public readership.[32]

Atwater's vision of a rationally managed, scientific society fit well with the Progressive impulse. His food economy provided more efficient ways of feeding poor Americans. More importantly, it offered stern advice and persuasive instruction for poor women. Educating married women about scientific nutrition could mean more vigorous male workers. It might also mean that these men and their families could be kept vigorous without an increase in wages. As with much Progressive thought, scientific nutrition offered solutions to social problems without disrupting existing power structures.

From Department of Agriculture home economists to private settlement houses, American nutritional input was increasingly *manageable*. This became more important as the United States entered World War I. In the war context, this nutrition management transformed from reform work with some federal funding to the actual advisory work of the federal government. As this work became more centralized and larger in scale, it also instigated a shift toward conflating the input of nutrition with the apparent product of that input—the size and shape of the citizen body. Atwater's research helped build the quantitative apparatus of the weight-oriented advisory state. In World War I, the labor of mothers and teachers would mainstream that apparatus.

Mother's Work and Children's Bodies

Scientific nutrition came with a political agenda. By focusing on quantified food composition, Atwater pushed the idea of nutritional equivalency. This meant that cheap cuts of meat could be nutritionally equivalent to more expensive ones, and stale bread just as full of needed calories and carbohydrates as bread fresh from the oven. As a result, the onus of nutritional health was firmly on the private realm. Wages did not need to be raised; food prices did not need to be regulated: the health and efficiency of American labor was in its own wives' and mothers' hands. Individual responsibility, not welfare state building or labor laws, was the adjustment Atwater's research justified.

Both Atwater's nutrition science and his politics directly influenced prominent home economists of the Progressive Era, members of the "dominion in reform" at the time. Early home economics activists, like Ellen Richards, worked directly with Atwater. Another generation, including prominent nutritionist Caroline Hunt, learned nutrition science by working under him. Other nutritionists, including his daughter Helen Atwater, based assumptions of their own research and writing on the senior Atwater's publications.[33]

The dominion of female reform, often discussed in the Progressive Era, included women's hands-on reform work, as historians have established, as well as the unrecognized work of the advisory state. Women doing this work sometimes moved from nongovernmental positions into the growing state apparatus of the early twentieth century. Home economists funneled into local and national government with the 1915 founding of the federal Office of Home Economics.[34] There, they worked toward changing American nutrition habits. Around the same time (1912), women entered the new federal Children's Bureau. Influenced by nutrition science—but also not bound by it—women of the Children's Bureau sought ways to optimize child health through promoting hands-on, proactive mothering.

Employees of the Children's Bureau shared the general concerns of Atwater, Atkinson, and Richards. They all sought Progressive reforms and had overlapping networks. The Children's Bureau emerged from the Settlement House Movement. Atwater had conducted studies on the children of Hull House, the same settlement house where Children's Bureau Chief Julia Lathrop had started out. In this era of maternalist activism, a women's reform network allowed middle-class women into politics so long as they centered their efforts on gender-specific reforms like those affecting children.[35] Progressive Era women, acting as mothers of society, carved a niche for themselves first in voluntary work, eventually catapulting themselves into local, state, and federal government through efforts like the Children's Bureau.

All parties worked within a Progressive Era framework of chemistry and social science, of expertise for a higher good, and of a belief in managing and controlling the country through quantification. The Children's Bureau embraced quantification as a means for improving the body, as other Progressives had done. Nutrition science supplied a language to bring the citizen body into the realm of policy, a language that made the individual body's weight and size manageable on a larger scale. Instead of calories, though, the Children's Bureau would champion height and weight measurement as the path to a stronger nation.[36]

At its 1912 creation, the Children's Bureau was charged with very specific tasks. It was to investigate and report on child health and welfare. Its staff was to collect statistics, perform studies, and publish their findings. The bureau would gain moderate authority in the area of child labor by the late 1910s. In the terrain of children's health and bodies, however, it only encouraged women to undertake its health proposals. The Children's Bureau was not supposed to involve itself in the medical aspects of health, including anything that had to do with disease or illness. That was the fiercely guarded territory of the growing American Medical Association and the U.S. Public Health Service. Barred from the world of disease, illness, and medicine, the bureau's campaigns relied on the quantitative language of height and weight as a stand-in for health.

Julia Lathrop and the Children's Bureau focused on the women's space of government–advisory state work. The bureau used the voluntary labor of mothers, teachers, and nurses across the country in its health measures.[37] They maintained influence with strict limits as to which aspects of human health and wellness were within the bureau's jurisdiction. The bureau addressed this problem through the adoption of height-weight tables. In turning the ambiguous concept of health into quantified, definitive, and expert height-weight tables, the bureau both broadened the scope of what concerns it could legitimately address and made it easier for nonexperts to voluntarily do the work of the bureau.

The Children's Bureau's advisory health projects were pioneering state interventions into the health and bodies of Americans. The bureau built networks of volunteers and reshaped the public discourse around child health and physique. It used maternal education, the voluntary labor of women, and Atwater-esque quantification of the body for events like child health conferences, Baby Week, and Children's Year. As Grace Abbott, Lathrop's successor at the bureau, later explained, they "furnished the facts on which action was frequently based."[38] With advertising and some cajoling, the bureau convinced middle-class mothers to show up at bureau events. Participation in such events was, of course, not a legal obligation, but it was a gendered social obligation. As such, participating in child health conferences and events became the women's work of government.

Julia Lathrop, the settlement house and juvenile justice reformer turned bureau chief, wanted to understand the ills facing American children. At the turn of the century, these were many. The 1910 census revealed that over 150,000 American infants died each year. Lathrop believed the census number, which left out many immigrant and poor urban citizens, was a severe undercount of the infant mortality problem. She estimated that 300,000 American infants and toddlers died every year.[39] More disturbing was that half of these deaths might have been avoided with modest child hygiene measures. For reformers like Lathrop, such measures included what they viewed as proper child nutrition, breastfeeding, cleanliness, and visits to physicians. According to Lathrop, child mortality rates could be solved "with methods which are in the reach of every community."[40] The women of the Children's Bureau, most of whom had come to government by way of reform work, focused on urban immigrants living in broken-down tenements and rural women raising children in poverty. The bureau became especially focused on the health of these children.[41]

The bureau's staff presented their ideas for improving child development to mothers and teachers with the expectation that these caregivers would opt to follow through on their suggestions. The bureau relied on the efforts of existing voluntary and professional networks of women, and attempted to shape local groups' and individual women's child health practices. The bureau itself could not require that this research, or any of the bureau's goals for child health and hygiene, be implemented. Instead, it succeeded in getting women's groups, teachers, and other local groups to fund and disseminate advisory policy. Using these tools of the advisory state—child health conferences, Baby Week, and the Children's Year—the bureau reached hundreds of thousands of American families in the 1910s and early 1920s.[42]

Quantification in the Advisory State

As the bureau set out to reach women, it needed otherwise untrained women to become authoritative figures on health and wellness in their local communities. It was necessary to do this quickly, and to do it convincingly. This would require a shortcut of some sort, since the bureau was in no position to send the thousands of women who would lead local community health projects to medical school. The bureau also needed a way to raise the credibility and authority of this army of (mainly) nonexpert women who would do the bureau's work of managing child health in cities and towns around the nation. These nonexpert women might seem suspect in a country increasingly obsessed with professionalism and expertise.[43] Finally, the bureau had to address health issues without upsetting territorial groups like the American Medical Association and the Public Health Service. All understood the woman-run Children's Bureau as a gendered helping agency, not a medical one.[44] Whenever the bureau crossed over the line and became too hands-on or was otherwise a threat to more established health and medical organizations, these organizations became vocal critics of the bureau.

Not unlike Atwater's hope that calorie charts could simplify human nutrition, the Children's Bureau came to rely on measuring children as a way of simplifying discussions of child health. Height-weight tables became a favorite tool of the bureau. The use of tables greatly simplified the idea of health for both the bureau designing health programs and those who were charged with implementing them. Charts suggested expertise and authority, but were still lay tools that did not encroach on medical territory.

The advisory projects of the Children's Bureau were enabled through the broad use of quantification and the promotion of physical standards. Height-weight tables were designed to allow a quick evaluation of physique based on the ratio of one's height to one's weight. Some described them as "slide rules" of nutrition.[45] Dr. Thomas Wood's height-weight tables provide an example of how these charts worked. The chart includes one axis for heights and another for boys' ages. In the Wood chart, a mother might evaluate her 64-inch (5'4") boy. On the left, she locates the 64-inch mark. She drags her finger horizontally across the chart, stopping her finger when it is below the boy's age. If her boy is thirteen years old, then, he might weigh 115 pounds. That would be average. Some list average height and weight, others list so-called ideal height and weight combinations. In the early twentieth century the average and ideal statistics were often handled the same way. When a mother or teacher compared a child's weight with its height using one of these tables, she generally hoped to find that the child was of average build. If the mother in the example just given found that her boy weighed more or less than the 115-pound average, then she would know he was above or below the average. In another decade, height-weight charts would begin replacing the single number (the 115 pounds) with a range of weights one might aim for. The charts of the 1910s and

1920s, however, were built on the understanding that a single number could indicate what all boys or girls of a certain age should weigh.[46]

With this knowledge, clear quantitative evidence that her son was too small (or, less frequently in these decades, too large), a mother could remedy the situation. With a tape measure in one hand and the Thomas Wood chart in the other, the mother was now responsible both for the boy's present physique and for improving it. This was the power of height-weight tables. They were simple columns of numbers that induced action by the women using them. The numbers looked objective and authoritative. The average weight allowed for each height and age left no room for error. It produced two categories of people: those with average or normal physique and those with above or below average—now defined as abnormal—physique. Although the average weight was not statistically correlated with ideal health, in practical use the average weight was used as the ideal weight on charts of the 1910s and 1920s.[47]

The Children's Bureau used these tables both to assess and to promote child health. The bureau adopted tables that were a mixture of Thomas Wood's and those of another child health researcher, Bird T. Baldwin.[48] Baldwin's tables focused on children under six years of age, while Wood's focused on children and teens between six and adulthood. The Children's Bureau adopted the unified Baldwin-Wood tables through the 1910s. The bureau would go on to use these tables in its publications and as promotion for its child health events. For the bureau, charts provided a simple way of assessing health. If a child was two or more pounds below the average weight for his or her age or height, bureau employees wrote, it "should be a warning that the child's nutrition is not normal."[49]

Height-weight tables simplified the complex subject of child health down to a series of numbers. But this was not what the tables were originally meant to do. The first chart that might be called a height-weight table was designed by Lambert Adolphe Jacques Quetelet in 1836. Quetelet, a Belgian mathematician, developed a Body Mass Index or Quetelet Index. His index, though, was not meant to assess individual health but rather to assess the weight of entire populations and to determine averages. It was a sociological tool, not a medical one.[50]

When the Children's Bureau conflated height and weight ratios with health, it solved some of its child health problems and created others. By the early 1920s, for example, statistician Louis Dublin wrote that immigrant children's bodies did not conform to the same standards as white,

native-born children. When public health workers measured Italian immigrant children to assess their health, he explained, they marked many of the
children as healthy when they were in fact malnourished. Along the same
lines, other researchers concluded that "the fact that an individual child
weighs less or more than the average is not conclusive proof that he is
undernourished or overnourished."[51] In a 1924 article bluntly titled "The
Use and Abuse of Age-Height-Weight Tables as Indexes of Health and
Nutrition," table cocreator Bird T. Baldwin argued that height-weight tables
were "frequently inaccurate in themselves" and egregiously inaccurate in
the hands of novice measurers.[52] He still supported the use of his own
Baldwin-Wood tables, but decried the use of other tables and what he called
the "inaccurate measurements" taken by laywomen, nurses, and nutritionists alike. While Baldwin's condemnation of female-led public health work
fits into the consolidation of medical authority happening at this moment,
more surprising critics of the tables also spoke out. Suspicions even
emerged from the Children's Bureau itself, an agency whose public health
identity was tightly linked with its dissemination of the charts. The bureau
promoted height-weight tables even though few of its employees believed
that the tables identified all the health issues they were meant to identify.[53]
The charts were political tools that *produced* the idea of the healthy modern
child as much as they assessed it.

Bureau promotions not only popularized weighing, but also constructed the practice as an unusually intimate advisory state activity. Weighing in and of itself did not require medical expertise, but it did take
equipment. Anyone could weigh themselves or someone else with little education. In the 1910s and early 1920s, public health and medical specialists
owned the proper scales, which might be borrowed for child health contests. Women's clubs interested in weighing and measuring children often
teamed up with public health officials as a way of accessing scales and
charts. By the late 1920s, however, it was much easier to find both of these
technologies. Retailers began marketing home scales as early as 1913, but
these remained too pricy for most.[54] Scales constituted a more reasonable
purchase for a school, though, and school nurses weighed children a few
times each year.[55] Most mothers could also be taught the basic graphic
literacy required to read height-weight tables and figure out if the weight
they calculated was too high, too low, or about right. With this number in
hand, a mother or teacher could pick up a nutrition book to fix the problem
herself. Or she might go to a clinic or physician, especially if it was a young

child who was not measuring up. The bureau inserted these charts into nearly every infant and child care pamphlet it published. Tables were not meant to be flawless; they were meant to draw women in.

Height-weight tables truly came to the forefront in the mid-1910s, when women's groups around the country had begun projects linking child weight, aesthetics, and health. Through baby health contests and other child health pageants, these groups hoped to draw attention to the importance of baby health as a step toward improving infant mortality rates.[56] Rural girls' and women's groups took the lead on such contests, at this moment when an increase of funding to groups like 4-H helped facilitate the growth of sex-segregated agricultural programming.[57] Mothers brought in their babies (and sometimes older children), and judges evaluated and ranked the youth. Ultimately, they named and honored the healthiest child and his or her mother.[58] In Louisiana, in 1908, the state fair included a Scientific Baby Contest.[59] In Iowa, in 1911, the Iowa Congress of Mothers put together a Better Babies Contest for their state's fair. The women added entertainment and prizes to their event, vastly increasing its appeal. This chapter of the Congress of Mothers—taking a little inspiration from popular livestock contests already at state fairs—sought to make child pageants that had some health reform programming built in.[60] The fairs already had some of the necessary accoutrements for weighing commodities. These better baby contests channeled a romanticized idea of the ruddy, rural child to a nation increasingly grappling with urban malnutrition and child labor in factories.[61] In this space, though, judges scored children from zero to a hundred points with this milk-fed and sunshine-grown health ideal in mind.[62]

The judges declared the children with the most points to be the healthiest, a term that blended racial, moral, and physical factors. Those children won ribbons. The American Medical Association's public health section cosponsored some child health contests, lending an air of professional legitimacy to events otherwise surrounded by prize pigs and pies.[63] In some cases, the contests included measures to more broadly improve child health, such as presentations and displays from public health nurses and clubwomen. Even when the contests did not have a specific health improvement section, they still had pedagogical intentions. Ranking infants and children in an ostensibly objective fashion required score cards. Score cards varied from event to event, but most employed similar conventions. Cards asked for the age, height (or length, for infants), and weight of the child. This was nonnegotiable. Other categories, ranging from plumpness to symmetry, might be included depending on the interests of the local groups running the contests.

Eugenicists shaped some of the first contests.[64] Like the Children's Bureau, positive eugenicists—those who encouraged the reproduction of the supposedly fit—often relied on educational measures mixed with strong social pressure to share their message. The eugenics movement was not unified in its methods. While some eugenicists did not believe educational methods would ever truly weed out the unfit, instead pursuing legislation and force, others relied on these measures.[65] Most of the better baby contests, intertwined with eugenic aims, were racially segregated.[66] Still, black middle-class women's concern about high rates of black infant mortality kept many of them engaged in the better baby contests.[67] The Children's Bureau was not especially eugenic, but it sought to translate the energy around these projects to their own ends.

There was plenty of energy to work with. Following the Iowa fair, club-women and public health workers in Colorado, Louisiana, Oregon, Washington, and New York developed their own competitions. In the years that followed, the competitions expanded still more, "sweeping the whole country," in the words of one reporter.[68] Some groups offered cash prizes, others only ribbons, local media attention, and, of course, maternal bragging rights. More important from the point of view of the reformers involved, the contests also included instructions on proper baby feeding and nutrition, an assessment of the child for obvious signs of illness or malnutrition, and lessons in what the clubwomen deemed proper hygiene. Discussions of what the contests accomplished slipped easily between eugenic and noneugenic language. The Illinois Medical Association justified the contests as a response to the "deterioration of the American stock."[69] While many eugenics groups focused on reproduction and the elimination of the unfit through genetic means, baby contests were centered on improvement of the unfit. As the decade went on, contest organizers embraced the language of health over the explicitly eugenic language of stock. This is a critical distinction. After eugenics fell out of national favor, the language of improved health allowed subtle projects around fitness to carry on with little controversy.

The Children's Bureau and the voluntary groups organizing baby and child contests shared the goal of assessing child health through physique, but the contests themselves frustrated the bureau leadership.[70] Julia Lathrop thought the contests were sometimes disorganized or loud and dirty, and lacked standardization.[71] She also did not approve of the prizes distributed at these contests. Commodifying child health with cash prizes seemed crass and unprofessional. It made the contests carnivalesque, and detracted from the serious health purposes Lathrop envisioned for the events. Even more to the point, an emphasis on rankings and prizes created an environment that encouraged a large attendance of mothers with already healthy children. Why would a mother bring her thin, sickly child to the contest when she knew the child did not have a shot at the $100 pot? Instead, the bureau wanted mothers of the thinnest, sickliest children to show up at child health events.[72] Based on the early work of figures like Ellen Swallow Richards, the Children's Bureau insisted their goals were backed by "euthenics" rather than "eugenics." Lathrop and the bureau were not alone in their insistence. Some medical professionals completely disavowed the contests, like the editor of the *American Journal of Diseases of Children* who said "lining up these human infants as if they were pigs or calves is exceedingly repulsive."[73]

Lathrop could not afford to dismiss voluntary energy around child health, though, so she set out to reform the contests. The middle-class bureau attributed thin children to well-meaning but ignorant mothering. Ignorant mothering could presumably be fixed by introducing these women to scientific motherhood. The bureau needed to create audiences of mothers interested in its child hygiene advice. The baby and child contest model had two things going for it that the bureau needed. First, the contest model attracted publicity and excitement. More importantly, the contests were run by a decentralized set of (mainly) voluntary agencies across the country. These were urban as well as rural women's clubs, public health groups, and teachers. They received some support from a variety of national organizations, including the American Medical Association's public health section, local and state government agencies, and the magazine *Woman's Home Companion*. The contests had created an informal infrastructure around child health and aesthetics, a way of reaching millions of women across the nation and influencing their ideas on child hygiene without spending much money or expending other resources.

Assessment and Advice

In 1916 the bureau tried to mobilize its informal network of female labor. These women, they imagined, would accept the bureau's child health conferences as the scientific alternative to baby contests. To this end, the bureau instituted a national Baby Week. The event consisted of nurses and volunteers examining hundreds if not thousands of babies in one busy week. The labor was dispersed. Local women examined local babies. The campaign included events in New York City, Pittsburgh, and Chicago, as well as in small towns and cities across the country. The number of children weighed, measured, recorded, and assessed was more than anyone had set out to assess before. One New York City reporter insisted that "Baby Week has done to New York's attitude toward babies what a large, active firecracker placed under the chair of a dozing grandfather might be expected to do."[74] Attaching the stamp of federal approval to these local events helped publicize them, and granted them political authority. Baby Week did not include the prizes and awards that Lathrop had deemed crass, which reduced the entertainment value of the events, but actually increased their credibility as scientific events. Baby Week events were held in around 4,700 communities.[75]

The bureau's Baby Week succeeded because of its combination of federal authority and quantification. Height-weight forms and measuring instructions offered an aura of scientific legitimacy to the project. They also made it simple for any laywoman to become an expert on child weight. While other height-weight materials and instruction existed at the time, the insistence that Baby Week was a project for the national good placed it in a different category. Historians have studied the power of the federal government to persuade—but not technically force—female citizens to comply with federal projects in roughly this period. By the time the United States entered World War I in 1917, there were programs to brutally repress and prosecute radicals, dissidents, and certain immigrants. There was also aggressive propaganda work like that of the Committee on Public Information (CPI), which made the Children's Bureau's requests for citizen action seem familiar and, by comparison, quite moderate.[76] CPI projects included campaigns encouraging women to do everything from monitoring their block for communists to buying war bonds. Not planting that victory garden might get a woman a sneer from her neighbor, but it was not likely to get her a police visit. Compliance was all about the responsibilities of good citizenship—and a little dose of guilt. In the end, though, huge numbers of Americans voluntarily grimaced through meatless Mondays and sent their kids out to collect scrap metal. It was both a responsibility of citizenship and a point of pride. Baby Week carried a similar mandate.

Baby Week was a way of encouraging women's voluntary groups around the country to put on child health conferences by suggesting one week would be set aside around the nation for such events. The bureau further encouraged women's groups by drumming up media attention for the events, and preparing more printed materials for groups that wanted them. During Baby Week, women's groups around the nation put on conferences using height-weight tables, and employed advisory technologies to assess children's height (or length), age, and weight. The intersection of these measurements marked the child as underweight, overweight, or acceptable in weight. These weight ratings could then be translated into health ratings: the child was read as healthy if it met the average and unhealthy if it fell short.[77]

The introduction of the 1916 and 1917 Baby Weeks encouraged mothers to take these child health ratings to heart. Through brochures and pamphlets especially, mothers were to embrace the new scientific nutrition daily, not just during the designated week. The bureau's printed materials reiterated the ideas of Baby Week, especially the idea that mothers did not innately know best.[78] They needed to learn, and they needed to embrace the new science of child health. The health of the nation, they understood, depended on it.

The Children's Bureau's 1914 *Infant Care* and 1915 *Prenatal Care* were designed specifically for mothers, social workers, and teachers. *Infant Care* would become one of the agency's most popular publications. The booklet advised women on such topics as ventilating the nursery, registering their infant's birth, and, of course, provided extensive details on weighing and measuring infants. Various iterations of the popular booklet remained in print for decades.[79] American mothers and women's groups hungrily consumed the federal pamphlets. According to Lathrop, the agency sent out over 100,000 copies of both *Infant Care* and *Prenatal Care* in their first year of publication. Most of the bureau pamphlets were sent in response to individual letters directly requesting either a pamphlet or advice related to pamphlet topics.[80] Many of the pamphlets and height-weight tables were available for free, or for just a few cents. Advice literature was exploding in popularity at the time, and women were open to experts.[81] For women with minimal resources and a genuine concern about how to keep their children healthy, this might be the best advice available. Pamphlets were often given to women directly, such as when they were leaving a Children's Bureau–approved baby conference (or even one of the more legitimately educational children's health contests of the period). Other women heard about the pamphlets from friends, neighbors, or public health workers, and then wrote to the bureau requesting copies.

Lathrop described the tone of *Infant Care* as "addressed to the average mother of this country."[82] Its voice, according to one reviewer, was "simple enough to be understood by uneducated women and yet not so simple as to seem condescending to the educated." The maternal voice was in part meant to comfort any mother reading the pamphlet, but that was not its only aim. The maternal voice also allowed the bureau to claim it was not going beyond the bounds of what it was allowed to do. Although Lathrop was proud that the booklet was based on health literature and discussions with nurses and doctors, she also noted explicitly that with *Infant Care* "there is no purpose to invade the field of the medical or nursing professions."[83] The booklet would by nature be advisory—all advice literature is. The bureau added an extra caveat to its booklet, though, with the explicit insistence that it was not a threat to other health organizations.

Baby Week was an ideal venue for disseminating publications like *Infant Care*. Baby conference score cards had begun the process of arming non-experts with tools of scientific assessment. Mothers, teachers, and nurses (in practice experts, but grouped with nonexperts since their skills were rarely taken seriously) could read a scale or ruler and fill in the blanks on a score card. The charts allowed supposed nonexperts to authoritatively do the work of experts in a simple, standardized, fashion. Lathrop thought that this quantification—the use of child contest methods alongside the more scientific-seeming advice à la *Infant Care*—was an efficient way of reaching as many mothers and teachers as possible.[84]

Still, Julia Lathrop struggled with getting her child health agenda in the hands of everyday women. She wrote about how "even many of the best educated fathers and mothers . . . have never read a statistical table, and never will."[85] Getting these parents to take statistical tables home and integrate them into their regular child health routine was critical to the maintenance of a height-weight program. Lathrop also wrote that, while she filled the Baby Week pamphlets with "facts about the dangers which beset American babies," she knew that parents would "successfully evade" them. Great success required a larger campaign, Lathrop knew, and that campaign would also need more active advising by the bureau.

The Great War and the Children's Year

During the first U.S. Baby Week, Europe became engulfed in a war both enormous and—for most Americans—distant. By the second Baby Week, in June of 1917, the Great War was no longer so distant.[86] Although the scheduled work of the Children's Bureau, including Baby Week, went forward, the U.S. entrance into the European war changed the bureau's aims. While funds for domestic programs were scarce, American state building increased. It also intensified the discourse around women's voluntary sacrifices and contributions. The new emphasis on women planting victory gardens, preparing wheatless and meatless meals, and rationing their shopping elevated the idea of voluntary action. It fit well with Children's Bureau politics. Here was an unusual moment, in which the rapidly expanding federal government kept pushing into private spaces, including the intimate space of the family meal. As propagandists like the Committee on Public Information pushed these voluntary actions as responsibilities of patriotic motherhood, though, such requests fit well with middle-class American women's existing relationship to the state. This seemingly paradoxical obligatory-volunteerism enlisted women's labor and allegiance without apparent federal overreach. It also helped construct a narrative of individual responsibility around food choices being beneficial to the civic whole.[87]

The need for so-called responsible food choices was not only the result of limited butter and sugar. As the Great War progressed, so grew an American anxiety over men too malnourished to fight. The medical statistics collected during men's draft examinations suggested a great deal of physical unfitness. In World War II, many more extensive height-weight and physical examination guidelines made for detailed health concerns, concerns that began even before Selective Service examinations did. In World War I, though, these examinations were more holistic than the specific quantified health data to come.[88]

The Children's Bureau then promoted an even louder call to improve child health. This was not simply to be for the sake of individual children (as baby contests often portrayed themselves) but for the good of the entire nation. It was a compelling opportunity for middle- and working-class women to demonstrate their patriotism in a gender appropriate manner.

Julia Lathrop declared that 1919 would be the Children's Year. This was a year-long campaign to promote child health. To create such a large and sustained campaign, the bureau enlisted the voluntary labor of swaths of Americans in order to promote child welfare and hygiene. The bureau's Children's Year campaign explicitly targeted "not only mothers and fathers, teachers, physicians, infant-welfare nurses, and other social workers who have to do with children, but men and women experienced in organization, and young people with leisure and good will."[89] All could be used in improving child health. Lathrop explained that the goal of the Children's Year was to save the lives of 100,000 children under the age of five, children who might otherwise die of preventable causes. Lathrop won support for this campaign based on the public claim that nearly 30 percent of World War I rejections owed to the long-term effects of childhood diseases or neglect.[90] With this incentive, an impressive list of local-level public health and hygiene measures came out of the bureau's Children's Year. In California, local participation sparked action to create seventeen permanent county health centers and positions for dozens of public health nurses and dental hygienists. Additionally, the state established a division of child hygiene with a $20,000 budget under the state's Department of Health.[91] The bureau argued that there was a similar outcome in every state, although this was an exaggeration. Still, following the Children's Year, twenty-one states created child hygiene divisions (nine states had already had such divisions). The bureau's voluntary, minimally funded, and decentralized program had more or less succeeded. Where the bureau had no power to build clinics or install teams of dental hygienists, it still managed to accomplish some of its goals during the Children's Year.

The bureau framed the project from the start as a project that would rely on voluntary agencies and women's cooperation. The bureau had no financial resources to offer to local events, but promised local communities that the events would be inexpensive and worthwhile. Free instruction from the bureau would be implemented through generous workers and volunteers. The Children's Year was a more ambitious campaign than either the 1916 or 1917 Baby Week, and over the course of the year it won greater participation, enthusiasm, and support than had previously been received. The first major event was a "nationwide Weighing and Measuring Test of young children." According to the bureau's publications, the support would come from a number of sources. In larger cities, the bureau would lean on city officials, city health departments and their child hygiene or child welfare divisions, women's organizations, school boards and teaching staff, and churches. They went so far as to optimistically anticipate that the mayors of some municipalities would get involved. Civic organizations were also enlisted. From infant welfare societies to the remaining settlement houses to the Camp Fire Girls and the Boy Scouts, charities could be of great use. While the actual workers involved with rounding up and measuring children were expected to be female, the bureau believed that men's organizations

The health of the child
is the power of the nation

APRIL 1918   Children's Year   APRIL 1919

UNITED STATES CHILDREN'S BUREAU AND WOMAN'S COMMITTEE OF THE COUNCIL OF NATIONAL DEFENSE

Figure 1. Poster from the Children's Year campaign, which sought to improve child health through child health conferences and the promotion of weighing and measuring children. Committee on Public Information, Division of Pictorial Publicity, Library of Congress Prints and Photographs Division, Washington, DC.

might get involved with promotions and financial backing. The bureau asked fraternal orders, labor unions, and chambers of commerce all to stand behind the weighing campaign. Many provided publicity and financial support. Once support for Children's Year was established in each locality, the bureau also provided instruction on how the groups should organize themselves. The bureau suggested local conferences be divided into publicity, finance, and enrollment committees. Another committee would focus exclusively on procuring the scientific equipment needed for measuring.[92] The bureau managed the Children's Year with a vision of truly shaping each event according to bureau expectations.

As part of the Children's Year, the bureau became an even more enthusiastic proponent of child measurement and standards. The mostly female volunteers at the events were instructed to draw heavily on the bureau's Baby Week and child health conference pamphlets for guidance. It issued pages of special instructions for the Children's Year weighing program. Children were to be weighed and measured with very specific equipment.

The bureau promised that "the equipment essential for the test is simple." This included a standard scale, a platform scale, a measuring rod, a good supply of tape measures, a 45-inch-long table covered in quilts, oilcloths, cotton sheets, paper towels, and a few other supplies.[93]

The instructions for actually performing the weighing and measuring were even more complicated. They required their own separate Children's Bureau pamphlet: Wash your hands. Undress children and wrap them in a thin towel. Take off their shoes. Hold a book or small box horizontally on top of the child's head when measuring his or her height (assuming a more scientific scale was unavailable). Lay babies down, completely relaxed with no bent joints, and measure their length with enamel bookends. There was even a science to filling in measuring cards. Examiners needed to use fractions rather than decimals, and round ages to the nearest birthday.[94] The women who participated in this work would ideally be aided by local physicians or nurses who gave of their time freely. Only a physician was allowed, for instance, to mark a child as "healthy and free from serious defect" or to provide recommendations to mothers in writing.[95] Most of the examiners, however, would be middle-class women active in the community. These women, the bureau advised, ought to "rehearse the procedure of weighing and measuring" before being released on the babies.[96]

After the actual weighing, the measurers had extensive instruction on how to record the data. The available height-weight tables represented a large number of average children, bureau pamphlets explained. Despite bureau apprehensions, local women conducting the measuring were told to treat the measurements as scientific fact. When actual children deviated from the average child weights on the tables by just two pounds, they were marked as abnormal. When the women found these divergences from the norm, even the mere two-pound ones, they were to advise parents to bring the child to a physician. In the bureau's plans for events of meticulous measurement and careful assessment, the bureau reiterated the importance of expertise. On the one hand, giving laywomen weight tables and putting them in a position to take charge of child health—both that of their own children and of the community at large—empowered these women. On the other hand, the growing insistence on experts undermined that empowerment. As the bureau further sold the importance of expert-validated quantitative child health, mothers increasingly accepted the bureau's message: it was their responsibility to assess and measure their child, and that was something the bureau could help them with. It was also now their responsibility to take the child for a true expert measurement and assessment. This was not something the advisory bureau could do for them.

The acceptance of the first part, the idea that women needed to take charge of their children's health through scientific means, can be seen through their participation in the Children's Year measuring test. As part of the bureau's promotion of the mass quantification event, it prepared a short film called *Our Children*. The film was produced as part of the Children's Year, but the Children's Bureau hoped it would have an impact beyond the one-year affair. *Our Children* began with the idea that children needed to be weighed as a response to the high American child mortality rates. Club women in the film were spurred to action simply by reading a newspaper article in which the Children's Bureau called for women to weigh their children. Clearly, the bureau believed itself to be so influential that a mere call to pay attention to a problem would lead to voluntary support. In the film, though, simply weighing children was not enough. Weighing needed to be careful, to be scientific.[97]

Without a home scale, the women in the film first tried to weigh a baby by sticking him on the scale attached to the back of a passing ice truck. The infant was not interested in this, however. He cried and screamed, and wriggled so much that the women were unable to get an accurate weight reading. The women then took the child to the grocery store for a produce-scale weighing. The results were not much better. Older children kept falling off the grocery scale.[98] This was no scientific motherhood. Finally, a group of clubwomen decided to invite experts from the bureau itself to come and assess local children. As might be expected in this propaganda for health quantification, only this expert guidance allows the women to successfully weigh their children. The pictured bureau and their nurses were adept at handling children, even more than their mothers seemed to be. They came equipped with scales designed especially for babies and children, and were meant to produce meaningful numbers. Only a numerical assessment of the child could provide the modern measure of health that the bureau valued. In time, these would become the measures that most women valued.

All this weighing was explicitly intended to measure and improve the health of children around the nation. It also served another purpose. The conferences would allow the bureau to create its own height-weight dataset on American child health. The bureau figured that collecting the weights and measurements of about 200,000 children would allow them to create

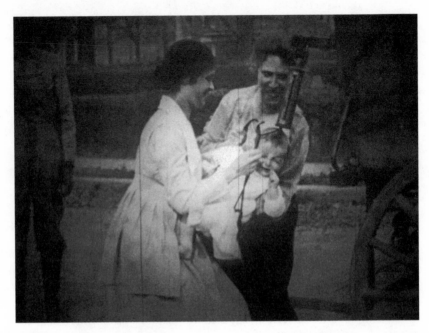

Figure 2. Still from the 1919 Children's Bureau film *Our Children*. The film encouraged mothers to embrace the scientific weighing and measuring of their children's bodies by illustrating the limitations of less-than-scientific attempts. Here, two women try to measure a baby on the scale of a passing ice truck. The baby squirms and they move on to find a more precise scale. Records of the Children's Bureau, 1908–1969, Motion Pictures, National Archives at College Park, College Park, MD.

new height-weight charts that would assess a larger number of children, and a more ethnically and regionally diverse set of children. One of the bureau's major complaints with baby contests had been the lack of consistent, accurate standards for assessing children.[99] With this new 1919 dataset, the bureau would have standardized numbers for future events.[100] To prepare this dataset, local conference organizers were asked to write in to the Children's Bureau for official child scoring cards before holding a conference. The measurement cards used in any weighing situation were meant to be torn in half. One half of the card would be given to mothers to remind them of where their child fit into the average, and where he or she ought to fit. If a child was deemed underweight for his or her height, the local women who put on the event were also advised to keep a permanent record of that child's measurement for themselves.[101] Mothers also were given a

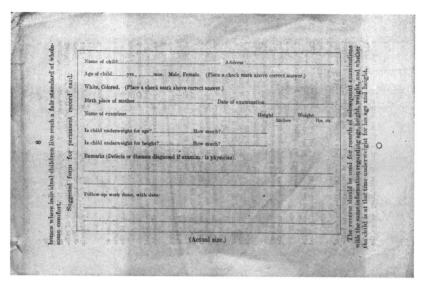

Figure 3. The Children's Bureau included this sample of a child's health record in a series of pamphlets designed to prepare clubwomen to hold child health conferences as a part of Children's Year. This was an attempt to standardize the conference experience and the definitions of child health, as well as allow the Children's Bureau to collect data. Children's Year Pamphlet No. 2, Part 3, Bureau Publication No. 38 (Washington, DC: Government Printing Office, 1918), 7.

more detailed physician's assessment of their child. The other half of the simple measuring card was to be mailed to the bureau for its own records.[102] Using the half-cards, bureau statisticians developed a set of height-weight charts divided by race (black and white only) and gender.

The newly created bureau height-weight tables replaced most of their predecessors, becoming the gold standard for child measuring, which in turn was the gold standard for child health. By the late 1920s and early 1930s, Americans moved most child health concerns from the community to the physician's office. The bureau could not stop this, nor did it want to.[103] It kept a toehold in child health, though, by setting the terms on which experts would discuss child health in the immediate future.

During the Children's Year, which ran April 1918–April 1919, the Great War ended. The Children's bureau encouraged the local women responsible for the weighing and measuring to pursue other child health measures. Once events like the Children's Year had brought women into the world of

public health work and scientific mothering, the bureau advised localities
to keep women in that world through continuous events. The bureau recommended that its pamphlets on topics like prenatal care and milk safety
be spread around communities. It also suggested that local women's clubs
hold lectures and meetings on the care and feeding of children. Local
groups might also introduce the next generation of mothers to weight and
health standards through Little Mothers' Leagues or school programming.
Above all other measures, the clubwomen who had participated in Baby
Weeks and Children's Year were encouraged to fundraise and campaign to
get at least one public health nurse in their community. The nurse must
focus on prenatal and young children's health concerns, and could be supported through private fundraising or by convincing the local government
to allocate funds.[104] In any case, the bureau made clear that women were
not to lose interest in the project of scientific mothering and health. Children needed to be weighed, the bureau told them, and they needed to be
weighed in a very specific manner. The continuation of that work, though,
was up to local women.

The Children's Bureau employed a variety of advisory state techniques
in the 1910s and early 1920s. The primary strategy of the agency was a reliance on voluntary networks, especially those run by women sympathetic to
the bureau's cause and accustomed to being called upon to do the family
labor of government. Middle-class clubwomen read child health conference
brochures, organized baby weeks in 1916 and 1917, and rose to the challenge
of running a series of Children's Year events. Through quantification and
standardization, through little score cards and straightforward scales, these
women likely internalized the values of scientific motherhood. In the process of accepting these values, they accepted that a careful measurement of
height and weight could be a stand-in for child health. Height and weight
measurements that fell within the normal range were evidence that a
mother was living up to the expectations of scientific motherhood. If a child
was above or below the normal range, perhaps there was something wrong
with that child. More to the point, perhaps there was something wrong
with that mother. At that point, it might become a public issue. It might
also become a professional medical issue, an issue for the growing field of
pediatrics.[105]

Projects like the 1919 Children's Year helped the bureau gain support
for its child health/child weight efforts. Soon after the bureau published
the results of its Children's Year, the 1921 Sheppard-Towner Maternity and

Infancy Protection Act passed Congress.[106] With it, communities found help getting the public health nurse the bureau told them to get, running the health lectures they had been asked to run, and making child weighing and measuring a regular affair. While the Sheppard-Towner Act suggested a new direction in child health matters, and a more involved and directive Children's Bureau, the short-lived program might be better understood as an anomaly in the primarily advisory work of the bureau. Pamphlets, quantification, and, above all, women's voluntary labor made the work of the Children's Bureau possible.

At the same moment the Children's Bureau was popularizing height-weight charts as a way of accessing information about children's health, they were also putting the charts in the hands of mothers and teachers. Height-weight charts then became popular ways for those women to measure themselves. Versions of such tables, claiming to offer medical insight, circulated in the life insurance business. They circulated in popular women's magazines. By the early 1930s, such tables would increasingly be used to assess adult men when they came in contact with the state. In the interwar years, the majority of which did not have an active draft, the men who ended up in intimate contact with the state were commonly low-income men. As the Great Depression expanded men's participation in social welfare programs, the physique of these men was analyzed according to the quantitative norms popularized in the 1910s and 1920s. The quantification that made these height-weight tests possible would now allow for the measurement of masses of young American men. Advisory techniques continued to guide the approach of state entities toward physique, but the specific demographics of those participating in this social welfare program also recast the boundaries of the advisory.

CHAPTER 2

Boys into Men: Depression-Era Physique in the Civilian Conservation Corps

"Have you ever seen a boy from your community leave for a CCC camp and then come home again six months or a year later?," the Civilian Conservation Corps director asked in the pamphlet *Now They Are Men*. "If you have," James McEntee continued, "you are almost certain to have seen a striking change in his physical appearance." The young man's posture was improved, his muscles hardened, his cheeks ruddy, and his scrawny body filled out. This boy, on average, "has gained ten or fifteen, perhaps even twenty or twenty-five pounds."[1] While designed as a social welfare program, the Civilian Conservation Corps (CCC) provided its aid through a literal reshaping of the male body. As one supporter explained, the opportunity to improve "physical development . . . will help [men] to wage a better battle for economic independence" even after they left the corps.[2] Using both advisory (weigh-ins and media) and more hands-on (calisthenics and hard labor) state body projects, the CCC set out to alter the bodies and circumstances of young, low-income American boys, rehabilitating them and transforming them into breadwinning men.

For those men living in CCC camps, the corps' body project could be coercive. Men labored, ate, slept, and exercised the CCC way. In different circumstances, such a direct, aggressive body project would have been unimaginable. For about 200,000 young men each year of the corps' existence, though, the American body project was an astonishingly intimate one. These young men, cast by the corps as malleable boys, could be subjected to hands-on body projects ranging from mandatory calisthenics to arduous physical labor. This was because they volunteered, because they were low-income, and because the language of body shaping was sometimes actually less insulting than the language of social welfare. The CCC was domesticating these boys, in their mind, turning them from imagined bands of vagrants and multiethnic drifters into productive protobreadwinners.[3]

The hands-on experience was meant to reform and rehabilitate these men, to transform them from welfare clients to self-sufficient citizens. One pamphlet called *The CCC Offers A Young Man a Chance* argued that "enrollment in the CCC may be the best opportunity many men will ever have for building up their health and strength."[4] Franklin Delano Roosevelt himself promoted the CCC by linking health gains with employment prospects and economic recovery. He said that "the clean life and hard work in which you are engaged . . . cannot fail to help your physical condition." Improved condition meant better individual and national prospects. "You should emerge from this experience, strong and rugged," he continued, "and ready for reentrance into the ranks of industry."[5]

The corps was not concerned solely with the bodies of those men it had enrolled. It balanced hands-on body projects within camps with widespread advisory body projects aimed beyond the camps. Corps leaders—from President Franklin Roosevelt on down—imagined their program shaping men far beyond the camps of select young enrollees. In this way, the CCC's directive body project also functioned as a wider advisory project for all young American men. Believing the American breadwinner model itself to be in crisis, the corps' leadership publicized corps men's physical changes. The CCC placed muscular bodies at the center of all its publicity, from pamphlets to photographs to movie reels, even to talks from President Franklin Roosevelt himself. "The only difference between us," Roosevelt told a group of Virginia corpsmen in a filmed speech, "is that I am told you men have put on an average of twelve pounds each. I am trying to lose twelve pounds!"[6] The CCC was one of the most popular and most publicized components of the New Deal, in part because of the great visuals that forest landscapes and strong male bodies offered. The CCC project combined building up white, male bodies with building a prosperous and socially stable nation. Its directors eagerly interpreted strength, able-bodiedness, and heteronormativity as markers of the nation they could make out of the ruins of economic depression and dependency. In specific camp settings the CCC could be directive, while in the broader public sphere the CCC cultivated an advisory body project.

The CCC in Brief

In March of 1933, a joint committee session of the seventy-third Congress met to consider S. 598, the bill that created the Civilian Conservation Corps. The bill promised a trade: "relief of unemployment through the performance of useful public work."[7] Men from around the country would be selected to work in camps for one-year stints. They would plant trees on national and state lands, exterminate agricultural pests, work to prevent soil erosion and flooding, and build, maintain, and repair trails in government parks. Most of the work would be done in the American West, far from the cities from which most of the recruits hailed. The federal government owned well over 100,000,000 acres in these western forests. Corps men would be paid up to thirty dollars each month (though they would not see most of it), and receive food, room and board, clothing, and medical attention. The corps enlisted about 250,000 men to start.

Secretary of Labor Frances Perkins described the Civilian Conservation Corps "as entirely a relief measure." Perkins endorsed the program but, given her position, clarified that she did not consider it a threat to organized labor or an expansion of federal employment.[8] Instead, she explained, these were not jobs "in the truest sense of the word." They should be thought of as projects that kept unemployed young men occupied. Not every unemployed man would do this work. Men with too many dependents or families they could not be separated from would not do this work, nor would men who were so malnourished as to not be physically up to the task. Perkins asked Congress to remember the voluntary nature of the projects that men would undertake. No men, she explained, would be "compelled to go" to work at a CCC camp. This was especially important when committee members questioned Perkins about the similarities between sweatshop wages and corps wages. Factions of organized labor were worried less about the well-being of corps men than the possibility that low CCC wages would depress all wages. The corps has to be understood as a sort of workfare, as Perkins understood it. This appeased organized labor groups. The emphasis on the voluntary and relief nature of the program also allowed the corps leadership to intervene in the bodies of its workers in ways few civilian organizations could.[9] In fact, as CCC publicity often focused on men's physical rather than economic transformations, these corporal interventions were practically necessitated.

Franklin Roosevelt appointed Robert Fechner director of the first CCC in 1933. The selection of Fechner was another attempt at calming unions and demonstrating how the corps was not a typical work program. Fechner was a labor leader, just off a stint as vice president of the International Association of Machinists. By April of 1933, Fechner had begun the recruitment process for the rapidly organizing corps. To be eligible to join the CCC, men needed to be unemployed, unmarried, United States citizens, and between the ages of eighteen and twenty-five. The first CCC recruits were chosen from a list of those who were already clients of another social welfare project. At least one young man wrote to the national office complaining that he was not able to get into the corps, since his father kept managing to find work. Only when the eager young man's father eventually succumbed to Depression economics and needed social services, was the young man finally able to enlist.[10] The main purpose of this eligibility requirement was for the CCC to save its own resources by using the current social welfare infrastructure, and having other agencies determine the neediness of clients. Men enrolling in the CCC were supposed to be up for physical labor, although underweight and muscularly underdeveloped men, even those who would not qualify for military work or private sector labor jobs, were accepted.[11]

Enrollees were entirely male. Eleanor Roosevelt, reportedly inspired by the creation of the CCC, pushed for parallel women's camps. A couple of years later, the Federal Emergency Relief Administration developed an experimental program like this, centered on one New York camp, although it primarily used women for sewing and forest nursery projects. It was still agricultural and conservation work, as the young women transformed a substantial surplus of cotton into sellable goods through sewing work. While derisively nicknamed "She-She-She" camps, these female workers did not join the actual CCC program. They never fit the corps' sense of itself, or earned the nickname—or wages—of "tree soldiers." Instead, CCC newspapers described the women as easily tired by their work, and as more likely to eat pastries than the manly rations of the CCC. To the extent that the corps was a project meant to strengthen the male breadwinner and craft a specific family model, a female corps was decidedly off-message.[12]

The CCC imagined itself making boys into men, not managing women. Some of the CCC leaders even feared inviting too many educators to the men's camps, lest this aspect of camp life disrupt the labor and man's work at the center of the corps. One military leader of the corps, worried that "we are going to be hounded to death by all sorts of educators. Instead of teaching the boys how to do an honest day's work we are going to be forced to accede to the wishes of the long-haired men and short-haired women and spend most of the time on some kind of an educational course."[13] The colonel's views on the subject were extreme; both Fechner and Roosevelt supported after-work schooling for CCC boys. What is striking about the colonel's statement, however, is his rhetoric. In his imagining, corps camps built masculinity through hard labor, a masculinity under threat from gender nonconformists. In this debate over education in the camps, the colonel could only understand the program in terms of gender and sexuality. The existence of women's camps reminded men like the colonel of the perceived threat from "short-haired women," ready to damage the white, heteronormative, male breadwinner, family model that the corps was so focused on strengthening.

This family ideal of the white, male breadwinner proved an especially uneasy model for enrollees of color. The actual legislation responsible for the corps explicitly stated that the program would not discriminate based on "race, color, or creed."[14] While black enrollment levels did not correspond with black Americans' relief needs, the fact that black Americans made up about 10 percent of the corps still suggested it was more racially inclusive than many other New Deal programs. At the level of individual states, numbers could be far less equitable.[15] Georgia would not enroll any black men in the corps until the federal CCC administration intervened. The state director of the CCC there explained that men were classified by need, and that no black men met the need threshold. Moreover, he explained, it is "vitally important that negroes remain in the counties for chopping cotton and planting other produce."[16] Mississippi, a state where more than 50 percent of its citizens were African American, enrolled a corps with only 2 percent black men.[17]

Although the CCC was actually more inclusive than many New Deal social welfare programs, it was still plagued with inequality and discrimination. The corps leadership was focused on improving the projected white family model; there was little room in this projection for black men. This reality was reflected in, and reinforced by, the place of racial minorities in corps publicity. As the white male body (ultimately including immigrant bodies made American through the CCC project) became a central point of New Deal propaganda, black bodies faded into a segregated, shadowy image. Employing and building up white male bodies and masculinity suggested national progress. Enhancing black men's bodies and masculinity was likely imagined as a danger rather than a service, especially to neighboring white communities who associated black men with crime and drunkenness.[18] Although some of the corps leadership did support black men's right to enroll in the program, intervening when the program excluded black men, the white American man remained the face—and body—of the CCC.

Debilitation and Rehabilitation

The end of World War I and the subsequent homecoming of large numbers of traumatized or physically disabled young men dealt a blow to the ideals of American masculinity.[19] The Great Depression dealt another. As the male breadwinner role of young, white American men was threatened, so, too, was the imagined family unit they anchored. CCC leaders argued that forest-based work camps like those of the corps could rebuild this beleaguered manhood. CCC camps sought to fix the male breadwinner family model that many saw as the backbone of American masculinity. The CCC thus pressured men into taking on a breadwinner role. The program sent the majority of a man's earnings directly to his family. The generally unmarried young men were meant to be supplementing their father's income, rather than supporting their own families. The leadership imagined men entering the CCC as scrawny, naive boys, while in the camps they became manly tree soldiers. It was only after CCC participation that they emerged as men ready to be the breadwinners for their own households. The CCC structured its welfare payments within the language of the breadwinner model, which distanced these payments from the fears of dependency often tied to social welfare.[20]

A decade of American agricultural depression, combined with the stock market crash of 1929, spelled economic disaster. By the early 1930s, about 250,000 young men wandered the nation in search of work. While these so-called drifters and tramps loomed large in the American imagination, a much broader swath of young American men were actually unemployed.[21] Around one-fourth of young men under twenty-four could not find any work, and another third of the same population could only find part-time work. The underemployment of these young men threatened to reshape American family dynamics. An early historian of the corps described this population as "bewildered, sometimes angry, but more often hopeless and apathetic."[22] The troubling image of these disaffected male youth was difficult to shake, especially as their equivalents in Germany and China radicalized.[23]

For politicians who understood men's relationship to the family unit as a civilizing force, these high numbers of unemployed men were dangerous. These men were undomesticated. Many feared that young men without work would become criminals, or join the bands of wandering tramps and vagrants. Worse still, they might totally—not just temporarily—abandon the idea of the breadwinner model meant to structure American society. One congressman discussing CCC expansion argued that "the young man who is unemployed and is forced into an unfavorable environment not of his choosing will eventually turn against society."[24] While the reality was that young American men came from all sorts of family units, the society at risk here was that of the idealized family unit—explicitly heterosexual, implicitly white and middle class, and containing one couple and their children rather than the multigenerational arrangements common in many immigrant and urban families. This idealized unit lined up with the breadwinner model for families. The male head of household was supposed to earn enough money to support his immediate family all by himself. In Depression-era America, with wages hard to come by, this already unrealistic model became fantastically impossible in the eyes of unemployed young men.[25]

As mainstream politicians of the 1930s saw it, young men not only needed to be stopped from political deviance but also from the related arena of sexual and gender deviance. Agencies regularly structured social welfare policy in this moment around the necessity of heterosexual attachment and the danger posed by unattached (or nonfamily) individuals.[26] In the eyes of supervisors like the first Civilian Conservation Corps director, Robert Fechner, unattached men inherently posed a threat to the social fabric. Another New Dealer explained, in support of CCC expansion, that young men without the responsibilities of a job, home, and family were "a volatile element in society."[27] "They have everything to gain by a change in the established order and nothing to lose."[28] When men could not support the family they had, they might desert their wives and children, leaving them as burdens on the budding welfare state.

In reality, working-class married women had long made money outside the home, and the pre-Depression American family was never such a simple economic structure. Moreover, camps created to domesticate men were at times also charged with overdomesticating them, as CCC men cooked and cleaned during their time away.[29] Still, changes in how Americans *imagined* families to work were as important as changes in how the unit actually functioned. When an unemployed man ceased to be a breadwinner, he ceased to be the head of the household. The unemployed man seemed undeserving of respect from his wife and children. Government planners imagined youth as increasingly delinquent and living in unstable family units. Women might need to work outside the home, undermining their husbands' authority while simultaneously leaving their children unsupervised (and, in turn, at risk of delinquency). Most men, the concerned parties worried, would not even get that far. Criminality and homosexuality were all imagined threats to the unattached man.[30] So long as young men planned to support a family, they had reason to find and keep jobs, to obey laws, and to reproduce. Without the taming influence of rigid sex roles, many imagined, there would be nothing to hold men back from their unsavory natural state.

This social welfare program was built against the backdrop of an emerging New Deal, but its supporters rarely framed it as welfare. The program instead emphasized its workfare approach, and the association with labor and male independence painted the benefits as earned (masculine) rather than as a feminized dependence on the state. They saturated the program with images and claims of masculinity. As workers, CCC men would be independent and autonomous. As so-called tree soldiers, these men would be muscular, obedient, and brave. The two models of masculinity, and the methods through which the different models were instituted, could at times conflict. In the corps, men were both the obedient trainees of a premilitary program and autonomous, self-defined independent men. The Civilian Conservation Corps had both an advisory and a hands-on role in the lives and bodies of its enrollees.

Within camp settings, making a model male breadwinner by physically rehabilitating a welfare client was a bold project. It would have been impossible without the advisory state body projects that came before it. In Atwater's turn-of-the-century laboratories, the idea that food could be carefully monitored to improve citizens' bodies blossomed. By the 1930s, the idea of the laboring body as a machine, with food as its fuel, had become widespread.[31] Likewise, the explosion of interest in height-weight measurement during the 1920s put poundage into the American vocabulary and made the bathroom scale a familiar object. Americans increasingly understood their bodies to be quantifiable, and to represent something larger about their social and political value. The advisory projects of the Children's Bureau provided an un-acknowledged foundation for corps projects. The Children's Bureau relied on advisory state methods like education, scientific expertise, and quantification. It had a relatively small budget and its leaders, especially the female leaders, had mainly indirect political influence. Given these circumstances, the bureau worked almost entirely through advisory mechanisms.

The CCC was founded under rather different conditions, which enabled the development of body projects that drew on but also extended the scope of the advisory state. The corps had more funding and more influence than the agencies that came before it. In 1938 the Children's Bureau asked Congress for $400,000 to pay its employees' salaries. The corps, during the same fiscal year, spent over $500,000 on denim jumpers alone. For 1938 the Children's Bureau requested over three million dollars be sent to the states for local child health and welfare programs. The corps, that year, requested just over three *hundred* million dollars.[32] Forty million dollars of that was just for subsistence. The bureau could give advice on food, but the corps could dish it out by the pound.

The corps, however, did not want to simply give away food, a move its leadership equated to mere charity or welfare. Instead, it explicitly sought to push its volunteer enrollees to rehabilitate themselves in both body and behavior. Social commentators at the time understood the problems of 1930s masculinity as stemming from economic issues. It was a problem of men unable to obtain and keep family-supporting jobs. The corps, in turn, provided such men with temporary jobs to reinforce the idea that male income was meant to support a family, though the program directors rarely spoke explicitly about the money involved in the program. Although the CCC was a social welfare program based on work, a program built on its opposition to charity or unearned welfare, openly discussing the program as workfare still reminded some people of welfare. In a culture that linked economic independence with masculinity and economic dependence with femininity, a focus on these young, low-income men as welfare recipients only further damaged their already besieged manhood. Instead of discussing changes to men's finances, CCC leaders often focused on changes to participating men's bodies.

Within camps the CCC helped men reshape their bodies, while outside the camps CCC publicity touted a narrative of the transformation of scrawny, urban male bodies into robust, able-bodied men. The extensive CCC use of film and newsreels focused on strapping, shirtless laborers reinforced this idea nationwide. "The fact that enrollees gain so much weight is proof that it is good for them," explained one corps pamphlet.[33] At a moment when the idealized female body was increasingly slender and weak, the idealization of young white men as husky and muscular spoke to a stark difference in social expectations. The built-up male body had only taken hold as a desirable aesthetic in the years just prior to the Depression. In the late nineteenth century, American reform movements advocated "Muscular Christianity," and pushed the use of gymnastics and bodybuilding as a means for avoiding urban temptations and isolation.[34] By the Progressive Era, this ideal of vigorous, embodied masculinity had gone mainstream. Figures like Theodore Roosevelt and G. Stanley Hall pushed the importance of well-off white men seeking fitness through "the strenuous life," and emphasized the relationship between racial and physical fitness.[35] By the 1920s and 1930s, under the wing of celebrity gurus like Eugene Sandow and Charles Atlas, fitness culture moved from highbrow to low-brow.[36] Big names in bodybuilding wrote books, opened gymnasiums, and sold training plans and products designed to build up the American man. This meant that the average CCC man was likely quite familiar with this muscular ideal long before he encountered it in camp rhetoric. Even men who did not aspire to such chiseled extremes absorbed changing cultural ideas about male bodies, notably the transformation of the stout male figure from successful to slothful.[37] Meanwhile, the CCC leadership embraced the idea that adding pounds to these young men's bodies could do more than improve them physically. This bulking-up project also functioned as shorthand for the transformation of a boy into a man poised as breadwinner, family anchor, and productive economic and social citizen.

At the same time that devastating Great Depression economics seemed to threaten American social roles, they also threatened the physical bodies of these same Americans. While middle-class American men might try to build themselves up in the image of Charles Atlas during the early 1930s, the more typical male body looked nothing like his. This was doubly true of the bodies of low-income Americans. Dorothea Lange's photographs captured the sunken eyes and hunger-stricken faces of Depression-era children. While they could not easily cut back on rent, Americans could cut back on the elastic expense of food when their money ran out. In the 1930s, the result of these sacrifices was malnutrition and sickness. Food relief provided by strained local charities was typically inadequate. Meanwhile, clients found early federal relief programs, with long public lines and goods they did not choose, embarrassing.[38] Malnourished children, urban and rural, haunted the national imagination. Visuals of breadlines and underweight children complemented a growing collection of scientific research on underweight American bodies. Researchers produced varied numbers, but most studies showed that about 20 percent of American children were malnourished. Some reports were more extreme, suggesting deficiencies in 70 or 85 percent of children.[39]

These underweight children were not the only undernourished people in the country. Single men were often ineligible for food aid, which was primarily distributed to families. In 1935, when a federal commodities program was set up to distribute agricultural excess to those in need, single men were excluded.[40] The federal Food Stamp Plan, initiated in 1939, explicitly barred "unattached men."[41] While women and children were imagined as innocents who might merit federal resources, many believed that men without families would only become more shiftless and irresponsible if they had access to benefits. At best, urban single men might find private charity through soup kitchens and breadlines. Outside the urban setting this organized relief was harder to come by. Hunger and malnutrition were filtered through gendered cultural lenses. The same political rhetoric that described hungry women and children as malnourished tended to describe underfed white men as weak. This language denied men's strength and autonomy, instead portraying low-income men as effeminate and sexually perverse.[42] This emphasis on their concurrent physical and moral states, so-called weakness, rejected the possibility of structural problems and instead placed the onus on individual men. Paralleling threats to men without breadwinning status, the poor physique of Depression-era men suggested men whose disability and dependency was written on the body.

Underfed bodies thus matched unrealized breadwinner status. In response, the Civilian Conservation Corps sought to both economically and physically improve enrolled men. As one enrollee told it, "things were going from bad to worse, when his honor, President Roosevelt, said, take the young man off the city streets, put the under-nourished in re-conditioning camps until they are capable of swinging [like] an ape."[43] The CCC paid men a little, but improved men's bodies a lot.

Changing Bodies in the CCC

James McEntee, the second director of the corps, explained that, while men did a variety of work in the corps, the end result was always the same. Whether they drove tractors, dug holes, or swung axes, they grew more masculine. "Whatever they do," McEntee explained, "it is toughening, a man's work. Their muscles grow strong under this daily work." The extensive exercise was only one piece of the hands-on body project. Press releases proudly stated that the average enrollee ate five pounds of food per day, and that the program used "more than 14,000 carloads of food each year." Additionally, the health programming of the CCC included vaccinations. "The health of enrollees is vigorously guarded," wrote one CCC enthusiast. "The food . . . is constantly under expert supervision. . . . [The enrolled men] are given careful physical inspections at monthly intervals by the camp medical officer."[44] The food served in the camps was basically the same as that served in domestic army and navy camps. The medical corps described the rations as "abundant," and explained that this food was nutritiously dense and would "speedily overcome the effects of moderate dietary deficiencies suffered by the enrollees, assist their bodies in returning to normal function, and increase resistance and ability to perform manual labor."[45] Control over food was an important component of the CCC body project.

Corps leaders regularly measured men, and used the statistics as evidence of the corps' success.[46] Since weight gain indicated masculinity, economic success, and future prospects, these numbers were critical to the CCC narrative.[47] According to one test, men averaged a thirteen-pound gain during their first eight weeks in camp. Another test conducted by the Office of the Surgeon General of the War Department said men gained an average of 6.04 pounds in their first eight weeks.[48] Frank Persons, special assistant to the director of the CCC, claimed that enrollees gained around twenty pounds in their first six months.[49] In a different report, Fechner proudly told Congress that the standard six-month weight gain for enrollees was an exact 7.2 pounds.[50] James McEntee also wrote confidently about the transformation of CCC men. Eighty-four percent of all the boys who were below the minimum at the time of enrollment gained weight rapidly, he said, because they ate beef, potatoes, and vegetables and drank milk. "This is why you notice so much difference between the boy who leaves for a CCC camp and the boy who comes home after his term of service is

Figure 4. Men perform daily calisthenics as part of their CCC activities. The official caption for this image notes that CCC men performed fifteen minutes of calisthenics outdoors every day except holidays and Sundays and that this exercise regimen helped "build strong muscles and strong bodies for the CCC boys." No. 587, Camp Roosevelt, F-1, Edinburg, VA, July 22, 1940, RG 35, Records of the Civilian Conservation Corps, National Archives at College Park, College Park, MD.

over," he explained.[51] The CCC reshaped low-income men, and average poundage served as the leadership's proof.

Mandatory exercise in camps supplemented this bodybuilding project. "Coupled with the toughening work in the field, the enrollees take a regular daily calisthenics drill," McEntee wrote. "Much of the field work develops only certain muscles. The calisthenics, scientifically planned by Army experts in body development, are designed to give each muscle in the body proper exercise."[52] The corps' plan for building strong men was about encouraging employment and breadwinning. At the same time, though, the phrase "building men" had a more literal meaning. All these projects were nested in a shell, in a New Deal image of muscular manhood. Building was about the intersection of economics, masculinity, and the physical body.

Director Fechner wrote that "two principal benefits [had] been received" by CCC men. One was better health, and the other improved employability. He reasoned that disaffected men left camps "with healthy bodies, with heads up, and capable of making their own way if jobs [were] available."[53] While Fechner framed the benefits to bodies and bank accounts as if they were separate, the relationship between the two was evident. As Fechner promised to build up men, he promised a whole package. A strengthening or building up of American men necessitated the development of one specific image of manliness. Fechner's intention for the program was to produce domesticated yet strong, skilled, and muscular men. One CCC pamphlet, *Builder of Men*, promised that enrollees "who are overweight and flabby lose weight in camp and soon turn their excess flesh into hard muscle."[54] While the pamphlet certainly meant this at the literal level, intending to directly improve the bodies of American men sent to corps camps, it also functioned as a metaphor. Corps bodies changed from social excess flesh—understood as masculinity gone soft and useless—into hard muscle, or breadwinning, virile, masculinity. This transformation stood at the center of CCC projects.

A 1936 promotional brochure published by the Government Printing Office and called, simply, *The Civilian Conservation Corps*, listed some of the benefits the CCC provided enrollees. First on the list was "muscles hardened," followed by vocational training and education. Publicity materials consistently conflated musculature and weight with health. Then, like so many body projects, they used health as a stand-in for a diversity of social and economic concerns.

That brochure went on to explain that an improvement in health and discipline made CCC graduates uniquely prepared to "make good in any kind of honest employment."[55] In an annual report on the 1938 corps, CCC leaders prepared further thoughts on the young bodies under its supervision. "It is significant that the average boy entering the Civilian Conservation Corps will gain between 8 to 12 pounds in weight during a 3- to 6-months period," the report emphasized. "The food which is furnished is wholesome, palatable, and of the variety that sticks to the ribs." While the authors of the report went on to explain that "the amount of attention devoted to food is almost bewildering," they also noted that food—and the associated improvement of the body—is the best indicator of social welfare available.[56]

Another pamphlet, *What About the CCC?*, further underscores the physical goals of the program. "The supplying of jobs to unemployed men is important," it explained, and "the building of men is also important." The pamphlet went on to make the relationship explicit. "Fortunately, the two go hand in hand," they explained, "the men need the forests and the forests need the men."[57] The corps was supported (and partially run) by the U.S. Department of Labor. The department supported the project not simply on the grounds of getting jobs for men but on the promise of strong and stable men ready to enter or reenter the paid workforce when more jobs were available. The Department of Labor's publications reinforced their belief in the relationship between economics and male physique. "The emergency conservation work provides the opportunity to build up men as well as to build trees [i.e. work]," the department wrote in a 1933 bulletin.[58] In a corps-issued report, called "The Nation Appraises the CCC: April 1933–September 1939," Fechner used similar language. The director insisted that "virtually every enrollee" had improved physically, and that the program's benefit to trees was "at least equaled by the results in improved health, mental outlook and earning ability of jobless youth." In this report, Fechner emphasized a familiar mantra: the CCC "has conserved youths of nation as well as land."[59] Conserving youth implied the often-touted physical improvements to the men. Senator Elbert D. Thomas of Utah made the relationship between the expanding state and the improved body explicit in his praise for the corps. According to Thomas, the corps "represents the first direct large-scale attempt by the federal government to bring definite physical and character benefits to its idle youth." As such, he continued, "it has been a successful program."[60]

The Advisory Corps

In its intimate regulation of food and physical activity, the corps' body project went beyond advisory state regimes in a way few programs aimed at white men could do. As the CCC aggressively changed the bodies of young men in camps, though, it also reshaped the broader American idea of what productive young male bodies ought to look like. Roosevelt, Fechner, McEntee, and other corps leaders imagined their message of physical, economic, and familial strength reaching far beyond the enrolled men within those camps. Through speech, statistics, and propaganda, the CCC cast the successful enrollee body as the physical ideal of the new American male.

In a nation often deeply suspicious of social welfare and expanding government, the Civilian Conservation Corps was a popular program. "Today you can ask any citizen to name what he likes in the New Deal and you will find practically everyone says The Civilian Conservation Corps," one newspaper reported.[61] That popular appeal enabled the agency to influence American ideas of body, family, labor, and masculinity. It indirectly reached those citizens whom the agency could not literally touch. Like Children's Bureau health conferences, advisory technologies made state power and influence both invisible and omnipresent. In this capacity, the corps was more than a hands-on body project only altering low-income volunteers. Instead, the corps revised general American interpretations of the body by using the stories, images, and statistics of the men in camps. It was an advisory state-based lesson for the rest of the country.

The weight, musculature, and physique of Civilian Conservation Corps men were part of the program's powerful narrative from day one. The national corps produced a regular newspaper called *Happy Days*. Individual camps also often produced less polished newsletters and papers. As those papers were meant primarily for the eyes of men at those specific camps, they got a bit salty. *Happy Days*, on the other hand, was aimed at both corps workers and their families. The editors even encouraged CCC men to get subscriptions for their "girl" back home. The paper thus functioned as an unofficial mouthpiece of the central office. The reporting in *Happy Days* was not necessarily what the administration thought, and the paper could also be internally inconsistent, but the majority of it aligned with the corps leadership's messages. Franklin Roosevelt praised the popular paper, explaining that "it has aided in making the men of the CCC conscious that they are doing good, useful work and proud of the fact they are doing it. It has assisted also, in making the young men feel they are a part of a great National Movement for the conservation of men.[62] *Happy Days* was as much corps publicity as it was a newspaper for the actual corps men for whom it was supposedly written.

Early issues of *Happy Days* were peppered with stories of weight gain, even though the camps had hardly been open long enough to merit the boasting. In a column called "Smiles," the editors reprinted a note from a Fort Washington, Maryland, camp. "I'm going to write home and tell Ma she might as well give my other suit away," the man said. "It won't be big enough for me when I get out of here."[63] Another story, "Leavenworth Grub Sure Must Be Good," praised the weight gain of men during their two-week conditioning camp stints. In mid-1933, men reportedly ate eight pounds of food each day at conditioning camps, and gained up to ten pounds during their brief stay.[64] The paper even printed a poem on the subject of improving physique, referring to the CCC men as "peavies"[65]:

> A peavie from out of the west
> was tremendously fond of his chest,
> he pounded and thundered,
> and bellowed and blundered,
> and ripped all the seams of his vest![66]

In one issue, they reported that a boy in a New Mexico camp gained eighteen pounds in a matter of months.[67] In another case, a corps man wrote to *Happy Days* to complain about an earlier piece on weight gain in the CCC. He was "surprised to see that the record holder has only gained 18 pounds. Pooh, pooh!" He went on to name a man he knew who had gained twenty-one pounds, and said the men of his camp could be nick-named the "Jumbo Elephants." He continued to describe camp weight gain, writing that "even little Elmer Wieland put on 19 and is now on a Holly-wood diet, trying to keep in form. What a form!"[68] The weight gain of the men was not only a symbol of repaired manhood, but of a manhood secure enough to laugh over its once shameful body. Likewise, in a poem written by a Tennessee enrollee, the tree soldier explained that he had "gained in weight a lot,"

> And my sweetheart even loves me better too,
> For the girls admire men
> Who tackle things and win.
> All the girls like husky guys who dare and do.[69]

The "daring" and "doing" suggested a desirable, heteronormative masculine independence, perhaps tied to economic success—and certainly tied to physical success.

While the discussion of weight gain was a primary way in which the corps leadership reached both their own enrollees and the nation at large, it was not the only approach. The corps also used photography to communicate the message of general male improvement. The extensive photographing of enrollees focused heavily on white, muscular male bodies, those that best represented the program's goal of improving male lives by improving male bodies.

Regular publicity photos portrayed men with large tools at work in the forest. In most photographs, the men are bare-chested, exposing the literal improvements brought to their bodies through the corps. The photographs themselves were not meant for men in camps, though. The men in the photographs were already in the fold of the CCC (though it surely flattered the specifically chosen men to become corps models, and perhaps encouraged their peers to work on becoming huskier). Instead, corps photographs were an advisory tactic. The images, sent to be used in newspapers, magazines, and corps publicity around the nation, portrayed the bodybuilding work of the corps in all of its glory. As with quantification, the stylized photographs of corps men made a complex set of CCC goals easy to disseminate. Embedded in the pectorals of the idealized white male enrollee were claims of masculine independence, breadwinner status, and freedom from feminized dependence on the state (even as he received a form of social welfare). Through quantitative weight, and to a lesser extent camp visuals, the bodies of CCC enrollees were not simply the objects of hands-on federal action but also the medium for far-reaching advisory state action.

Letters from the Forest: Hands-On and Advisory States in Conversation

The mutual reinforcement of hands-on and advisory approaches to the enrollee body is best illustrated in a series of "benefit letters" composed by corps enrollees in 1935 and 1936. Corps leaders worked to justify the continued existence and even potential expansion of the corps. To help their case, they asked CCC men to write letters about their experiences in the program. Stacks of letters with titles like "How the CCC Has Benefitted Me," "What the CCC Has Done for Me," and "How I Benefitted by My Enrollment in the CCC" poured in for Director Robert Fechner.

These letters were guided by the needs of the corps director, and their words were both carefully solicited and monitored.[70] The authors of these persuasive benefit letters did not necessarily want to write them. A Minnesota camp's educational adviser tried to encourage letter writing with a contest for the best story from each barrack. The prize was a "Flat Fifty" of

Figure 5. A Pennsylvania enrollee poses shirtless with his physique on display. The official caption for this photograph is "Work Makes Brawn" and states, "This youthful CCC enrollee, engaged in a drainage project, is typical of the husky young men developed in the CCC. He works hard, eats well, keeps regular hours in camp." No. 143—"Work Makes Brawn," Port Hunt, VA, Camp NP-6, June 4, 1940, RG 35, Records of the Civilian Conservation Corps, National Archives at College Park, College Park, MD.

Figure 6. The young man in this CCC publicity photograph is shown shirtless, holding a sledgehammer. The image is typical of posed CCC work photographs, which often feature a shirtless white young man holding some sort of tool: a pipe, a shovel, a sledgehammer, a pickaxe. Records of the Civilian Conservation Corps, entry 6: Photos taken by Walter J. Mead, box 16, folder: Health 16-C, National Archives at College Park, College Park, MD.

cigarettes (a flat tin holding fifty cigarettes).[71] At one North Carolina camp, the educational director submitted a formal report on benefits to federal headquarters instead of asking his men to write their own letters. The letters, then, do not give us access to the feelings of actual corps enrollees toward the camps. What they give us, instead, is access to how enrollees adopted the goals and language of the corps directors when discussing how the CCC had benefited them personally. Enrollees wrote frequently about their weight in these letters, often adopting the corps' reliance on quantified weight numbers to stand in for improved health.

Many of the men's stories emphasized their personal weight gain. These letters were usually described as if they represented the unmediated voices of enrollees. In fact, weight gain and bodybuilding narratives were carefully crafted from above. While the beliefs of individual men were surely embedded in the stories, they are inextricable from the guiding hand of CCC officials. Rather than read these letters as a narrative of enrollee obsession with weight and bodybuilding, we must read them as evidence of an organizational obsession with those body projects. Weight gain was referenced over and over in CCC letters. In a set of December 1935 letters from a central Pennsylvania camp named Stone Creek Kettle, men testified to their improved bodies. Herbert Walker wrote that "the diet we received has increased my weight 27 pounds." Dale Lohman wrote, "I only weighted 135 when I came here—now 148 pounds." William Howry "picked up" twenty pounds at a North Dakota camp, and John Curry gained thirty-three pounds at a South Carolina camp.[72] Other men focused on their musculature. In addition to gaining twenty-five pounds, enrollee Paul A. Crouch said, after a year and a half in the corps, "I have ceased to be the weakling that I was before enlistment. My muscles are harder, and in general 'I can take it.' "[73]

Men regularly described a transition from being a weakling to becoming a strong man. One peavie explained that, "when I left home . . . I was 6ft and wade a hundred fifty pound. . . . I look like a banana with a pair of felt boots on." One man praised the camp food for changing him "from a skeleton-like person to a healthy-looking youth."[74] Another wrote that, "at enlistment I was what most people would call a bag of bones." The young man, according to the weight gain narrative of his letter, quickly put seven pounds on those bones.[75] Another said that when he entered the corps he "was pretty much a weakling." After his time in the corps, though, he said, "I can truthfully say that I am able to keep up."[76] One CCC man described his previous body as that of "a drug store cow-boy." Now, though, he was fit.[77] In letter after letter, individual men recounted their physical transformation as one of the primary benefits of corps enrollment.

Physical benefits like weight and muscle gain were almost as central as economic benefits in the letters of the corps men. Building men meant building financial independence. One often-discussed concern about financial independence was ensuring that young men had the strength and stamina for long hours of physical labor. The importance of the breadwinner role in building manhood was usually symbolic, but it could also be quite literal. One man beamed with pride at actually being able to feed his family through his labor. The corps man explained that not only had he built up his own body, gaining twelve pounds while at his camp, but the money he sent home had also allowed his entire family to gain weight.[78] The economic and physical goals of the corps men were inseparable.

This relationship was reiterated by the reports written by educational directors of the camps, and included with some benefit letters. Like that North Carolina director who wrote on behalf of his men, most of these formal replacements of or accompaniments to benefit letters focused on the economic and physical gain of enrollees. One explained that, "of forty two members whose weights were checked, only two showed any loss of weight." These enrollees were identified. Also identified, though this time for praise, were the men who gained the most weight. "The largest individual gains in the group were made by Members Garland Core and Thomas Stanley," the director wrote, "both of whom gained twenty five pounds during the year in which they were here." Another man who arrived underweight gained twenty-five pounds, became a talented boxer, and then left the corps for the army. Two other men were lauded for gaining large amounts in just three months at the camp. He went on to calculate averages divided by length of stay. Although he admitted his calculations were "not a scientific experiment," he still proudly produced his research, which showed an average of ten pounds gained per man per year. From this, the education director drew some broad conclusions. First, he explained that, among hardworking men, "this gain in weight is indicative of better health and runs hand in hand with increased strength." Echoing the conflation of weight with health in the 1910s and 1920s, the director used weight gain statistics to demonstrate that "a boy makes a change for the better by serving in the Civilian Conservation Corps."[79]

One cartoon from a 1933 issue of *Happy Days* illustrates the difference between the rhetoric of the corps about male transformation, and the sometimes disappointing reality of those transformations.[80] The first three cells of the cartoon tell a CCC story that could be right out of one of Fechner's brochures. First, a young man named Pete writes home. "Dear dad," his letter begins. "Boy is this a swell place! Have gained a lot—coming home on work leave, will be there tomorrow." In the second cell, Pete's father interprets the comment about his son's "gain" as he has been trained to by corps publicity. The father immediately takes the reference to his son having "gained a lot" to mean weight gain. The thought bubble above the father's head fills with an image of a brawny, muscular man, his son's head on the body of a CCC Adonis. His proud chest thrust outward, the father smiles ever so slightly: the scrawny boy he sent away now has the physique of a man. In cell three, the boy, clad in a large overcoat, greets his father with a handshake.

Pete enters, and his father quickly sizes him up, exclaiming: "Gosh son youve really filled out." "Yep," Pete agrees. In cell four of the cartoon, however, the story takes a turn. Pete removes his bulky overcoat and reveals his body. Pete, it turns out, is an embarrassing "almost 110 pounds." His father falls to the floor with a big "PLOP!" The CCC had not made Pete into the man his father had imagined, or the man corps publicity had promised. The cartoon, with its emphasis on camp rhetoric and enrollee letters, reiterates how critical the discussion of the male body was to camp directors. It also reminds us of how that language shaped the language used by enrolled men to discuss their participation in the program. Even when it did not reflect the reality of their time in the program, the cartoon suggests, men in the corps understood their participation to be mostly about weight gain and growth. They had so internalized this idea, that the reality of their actual growth hardly mattered. Here, we see the limits of the hands-on state. Certainly not everyone grew under the care and feeding of the corps' program. Physical bodies, metabolisms, and hormones are all different. In notable ways, then, it was the advisory message of the corps that shone through. As it altered the imaginations of corps men at least as much as their actual bodies, the advisory components of the CCC may have been even more meaningful than the directive components of the program.

"After two years in the Civilian Conservation Corps I have learned to take care of my body," wrote enrollee Victor Pesek.[81] Another enrollee recounted how he observed "the weak and sickly shirker develop physically."[82] The corps not only tried to make men physically stronger, it also tried to make them better workers and shut down any tendency toward

Figure 7. The CCC language emphasized weight gain and bodybuilding as evidence of success for both the program and individual young men. This language became such a central tenet of the program that, as shown in this cartoon, those at home simply came to expect that men would gain weight while working for the corps. This was not always the reality, as the cartoonist illustrated. The assumption of weight gain nonetheless became ubiquitous in the program. Joe Campbell, *Happy Days* 1, no. 9, 21, April 1934, RG 35, Records of the Civilian Conservation Corps, National Archives at College Park, College Park, MD.

shirking. The successes of the corps were discussed often. The CCC became one of the most popular programs of the New Deal, and still holds a vaunted position in New Deal memory.

Building on the advisory body projects of agencies that came before, the CCC used the unique economic and political circumstances of the New Deal to implement a hands-on body project. The corps housed, fed, clothed, paid, and supervised men in camps. In the CCC's body-shaping project, there was no clear distinction between interventions to improve young men's job prospects, young men's behavior and morality, and young men's bodies. Yet altered bodies were not simply incidental, they were not a mere side effect of providing men with ample food and demanding physical labor. Rather, the muscular form that many CCC bodies took on was a directive at the center of the corps' aims.

The Civilian Conservation Corps was also an advisory agency. The corps photographed, wrote about, discussed, and otherwise heavily publicized the bodies of male enrollees. A young, white, muscular body at work came to symbolize the social and economic possibilities of a post-Depression nation. Corps publicity emphasized connections between one's muscles and one's ability to provide for a family. As the leadership prepared materials promoting the corps, they also promoted this physique and lifestyle as a model for all American men. In the case of the CCC, the hands-on and advisory projects of the agency complemented one another. As the corps produced more and more material linking muscles to economic success, it argued that all American men needed building up.

Once the United States entered World War II, however, a congressional committee met to discuss terminating the corps. "The time for frills in Government passed on December 7, last," one man told the committee. On the other side, an administrator from the National Security Agency argued that the corps could be adapted for a wartime context. Men in the CCC, he argued, learned discipline, work habits, and hygiene. The camps also "provide[d] an excellent rehabilitation service in preparing men for the Army. Numerous selective service rejectees," he explained, "are physically fit for service in the Civilian Conservation Corps. With proper diet, regular habits, and incidental corrective treatment large numbers of them are enabled to overcome their physical deficiencies and are made available for military service."[83] Those who understood the corps as primarily a social welfare or employment agency believed that the CCC was no longer needed. Those, including the corps administration itself, who conceptualized the CCC as a broader program of building men up physically and socially saw a continued need for the corps. In the end, as the war intensified, the former group won. There were cheaper ways to ready men for war. In the context of total war, moreover, all men—not just low-income men already using social welfare programs—were within the state's reach. Still, a large contingent understood the CCC as a critical man-building program, even worthy of coexisting with the greater man-building program of an army going to war.

Although the CCC did not last beyond the war, it set a precedent for hands-on programming focused on the young male body amid national emergency. The corps' ability to shape the bodies of its enrollees provided a model for some of the physical rehabilitation plans designed for men who did not live up to World War II recruitment standards. The corps also presented a new model for what a patriotic, masculine, white American body ought to look like, and how one could get that body through a combination of federal aid and individual initiative.[84] The CCC sold a muscular image of American masculinity and tied it to independence and citizenship. For select men, the CCC offered a hand in meeting the corps' imagination of the breadwinning male body. For all men, the corps advised the development of a muscular, weight-gain based, and labor-intensive American masculinity.

CHAPTER 3

Men into Soldiers: World War II
and the Conscripted Body

As a teenager in the late 1930s, Raymond Hackney grew infatuated with joining the U.S. armed services. He went to a local recruiting station, but was rejected as "underweight." Hackney was undeterred. When the United States entered World War II in 1941, the sudden demand for manpower improved Hackney's chances. He went to the recruitment station again. They recorded his weight at 113 pounds, still 7 pounds under the service's minimum weight of 120 pounds. In the modern military, these numerical requirements mattered. In the war context, though, just how the requirements were met mattered far less. A recruiter recommended that Hackney eat seven pounds of bananas, then top it off with as much water as he could stomach—then revisit the examination scale. He listened to this advice, and soon returned with a bellyful of bananas. "I weighed in at 120.2," he recounted proudly.[1] Hackney enlisted.

Many men did as Hackney had done, as the need for manpower increased amid the lead-up to U.S. involvement in the Second World War. President Franklin D. Roosevelt issued the first peacetime draft in 1940, beginning a gradual mobilization.[2] With the Japanese attack on Pearl Harbor in December of 1941, that mobilization sped up. The World War II body project entailed the examination of about twenty million men set to mobilize. Half of those men were successfully inducted, while the Selective Service found the other half wanting during the extensive examination process. Though the Selective Service used psychological, educational, and physical factors (which sometimes overlapped) to determine the war readiness of men, here, we will focus on the physical requirements and physical examinations. The public expressed the most interest in and engaged in the most vocal discussions about the physical properties of American soldiers, typically using physical fitness as shorthand for the general acceptability of potential recruits.

The need for such a shorthand came about because the huge number of men under examination—about twenty million—made comprehensive and holistic examination impractical. The Selective Service focused its examination process, asking local doctors to use simple measurements partnered with standardized tables as proxies for declaring men's fitness for war. As a result of this reliance on mass measurement, height, weight, pulse rate, and blood pressure became some of the most important yardsticks of the Selective Service physical examination. The development of standardized acceptable weights, heights, and other medical data grew in tandem with the necessity of mass measurement. Using these standards, during World War II, the Selective Service rejected about 2 percent of the men specifically because of their weight. For many others, inadequate weight was a noted but secondary reason for rejection, taking a back seat to other physiological or mental issues. While this is a far cry from standard weight as a huge qualifier or disqualifier of men, the centrality of measurement as a major, directive undertaking signaled how different wartime and peacetime body projects could be.

The fact that the U.S. government had promulgated body standards for use in advisory state work in the decades before the war ultimately made the implementation of stricter wartime standards possible. Rather than circulating standards among mothers, teachers, and medical professionals for their own education, the government itself now took the reins from those voluntary agencies. Physical examinations, mandatory for those choosing to enlist and those called up under the draft, reached more men than advisory measurements had. They also demanded far more of the men than voluntary measurement systems did. Adult men called in front of the board were required to open their mouths so someone could count their teeth, to read an eye chart, and, of course, step on the scale. After that, officials used standards to assess, classify, qualify, and reject American men's bodies. The results had material consequences. Men who failed to meet the standards would be embarrassed, often before the local doctor and in their own neighborhood. Men who passed, meanwhile, were likely going to war.

The application of physical standards to large populations was a wartime anomaly. This story is the exception that proves the advisory state rule: the moment of rare aggressive state intervention grounded in smaller-scale projects like those of the CCC, and made possible on this large scale only by the extenuating circumstances of wartime. World War II produced new obligations of citizenship. For many men, those obligations included physiological, mental, and intellectual examinations for the military. The tests themselves were not radically new developments, as the mass mobilization of male bodies in World War II relied on measurement tools and techniques of the Progressive Era advisory state. It was the widespread use of the tests, especially on those men who had not volunteered to serve, that proved the most forceful aspect of this intervention.

The aggressive approach taken by the Selective Service during World War II fits uneasily into the history of American masculinity. As male autonomy and self-definition grew in importance over the course of the twentieth century, the idea that white, middle-class men would be prodded, rated, and even told to change their physical bodies appears as a substantial challenge to notions of white normative masculinity in the period. And yet, while there were many contests over what the standards entailed, there was no real contest over whether it was appropriate to measure these men. Most federal expansion during World War II went unchallenged, as both the reach and responsibilities of the state grew exponentially.[3] American men in the 1940s found themselves in a mandatory intimacy with the state, their masculinity predicated on their submission to federal authority. Following the historical normalization of measurement and the growing acceptance of the idea that deference to a state at war was as manly as autonomy from that state, young men across the nation accepted this newer model of wartime masculinity.

This submission to the state was made possible not only because of the wartime context, but also because of the thirty years of advisory state preparation that came before it. These men had grown up with exposure to weighing and measuring. Some of this familiarity might have come from interactions with voluntary agencies, medicine, and popular culture, but interactions with agencies like the Children's Bureau also introduced many to weight standards. The Selective Service's weighing and measuring efforts promised a greater challenge to American masculinity than child health conferences did. Perhaps to downplay the difference between such endeavors, though, many Selective Service examiners described recruited men as "boys." That small rhetorical trick suggested these recruits were less likely to be undermined by state intervention. This is especially prominent in the literature on men failing physical exams.

Those who failed were "boys," scrawny and underweight, perhaps need-ing even further federal intervention. Those who succeeded might be deemed either "boys" or "men" depending on the situation.

Those men whom the Selective Service measured as physically accept-able often recast the whole process of a physical examination as their own choice, part of a narrative of patriotic participation in the war. They over-whelmingly rejected any narrative of federal reach (or overreach) on their bodies, especially narratives that might cast doubt on their masculine autonomy. As American men accepted the growing centrality of physical standards in their military service, they also deeply accepted something standardizing agencies has been promoting for decades: the idea that physi-cal standards were scientific. The mass application of these standards in wartime, and the cultural importance placed on them serving as an objec-tive and unemotional basis for determining men's fitness, helped obscure the intimacy and the irregularity of the measurement process.

America Goes to War

To fully mobilize the nation for World War II, the military required the induction of about ten million American men between 1940 and 1945. While some men joined voluntarily—especially just after the December 1941 bombing of Pearl Harbor—young male troops were in such high demand that voluntary enlistment could not meet U.S. Army needs. The Selective Service and Training Act of September 1940 was issued as the first peacetime draft in U.S. history.[4] Forty-five million American men registered for the draft, essentially making their presence as a male citizen visible in the eyes of a militarizing state. Of those men, about nineteen million were called up, and subjected to physical, mental, and moral examinations. About half of the men passed, and about half failed these examinations as the Selective Service attempted to sort America's fit from its unfit.[5] This culling process was hands-on state work, with the active examination and assessment of American men transformed into a mandatory component of masculine citizenship through the draft.

The draft brought thousands of men into contact with these standards, by what historian James Sparrow describes as the "three bureaucratic gates" a man passed through on his way to war. First, men went to their local examining boards. Then, they went to federal induction stations. And, finally, they attended boot camp.[6] Each interaction with the state came with examination and assessment of the man's physical and psychological health, as well as his education and morality. The two sites at which examiners extensively used weight and height standards were the local examining boards and the regional induction stations. As a result, those are the bureaucratic gates we must closely consider in our attempts to understand how this temporary project of the high-stakes measurement of male bodies was possible under the World War II state.

Politicians and bureaucrats worried about manpower in the years leading up to the war. General Lewis B. Hershey, a former army captain and the head of the Selective Service System, complained about the men available to him. In a dig at their masculinity, he explained they were only "half men."[7] Hershey's annoyance with American men's fitness especially became a recurring theme. "We nationally should be thoroughly ashamed" of our physical condition, he said.[8] The Selective Service director vocalized this complaint before, during, and after the U.S. involvement in the war. While Hershey was a prominent and powerful critic of American men's physique, he was certainly not alone. Just prior to official U.S. entry into the war, for instance, the War Department declared 60 percent of army reservists physically unfit for active duty service.[9] Physical unfitness was a continuing concern.

At the outbreak of war, even with the draft promising high numbers of men available to fight, the concern about the quality of such men remained. Meanwhile, the actual standards applied to men relaxed to allow more bodies into the armed services. Hershey and the men working under him sought to weed out the fit from the unfit without trampling on local power, without taking too many men away from industry or agriculture, and without upsetting those already worried about the politics of conscription in a democracy.[10] An elaborate series of classifications, including those of physical fitness for service, became the Selective Service's main response.

The Selective Service had cared about standards before, but World War II made height, weight, and other quantitative physical assessments more urgent than they had ever been. Lieutenant General Leonard D. Heaton bluntly described the heavy use of standardization by the World War II–era Selective Service as a way of "classifying and easily describing physical capacities of individuals."[11] Standards made mass mobilization possible, and physical standards made the mass examination of recruits possible.

Mass examination did not only apply to men, but here the focus is on men. This is because the number of male bodies formally mobilized in World War II was dramatically higher than the number of female bodies, and because the expectations for female interactions with state authorities were much different than those for men. During the war especially, American women were expected to submit to the good of the whole over the good of the individual through pseudovoluntary means. This submission ranged from cooking without butter to working as a "Rosie" on the war assembly line to joining the Women's Army Corps or its Naval equivalent, the WAVES.[12] Women who joined the Women's Army Corps (WAC) experienced a version of the mass examination that their male peers experienced, but there were also some fundamental differences between the practice and purpose of the tests. The examinations were focused on women who would be sent overseas, rather than all women volunteering. Above all, army physicians wanted to be sure that WACs headed overseas were not pregnant. This created its own controversy, as the pelvic examination given to women was much more invasive than the quick, standardized examinations given to men. While the WAC director Oveta Culp Hobby argued that the pelvic exam was unfair when only given to women, the exam was ultimately thrown out because it took too much time and was often ineffective at determining early pregnancies.[13] Beyond concerns over pregnancy, the weight of women in the army was only occasionally discussed. In one instance, a colonel was convinced WACs were too often overweight—and inadequately feminine. In response, he set up what he called a "birdseed table" of low-calorie food at the WAC training center for those "whose weights seemed to him to require it."[14] Women's weights were sometimes a point of contention in the WACs, whether over the "birdseed table" or Director Hobby's insistence that physical standards should not be too high for WACs, since many performed sedentary work.[15] In stark contrast to the men's enlistment process, there was little concern over women too underweight to serve. The comparatively small numbers of women serving in the WACs, and the lack of a Selective Service process for women, meant there was not the same urgency around height-weight tables and other medical statistics as there was in the men's army. When women's physique was assessed in the military, it was understood as part of a relationship with the state those women had opted into, rather than the relationship cultivated by the draft. Both because of the lower numbers of servicewomen and the lack of a need to prove any scientific or objective role for the state in such an intimate assessment, U.S. Army height-weight standards in World War II were decidedly more about managing masculinity than maintaining femininity (other aspects of the WACs managed that).

While women's submission to state authority was the expectation, men's submission was a messier affair. Now every adult man of qualifying age might be touched by draft, induction, and examination. Every man's height, weight, and musculature became critical clues to what that man's wartime role would entail. Each of the nineteen million men examined (of whom about ten million would be accepted and inducted) felt the arm of the state as they stood naked on the scale of a local draft board's station, and as they received their new identity as a classified man, a man whose value was boiled down to a number and a single capital letter: 1-A, 4-E, or 4-F. In the process of drafting, inducting, examining, and classifying, the typically advisory state began giving orders in a way that rarely seemed possible in a white male body project.

Examination board height-weight standards promised an objective take on the situation—they could weed out shoddy male specimens with scales and charts. The dream of objective measurement was never a realistic one, though.[16] The early 1940s saw many disagreements over what numbers constituted the fitness of American men. As this aggressive state intervention into the body became widespread, the limits of this arrangement came to the fore. The Selective Service introduced what it called fitness standards (actually basic physical standards) for entry into the services. When Lewis Hershey's Selective Service System—with nearly 200,000 workers—enforced physical standards, the application of those standards proved uneven. Even against the backdrop of a nation at war, local examiners refused to march in lockstep with the federal Selective Service aims. The height-weight tables, meant to seem objective and scientific, were regularly exposed as subjective assessment tools. As the Selective Service tried to determine both the numbers that connoted fitness and the rules it would impose on those doing the measuring, the process exposed diverse ideas about the physique and weight of the fit-for-war American man.

Lewis Hershey brought Dr. Leonard G. Rowntree on board to head the medical division of the Selective Service. Rowntree, a medical researcher who had spent over a decade at the Mayo Clinic in Minnesota, specialized in kidney disease. For most of the 1930s, he had served as director of the Philadelphia Institute of Medical Research, before being tapped to manage military health standards. Rowntree's duty as chief of the medical division was to manage the work of 17,000 doctors around the country, almost all volunteers, as they conducted examinations of inductees.[17] Rowntree was thus partially responsible for setting numbers for height-weight standards and other classifications.

Rowntree directed Selective Service physicians to use existing army standards around the country. Physicians at induction stations adopted those standards, albeit to different degrees of precision. Nearly 70,000 men were rejected during World War II because of their weight. Many others were rejected for multiple reasons, of which weight was only one. Despite the prevalence of so many statistically greater causes of rejection, like mental illness and venereal disease, though, this 2 percent of men (typically labeled underdeveloped) garnered a disproportionate amount of media interest and attention. Hershey, Rowntree, and the national press all wanted to know why American men were underdeveloped.

The media represented physical unfitness, a term that encompassed a number of possible problems, as the cause of the high overall rejection rate.[18] When one committee of the Federal Security Agency discussed American fitness during the war, they explained that, in order of importance, mental disease, mental deficiency, musculoskeletal defects, syphilis, and heart problems were the primary causes of draftee rejection. The agency then went on to explain that many of these rejections "could have been prevented or cured if the community had been aware of the importance of physical fitness."[19]

"Physical unfitness," referring most commonly to weight, strength, musculature, and stamina, became the primary term employed to discuss the shortcomings of American young men's bodies. Despite the measly 2 percent of rejections attributed directly to weight, the popular discussion focused heavily on weight, strength, and musculature as causes of American military weakness. Physical unfitness was easy to picture and explain in ways that the far more common rejections for mental illness were not. It was relatable. It also seemed vaguely under the control of individual citizens, and maybe even under the control of the state. In contrast, syphilis was a common cause of army rejection and a fixable problem, but it required medical intervention. Moreover, as the number one cause of black men's rejection from the services, syphilis was an uncomfortable topic for white America. Media discussions of unfitness appear to have hopped between the specific language of weight and the general language of unfitness as a way of implying concerns about sexuality (especially black men's sexuality) without making explicit references to the issue. After all, in the aftermath of eugenics, many understood physical and moral unfitness as deeply related.[20] Finally, weight could be analyzed as a highly individual problem while a common disease could not as easily be discussed. Weight measurements were thus framed as reflections of individual men's health choices.

Additionally, monitoring weight, height, and musculature served a gender and sexuality policing agenda. Army psychology suggested that sexual deviance would be inscribed on the body. First, soldier bodies were assumed to be male. While women actually served a number of roles in the war, including as soldiers, soldiering was considered male work.[21] Second, these male soldiers were also assumed to be masculine, in a fashion that explicitly excluded the military service of men deemed homosexual or otherwise sexually deviant. While some histories suggest that wartime allowed unusual freedoms for people to assert gay identities and behaviors, this situation did not apply to the draft, induction, or the examination process.[22] In fact, examination boards medicalized homosexuality to an unprecedented degree by replacing degeneracy language with the psychoanalytical language of homosexual identity. Board psychologists categorized homosexuality as sexual psychopathy, and a danger to other men in the service.[23] Less than their actual sexual behavior, an obsession with policing "sissies" and purging the service of effeminacy and gender deviance seem to have been at the center of Selective Service concerns. Later, the Veterans Administration would also worry about providing GI Bill benefits to such men, fearing a large psychiatric caseload.[24] Men with "broad hips," pubic fat, or a "scant and downy beard" exhibited physical signs of failed masculinity, which examiners might read as evidence of homosexuality.[25] Weight examinations similarly marked the below-standard man as frail and effeminate. The Selective Service understood subpar weight and musculature as subpar masculine vigor. Increasingly, the overweight (over standard weight) body was also associated with failed masculinity. Selective Service officials described the overweight boy as doughy, soft, and not a full man.[26] Leonard Rowntree made headlines in 1944 when he told a congressional committee that the average American boy was "somewhat flabby and soft."[27]

As the defined musculature of Civilian Conservation Corps poster boys showed, the range of possibilities for the American male body narrowed in the 1930s and 1940s. The widespread physical examinations initiated by the draft meant most American men would interact with this unforgiving system of measurement. Concerns about federal interventions into the body, including physical examinations, were then filtered through these results. The men deemed physically unfit because they were over- or underweight were the men whose interactions with the draft boards would be remembered. Those whose bodies met the physiological minimums of manliness had fewer interactions, which minimized their sense of state intervention.

Local examinations were the first level of exams, and were meant to be conducted close to where the recruited men lived. The surgeon general's manual on mobilization regulations, *Standards of Physical Examination During Mobilization*, was issued less than a month prior to the issuance of the Selective Service Act of 1940. The six thousand local boards around the nation rushed to learn their new equipment, forms, and examination procedures. Governors from each state, at the behest of the Selective Service System, called on privately employed doctors, dentists, and (in cities) psychologists, to conduct the medical portion of exams in accordance with Selective Service standards.[28] This division of labor remained in place through 1942, when the army decreased the power of the local boards to assess men.

In the first years of the war, physicians and a few other board members (such as those who might assess the familial or employment status of the draftee) were to classify each man according to printed standards.[29] From height-weight measurements and a series of other tests, the doctor would assess the man's fitness for service. A man would be assigned to class 1, 2, 3, or 4, followed by a letter between A and F, based on social, political, and physical concerns. The most famous rankings of the time were 1-A (fit for duty), 1-B (fit for limited duty), 4-F (completely unfit for service), and 4-E (conscientious objector). A 4-E or 4-F classification was not simply a marker stating that a man would not serve. It was also evidence of his failed masculinity. A conscientious objector was a "sissy," a man who would not protect his nation. A classification of 4-F, though, may have dealt an even bigger blow. While conscientious objectors had religious motivations, there was no way to turn a 4-F classification into a moral or ethical stance. The 4-F, instead, was a sign of a man's failure that might be attached to him for life.

The written standards asked a lot from local boards. In the name of objectivity, army medical standards offered detailed guidelines as to how physicians were to measure potential soldiers. Measuring height in particular required extensive instruction and a moderate amount of equipment.

Examiners were to use "a board at least 2 inches wide by 80 inches long, placed vertically." The manual then explained that "the registrant should stand erect with his back to the graduated board, eyes straight to the front."[30] The potential soldier was to be completely undressed for the weighing. The scale did not need to be a specific model, but it did need to be "known to be accurate."[31] The examination process was designed to ensure national uniformity in such an enormous examination process that army doctors and facilities alone could not handle it.

The war context altered men's relationship with the state, simultaneously increasing surveillance and pushing state institutions to look away from some of what they now saw. This was true about sexuality, and it was also true in the related realm of body politics.[32] The so-called unfit body was a problem, but overpolicing physical or moral fitness threatened to create manpower shortages. At the very least, it could lead to a bureaucratic mess. In cases where local board physicians could not decide on a particular draftee's physical condition, they might send him to a special Medical Advisory Board where a specialist would assess him. There were over 650 specialized Medical Advisory Boards in action during World War II. Those boards focused on body parts like eyes, ears, nose, and throat, and on orthopedics and psychology.[33] Sending men to Medical Advisory Boards could take days, though, making it an impractical arrangement during wartime, and most men were simply approved unless they had noticeable defects. As a result, height and weight—among the more obvious of potential defects—became the spaces where local boards had the most power.

With almost 6,500 local boards across the country, manned by nearly 30,000 (mainly civilian) physicians, it was difficult to claim uniform examination.[34] Exams did not always happen as dictated, especially in the high-pressure context of total war. The debate over what makes an appropriate martial male body is best evidenced, in fact, in the difficulty higher-ups experienced in getting boards to understand and adhere to both the actual written standards, and the unwritten rules for defining men's fitness or unfitness.

The overweight and underweight were both at risk of rejection, though managing underweight was a far greater concern. These charts provided two-tiered categories for acceptance and rejection. The first was an absolute minimum standard. Men shorter than 5′, taller than 6′5″, or lighter than 105 pounds were supposed to be immediately rejected with a 4-F classification.[35] Of course, this did not always happen—for instance, as with the young man who was told to binge on bananas at the beginning of this chapter—but it was the most clearly written of the classification rules. Assuming a man passed those cutoffs, he would be compared to the chart. The man would then be expected to meet either minimum or standard measurements.[36] To reach minimum goals, a 5'10" man had to weigh at least 133 pounds. Standard goals, based on height-weight ratios, were even more difficult achieve. The more desirable weight for a man of this height, according to the army tables, was about 152 pounds.[37] Thus, between 105 and 132 pounds, he was supposed to be rejected during peacetime, but might be accepted when reserves were low during war. Between 133 and 152 pounds, the man was supposed to be accepted conditionally, perhaps with the understanding that he needed physical rehabilitation before he could serve. In the midst of a national emergency, the same man would be accepted without any caveats. While men under 105 pounds were supposed to be rejected no matter what, there was also pressure to accept men who appeared to be able to handle the experience. It was often unclear what exactly local examiners should do with a man who whose weight was borderline. Such a man was unacceptable in peacetime, but might be fine in the pinch of wartime. The decision of just how slavishly doctors should read the scale was now one for local boards to make.

In the examination process, the ambiguity of the standards produced confusion but also allowed local boards to apply their own definitions of fitness and unfitness. Some rejections were simple. One man, Jiddle Jaffe, was rejected by a Tennessee local board for weighing 102 pounds. The same board rejected twenty-nine-year-old William Jordan, who weighed 104 pounds.[38] Underweight was the reason listed for their 4-F classifications. Even a diagnosis of extreme underweight would not necessarily stand in the way of acceptance if the local board could figure out a way to accept a man while still following the letter of the Selective Service standards. At least two men from Baltimore City, both three pounds underweight, were sent through a costly rehabilitation program before they were allowed to serve. Lawrence A. Miller spent thirty days in such a program after he was measured at five pounds underweight.[39] Such treatment, according to Hershey, the Selective Service director, could cost up to $60 (about $800 today) per man. The Selective Service paid one-third of the cost for that rehabilitation.[40]

While rehabilitation programs increased federal involvement with individual men's bodies, standards themselves often just confused it. In the

Height (inches)	Standard Weight	Standard Chest measurement at expiration	Minimum Weight	Minimum Chest measurement at expiration
	Pounds	*Inches*	*Pounds*	*Inches*
60	116	31¼	105	28¾
61	119	31½	107	29
62	122	31¾	109	29¼
63	125	32	111	29½
64	128	32¼	113	29¾
65	132	32½	115	30
66	136	32¾	117	30¼
67	140	33	121	30½
68	144	33¼	125	30¾
69	148	33½	129	31
70	152	33¾	133	31¼
71	156	34	137	31½
72	160	34¼	141	31¾
73	164	34½	145	32
74	168	34¾	149	32¼
75	172	35	153	32½
76	176	35¼	157	32¾
77	180	35½	161	33
78	184	35¾	165	33¼

Figure 8. This table illustrates the standard and minimum acceptable height, weight, and chest measurements for World War II inductees. The standards allowed some flexibility—for instance, those "whose weight is greater than the standards indicated for the height, provided the overweight is not so excessive as to interfere with military training" could be accepted for general service, and others found "generally physically fit" could be accepted for limited service. The standards included some hard cutoffs, though, including the strict exclusion of those under 60 inches in height or 105 pounds in weight, and those over 78 inches in height. As for bodies deemed overweight, rejection was pegged to any "overweight which is greatly out of proportion to the height if it interferes with normal physical activity or with proper training." Issues related to the 105-pound minimum proved the most common of height-weight problems. *Physical Standards in World War II*, Editor in Chief Colonel Robert S. Anderson; Editor for Physical Standards Charles M. Wiltse (Washington, DC: Office of the Surgeon General, Department of the Army, 1967), 164–165.

absence of more holistic medical examination, these measurements of weight and height took on increased importance. Lacking other medical information, this limited set of data served as proof of physical fitness or unfitness. One army medical examiner complained of a ridiculous adherence to standards and bloating of military bureaucracy in the service's search "for the 'perfect man.'" A better way to approach standards, the army major explained, was to just look for men who generally seemed like they could probably handle service—no fancy examinations or standards required.[41] One colonel evaluating the examination procedures accepted federal standards, but thought they should be taken as guidelines rather than rules. Rather than reject all those men who were just three pounds under minimum, Colonel Bennett G. Owens thought most examiners should break the rules to approve men weighing as little as a hundred pounds on the assumption that the men could gain five pounds by induction.[42] On the other hand, he believed rules needed to be stated more clearly on the Selective Service forms, since quite a few men under 105 pounds were making it to induction stations. Owens seems to have thrown out the subjective height-weight standards entirely in favor of the simple cut-off, a rule that he already found too strict. A year into World War II, Owens's choice to emphasize the bare minimum weight for rejection rather than the open-to-interpretation height-weight standards became the normal rather than exceptional approach. By late 1942, even the medical director for the Selective Service backed down from the published standards. He explained that, "in view of the urgent need of manpower, mild degrees of underweight carry less significance than in the past. . . . Unless the underweight is very marked, a large proportion of individuals will probably be accepted by the army."[43] He included this explanation in a two-way correspondence with a Hawaiian Selective Service representative, not as part of a public announcement. It was, moreover, not accompanied by any official reworking of standards. The written standards remained the same.

Standards were designed to allow for uniform, objective judgments across the nation, but more realistically provided examiners with tools of judgment and the authority to make their own decisions on behalf of the state. Height-weight standards put out by the army were themselves uniform (if open ended), but they were not uniformly applied. Local physicians and their examination boards still defined physical fitness for themselves as they determined whose examinations could be fudged and whose numbers should actually bar them from the services. On the one hand, this was a contestation over local versus federal power, but more simply it was a dispute over what the fit male body actually looked like. Private physicians took on the work of the expanding state and had to decide how closely to follow printed federal standards.

Contesting Weight

The uneven application of standards provides a lens through which we can examine some of the tensions between a growing federal bureaucracy and the local officials throughout the country charged with assisting it. Numerical standards seemed to offer a straightforward, uniform method of assessing potential soldiers. They would fulfill federal interests across an enormous, unwieldy nation, and keep local administration in check. But standards could not erase the importance of individual administrators and local boards, or what an irritated adjutant general called the "personality factors" of examiners.[44] Demarcations of male physical fitness were first made in the creation of standards, and made again "by those who appl[ied] the norm to the individual case."[45] Moreover, a subjective assessment of these bodily measurements was beyond the control of federal officials. As several historians have shown in the context of marriage law and New Deal policy, laws as they existed on the books could be quite different from the law as applied by local bureaucrats.[46] While the work of measurement was beyond the advisory state in this case, the reliance on local actors to do the work of the state mimicked the advisory tradition.

Some local boards did not merely misuse Selective Service examination standards, but appear to have skipped recording (or perhaps even performing) portions of their own quantitative assessments. In 1941, up until Pearl Harbor, local boards left off applicants' weights on almost 4,700 forms, and the height blank on nearly 4,600 (almost certainly overlapping) forms.[47] Local boards may also have misreported statistics, especially for draftee height. Selective Service statisticians determining the average heights and weights of enlisted men explained that their numbers skewed low due to bad record keeping. Some boards, they explained, wrote that 5'6" men were 56 inches tall. The statisticians determined that they would try to correct these errors in the statistics for accepted men (based on the premise that men under 60 inches tall should not have been accepted). They could not, however, make such assumptions with rejected men, and instead just generally distrusted the recorded measurements for those men.[48]

There is also evidence that local boards measured but did not use army standards when it came to assessing men who might qualify as overweight. Vague federal guidelines stated that overweight men could be accepted as long as their bodies were (subjectively) proportionate and as long as these men could still train. This baffled some local examiners, perhaps because it was subjective in a sphere obsessed with objectivity, or perhaps because it called on local boards to interpret overweight as a health problem at a historical moment when concern was usually reserved for underweight. Harry F. Besoda, for instance, who had been directing local examination efforts in Puerto Rico, wrote to the Selective Service System about his confusion over the absolute height and weight cutoffs. He asked whether a man must be rejected simply because he was under five feet tall or weighed less than 105 pounds, or if the man must meet *both* criteria to be classed as 4-F.[49]

In 1940 Edward A. Beckwith, South Dakota's director of the Selective Service, also turned to the national Selective Service to help guide him through the confusing terrain of determining how much weight was really too much. With no explicit cap as to the amount an overweight man could weigh while still being acceptable for deferred or limited service, Beckwith was unsure what to do with a 230-pound enlistee. At about 5'11", the man weighed almost twenty pounds above what was listed as an appropriate weight for his height. And yet, Beckwith explained, the guidelines for rejection owing to overweight were only "vaguely stated."[50] After all, at many boards men far below their appropriate weights were still accepted without question so long as they were above 105 pounds. Why would boards pay attention to height-weight ideals for the overweight when they often ignored them with the underweight? Robert A. Bier, captain of the Medical Division of the Selective Service, responded with even more confusing advice: so long as "the weight is fairly well distributed over his entire frame," this case of overweight should not prevent the enlistee's acceptance.[51] In this instance, then, even a request to the standards-setters to provide a more uniform regulation elicited further subjectivity. Now, local judges had to guess at whether an unacceptable weight was actually a rejection-worthy weight based not only on numbers but on how the weight sat upon the body. The dream of objectivity was undermined by conflicting ideas of what fitness meant, and whose quantification of fitness should prevail.

Raising the stakes of this confusion, men might be accepted by a local board despite some defect, and then rejected once they reached the induction boards at army bases. When the standards were first put in place, enough physically unfit men were still sent ahead by local boards that Selective Service medical officers complained. When some of the acceptances proved particularly unreasonable by Selective Service standards, the federal agency expressed a mix of concern and irritation that the local "physicians did not comprehend the physical standards" or were conducting inadequate examinations. In Pennsylvania, as one example, 15 percent of the men whom the local board physicians found acceptable went on to rejections from induction board examiners—examiners who were theoretically conducting the same exam and using the same standards tables.[52]

Federal induction stations often took recording "weight deviance" more seriously than local boards. A number of men still made it through local boards only to be rejected for their weight once they reached induction stations. About 1.5 percent of all rejections made by January 1943 were attributed to men's position outside of weight standards (both under- and overweight). This is a small percentage, of course, but it still represented a sizable number of men. Three percent of rejections made at the second step, the induction station, were attributed to concerns about a man's weight.[53] While weight was not a major cause of rejection for local boards, it was of concern to the national board. The discrepancy in rejections owing to weight suggests that this aspect of the soldier's body was difficult to negotiate.[54]

Neither the attempted standardization of physique, nor the implementation of objective weight tables, nor the use of these standards to manage normative masculinity came as easily as the Selective Service intended. Local and national boards could not agree on how strictly height-weight tables were to be used. Neighborhood examiners did not judge men the same way external examiners judged them. This assessment of these millions of young male bodies, this aggressive intervention into male citizens' bodies, was a project only conceivable under the circumstances of full mobilization. Quantified, scientific measurement was meant to legitimize the intervention and minimize its importance in the lives of fit men. At the same time, the Selective Service issued increasingly careful body standards for men to meet, though it often looked away when local examiners skirted those standards. The federal rhetoric hardened and the Selective Service used both special measurement tools and compelling circumstances to craft the body project it needed. In actual practice, the use of some advisory measures in a directive moment meant the Selective Service lacked ultimate control over its recruits. But it also meant that the agency had the flexibility and ability to live with contradictions that allowed it to acquire the manpower it needed.

After the War

The Selective Service project was one of assessing and managing bodies. What to do about the failed bodies, the failed American masculinities, was another story. In the years toward the end of World War II and in the immediate postwar period, Americans from military, medical, and political positions encouraged projects that would prepare American men—and American bodies—for the next national crisis. Once the war ended and Selective Service standards no longer mattered in most men's lives, many programs moved away from trying to fix weight and musculature and toward trying to fix a more general, often ambiguous, American weakness. As enforceable body standards became a less urgent project, the circumstances that made the unusually directive work of the World War II Selective Service possible dissipated. Plans to intervene in American bodies would be most successful when they were applied in voluntary and educational ways—through advisory state techniques. Anything more forceful was interpreted as a political threat in a moment of anti-Communist hysteria. The draft itself continued through the Korean War and the Vietnam War, which meant that the coercive project of measuring, assessing, and shaping the bodies of American men continued for another thirty years after V-Day. World War II practices normalized the role of fitness assessment in the Selective Service.

While questions about military fitness and a reliance on quantification lasted, the mass mobilization and examination processes of World War II would not be duplicated in the postwar era. Likewise, postwar military examinations would not receive World War II–level attention. This was not because American men's bodies were better matching printed fitness standards. The Selective Service tested programs designed to rehabilitate men's 4-F bodies after the war.[55] Officials debated whether such programs should be made voluntary or mandatory for men with remediable defects.

At the same time, concerns about unfit men spurred a number of civilian physical fitness programs, the most extensive of which was run by the Federal Security Agency.[56] Both rehabilitation and civilian fitness programs provided the grounding for the physical fitness campaigns of the 1950s and 1960s. Moreover, they linked the bodies of civilian men—and women working in industry—to the needs of the nation. They emphasized a specific image of fitness, and tied the work of maintaining one's individual body to one's civic duties.

As Americans began to prepare for postwar life, General Hershey opposed the return of this male body project to the advisory sector, proposing continued military training for civilians. Congress disagreed.[57] Instead, most attempted interventions in the postwar period were voluntary, and educational channels once again provided a practical method for state entities trying to improve the citizen body without appearing to do so. World War II had drawn attention to the apparent unfitness of men aged eighteen to twenty-four, the most desirable demographic for new soldiers. The Selective Service and other critics then quickly identified American high schools and universities as sites of both fitness problems and possible solutions. One branch of the New York State Education Department declared that physical fitness was necessary "for the very existence of our Nation," and explained that preventive fitness was necessary since the war proved American men were "careless about the follow-up and correction of remediable defects."[58] Increasingly, the desire for a quantifiably fit young man became an educational rather than explicitly military pursuit.

While advisory approaches shaped postwar fitness programming, this was never the inevitable course of action. During the war, New York mayor Fiorello LaGuardia called such programming "sissy stuff," preferring hands-on arms training to educational and health programs.[59] A few possibilities for mandatory physical training emerged in the postwar nation. The most famous were plans for Universal Military Training (UMT) in the late 1940s and very early 1950s.[60] The revival of a post–World War I plan, UMT would require all American young men to engage in basic military training. A large and well-trained army, officers hoped, could prevent future wars.[61] The idea made for intense debates, as many argued that UMT violated democratic principles and the American ideal of a voluntary citizen army.[62] Arguments for UMT, in any case, appear to have focused more on the need to train men for combat itself rather than the need to improve their physical fitness. A more limited plan, which did emphasize physical preparedness rather than training itself, focused on spreading examination and physical testing, with an effort to catch potential defects before young men (and in some plans, women) might be needed for service. Democratic Representative Samuel Weiss, for instance, called for such mandatory physical exams for all kindergarten and school-age children.[63]

In conjunction with Weiss's plan, Representative Fred Hartley, a Republican representing New Jersey, argued unsuccessfully for universal training "beginning at an early age."[64] His version of universal training was no UMT, and used a decentralized model in which schools would be responsible for managing compulsory physical training. Its purpose was primarily to design and fund state and local-level programming. The official plans did not include requirements for examination. Even with these limits, Weiss and Hartley found themselves in front of Congress explaining that their bill "[did] not set up a 'Hitler youth movement' idea."[65] The funding aspect of his failed proposal meant it would have had more teeth than most, but it still was ultimately a plan based on volunteerism and a belief that American citizens would agree to improve their bodies in the name of national security.

The aggressive work of the Selective Service stands out at a moment when almost all other American projects on white male physique and body weight were managed through advisory means. In the post–World War II era, similar body projects would once again be advisory. This aggressive work was carried out for only a very brief time. Even then, we find federal power was undercut by the system of dispersed local boards and the vast network of examining doctors who did not always understand these body standards in the same way that the Selective Service leadership did. Moreover, the reach of the state was somewhat camouflaged by the use of standardized measurements. Once the war was over and the expansion of the wartime state proved beneficial to most of those who had survived the ordeal, much of the unpleasantness of the Selective Service experience—including the intimacy of mandatory examinations—was forgotten. War participation, even for the drafted, morphed into a story of male autonomy rather than boyish submission to the state.

CHAPTER 4

Selling Postwar Fitness: Advertising, Education, and the President's Council

In his novel *1984*, published in 1949, George Orwell warned of government control over civilian life. An example of this appears early in the text—mandatory, daily calisthenic exercises for all civilians. While the requirement at first seems trivial in a world that involves a constant fear of death and a prohibition on love, the scene is memorable. A young woman shouts through the television, guiding drills while admonishing her viewers: "Comrades, put a bit of life into it!" The novel's main character feigns a smile during a wretched series of toe-touches. With federal cameras surveilling him at all times, the uncomfortable routine illustrates a mundane yet evocative form of government intervention. As Orwell's citizens move their bodies in time with a television character, boundaries between the public and private grow hazy. The home and television become sites for building up strong workers and soldiers. The individual citizen begins the day by acknowledging that his body belongs not to him, but to the state.[1]

Orwell's dystopia resonated in early Cold War America. In Orwell's fictionalized Soviet state, even the most intimate space—the individual body—was to be planned, monitored, and shaped by government. Americans accepted the interventionist state for men in the World War II military, but in the aftermath of war, body projects were rechanneled through the advisory state. Now, the image of a regimented, totalitarian approach to fitness, however exaggerated, provided a model against which American body projects could be defined. During World War II, some aggressive body projects had been possible in the United States. In a context of emergency, male American civilians submitted to physical examinations and assessments in the name of national security.[2] In the aftermath of war, though, interventions into American weight and physique would resume an advisory format. Postwar fitness efforts would echo the Children's Bureau's 1920s focus on children and the use of advisory literature, school curricula, and voluntary (usually maternal) labor. This was no Soviet state, but that did not mean the United States was any less invested in the bodies of young Americans. Fit soldiers and workers were vital to the escalating Cold War. Advisory state techniques would thus be central to distinguishing the U.S. path to youth fitness from the Soviet path.

In the postwar era, Americans flirted with more interventionist programs like Universal Military Training. With the critical exception of the draft, though, political interventions designed to repair American manhood—to improve laborers, providers, or soldiers, say—could not be directive without undermining autonomy and independence as central tenets of white masculinity.[3] Ultimately, these programs were inconsistent with the postwar political reality. This meant new space for an advisory approach, led by The President's Council on Youth Fitness. It was originally aimed at children, but under President John F. Kennedy the Council was expanded to bring attention to adult men and—for the first time on this large a scale—adult women's fitness.

While much of the discourse around strength, muscularity, and manly independence was centered on how the postwar American man should navigate the changing world, the Kennedy and Johnson administrations introduced programs and materials that reached out to girls and women as well. While women's and girls' programming still emphasized the centrality of marriage and motherhood to women's lives, by the early 1960s it had also identified young women as paid workers. In the Eisenhower years, white women's relationship to paid work was deeply structured by Cold War expectations of family unity and women providing the "warm hearth" against the specter of nuclear annihilation and cold Communism.[4] The reality of women's work, however, was more complicated. Many women, especially lower-income women and women of color, worked outside the home even after (or instead of) marrying and having children.[5] As policy makers concerned with American fitness planned programs, especially in the early 1960s, they recognized the growing visibility of white women in the remunerated workforce, and adapted policies concerned with worker bodies to include these female bodies as well.[6] As white stewardesses and stenographers joined the pool of American "manpower," physical fitness programming increasingly added woman-friendly variations of exercises to pamphlets and jump-roping girls to their advertising.

Even as the practical interest in women's fitness grew, the language of the program still typically focused on men's labor and anti-Communist ideology. Bud Wilkinson provided some of the most explicit arguments about the connection between American physical fitness and American liberties. John Kennedy appointed Wilkinson, head coach of the Oklahoma Sooners football team, to the President's Council on Youth Fitness in the early 1960s. As a celebrity spokesman for the President's Council in the mid-1960s, Wilkinson argued that "no free man can admire the Soviet system" of calisthenic drills, but still acknowledged "the system has its strengths."[7] Wilkinson would now be tasked with finding an equally effective fitness system aimed at the free man, the American man.

This search for a new fitness regimen did not, by any measure, mean the political desire for strong, heterosexual male bodies was on the decline, or that American politicians were not worried about men's fitness practices. Rather, by the 1950s, a number of Americans in government had become preoccupied with the American body shape and strength. Wilkinson, for instance, worried that American boys would not be as fit "as the Russians who will challenge them in the years to come." He decried the poor stamina and "flabby muscles" of American youth, and complained that key American values like vigor, sacrifice, and work were emphasized less and less. He was not alone. At the end of World War II, the Federal Security Agency argued that "Japan would not have dared attack us if she had not known of our physical softness and lack of fitness."[8] General Lewis B. Hershey, director of the Selective Service System, reflected on postwar bodies. While he had never been pleased with American fitness, he now declared Americans were "a Nation of Weaklings."[9] Similarly, Republican Representative Fred Hartley of New Jersey said that American "weakness in physical condition" had been responsible for some of the loss of life in World War II, and that Americans were continuing down the same path in the 1950s.[10] Manly American strength would protect the nation, and would be critical to any lasting postwar peace, these leaders suggested.

In the early Cold War context, the political, sexual, and physical weaknesses of American men were discussed interchangeably and, as the nation tried to recover from one war and prepare for another, the urge to eliminate them grew quickly. Wilkinson, Kennedy, and other Cold War liberals seemed to see Americans lagging in physical fitness everywhere they went. Like the softness of the Civilian Conservation Corps men and of World War II rejectees, this postwar concern over unfit Americans was about politics, gender, and sexuality as much as it was about actual physique. At a moment of fierce anti-Communism, being too far to the political left might suggest Communist sympathies, and with it anti-Americanism. To be "soft" on Communism was to position oneself against the rugged individualism that was at the core of American self-definition in the 1950s and 1960s.[11] Additionally, Cold War masculinity imagined "softness" not simply as the opposite of manly "hardness," but also as being at risk of Communist penetration.[12] The unfit body was now doubly dangerous, and the rampant use of softness rhetoric emphasizes this. In 1949, public intellectual and future Kennedy speechwriter Arthur Schlesinger described some progressives as "Doughfaces."[13] Joseph McCarthy conflated such softness with sexuality when he suggested any man against his crusade was a "Communist or a cocksucker."[14] Not just rhetoric, red-baiting of the early Cold War included campaigns to purge homosexual men from the State Department based on the assumption that those men could not be trusted with the nation's secrets.[15]

President Dwight D. Eisenhower, and later President John F. Kennedy, responded to the perceived weakness of American bodies though the development and expansion of the President's Council on Youth Fitness.[16] The council relied on a public-private network and on media partnerships to spread its messages and advice without alarming those concerned about state overreach. While the U.S. federal government expanded its reach in the 1950s, especially through defense spending during the Cold War, concerns about keeping the United States a democratic, non-Communist nation grew.[17] When discussing how to best institute an *American* fitness program, then, experts emphasized the importance of avoiding "mass regimentation."[18]

The council relied on a public-private partnership to disseminate its fitness message, as it attempted to address what many believed to be a serious American unfitness problem through advisory state mechanisms. Always contrasting its project with the body projects of the Soviets, the council embraced capitalism, consumer culture, and notions of individual choice to promote changes in American physique. In the Eisenhower years, it encouraged parents and teachers to take charge of their children's weights and fitness levels. It also leaned on groups like the Boy Scouts, religious organizations, and community centers to take up its project. Later, under Kennedy, the council used the mass media to get these messages across. A public-private partnership with leaders in the advertising industry meant that advisory state work would now be done with the uncompensated assistance of professionals. This relationship made capitalism and the market central pieces of the President's Council's campaigns, and helped position a growing advertising industry as the key mouthpiece of the new advisory state.

The Problem: The Muscular State of the Union

In the early 1950s, politicians feared that average Americans did not have the bodies that a superpower's citizenry ought to have. In 1955, publications from *U.S. News and World Report* to the *New York Times* to *Sports Illustrated* fixated on the unflattering results of an international fitness test. *Sports Illustrated* editors concluded that physical unfitness in the United States "[went] far deeper and [had] more serious implications for the future of the nation" than most thought.[19] Nutritionist Jean Mayer described the "muscular state of the union" as "flabby" based on the test.[20] Although reports like this one occasionally substituted unfitness or softness for weight-based concepts like overweight or underweight, they more commonly adopted some vaguer language about musculature without a direct weight reference. President Eisenhower and his advisers supposedly pored over the results, ultimately deciding they had to take action.[21]

Even as media reports deemphasized poundage, they increasingly relied on health statistics and quantitative evidence of bodily strength. The most publicized report was about the Kraus-Weber tests, the work of sports medicine professor Hans Kraus and posture expert Dr. Sonja Weber, which *Sports Illustrated* featured in 1955.[22] The pair had studied American boys and girls in the late 1940s and early 1950s. Their tests compared American and European physical fitness. Kraus and Weber included about 4,000 American children and about 3,000 European children (selected only from Austria, Italy, and Switzerland) between the ages of six and sixteen. Children performed sit-ups, toe-touches, and four other exercises for the lower back and abdominals as part of the test. Kraus and Weber included five muscular strength tests and one flexibility test in the battery.[23]

Almost 60 percent of American children sampled failed at least one of the six tests. Forty-four percent of American children failed the flexibility test, while fewer than 8 percent of European children failed that test. The children on both continents fared better on strength tests than flexibility tests. Still, about 36 percent of Americans failed at least one strength test although only about 1 percent of European youth failed.[24] According to these tests, which Kraus described as studies of the "minimum" rather than optimal levels of fitness, American youth were falling far behind their European peers. Just out of a war in Europe, their comparative unfitness took on new significance.

The Kraus-Weber tests probably said far less about American fitness than its creators claimed. In the years immediately following the publication of the tests, some fitness researchers attempted, without success, to replicate Kraus's results. Marjorie Phillips at Indiana University tested about 1,500 American children and found the children passed at far higher rates than Kraus-Weber had stated.[25] Their back strength and abdominal exam results proved far better than what Kraus had found. Phillips would not wholly denounce the Kraus-Weber tests, but argued that there had been a "serious misrepresentation of true conditions," which she attributed to "inept analysis" and "irresponsible reporting."[26]

Accurate or not, the Kraus-Weber tests and other statistics making the rounds played into existing anxieties about American softness, in all its meanings, and the Kraus-Weber write-up was "the report that shocked the president."[27] The report actually seemed to prove what many already believed about American unfitness. The results received a great deal of publicity, and the efforts of the minority of scientists and researchers who tried to disprove them only further evidenced the influence of the tests.[28] The tests were also only one piece in a growing cultural obsession with male softness and unfitness after the war.[29] In the years following the release of the test results, headlines increasingly insisted that "overweight is . . . a very serious health hazard" and that obesity is "the greatest problem in preventative medicine in the United States today."[30] As American political leaders tried to adapt to a postwar culture that would emphasize national security and heteronormative, male-headed nuclear families, the idea that they lacked men who were adequate to head these postwar families was unacceptable. The tests proved what American politicians already believed about American men's bodies—that they were too soft, too queer, too flabby, and that they required intervention.

The Kraus-Weber tests proved especially irksome to President Eisenhower, himself both a health fanatic and a believer in the need for martial fitness. Eisenhower had made a personal hobby of weight and fitness, and was as primed as anyone to act on these test results. While in office he encouraged the weight-loss efforts of friends and colleagues to the point of hosting weight-loss contests. He wrote about the benefits of a lower carbohydrate, lower fat diet for weight loss and general health.[31] He had also been a five-star general during World War II, and had not forgotten the shame of a nearly 50 percent rejection rate from that war's draft. Eisenhower described the Kraus-Weber results as "alarming" and a sign that the nation was in "a very serious situation."[32] He then called for a public response to the problem of children's unfitness.[33] As its first public event to address anxieties over unfitness, the Eisenhower administration hosted a luncheon discussion on American physical fitness in the summer of 1955.

Eisenhower and the Creation of the President's Council on Youth Fitness

The first federal luncheon on youth fitness included ample discussion of advisory state fitness measures, and limited discussion of federal intervention in the form of either resources or rules.[34] Eisenhower appointed Vice President Richard Nixon to head early discussions of unfitness. Nixon later emphasized the glory of mass consumerism, especially the same modern conveniences that critics increasingly linked to national unfitness (his famous "Kitchen Debate" at General Mills' Betty Crocker model kitchen, for instance, featured cake mix, Cocoa Puffs, and Trix cereal).[35] Nixon, who was unexcited about spending his energies on a physical fitness campaign, focused on the role other organizations could play. Nixon wanted to encourage other groups, especially schools, to do more while minimizing the role of the state in the fitness project. The experts in attendance ranged from Dr. Kraus and Dr. Weber, to Kraus's friend and fellow fitness crusader Bonnie Prudden, to sports celebrities like baseball hero Willie Mays.[36] The group drafted a number of recommendations meant to improve child fitness. They suggested a daily physical fitness period and recess twice a day for students from elementary through high school. The group also argued that better recreation facilities must be built throughout the country if these fitness plans were to be properly implemented. For example, school gymnasiums and pools should be open twelve months a year, and to the public. However, the declaration that better gyms and basketball courts and playgrounds should be constructed was not accompanied by a plan to allocate federal funds for local project grants. Likewise, there is no record of any

attempt to engage legislators or promote legal regulations around school
fitness. Instead, the luncheon attendants put the onus of such programming
and facility development on local community organizations and individual
educators. YMCAs, Kiwanis clubs, the American Legion, industrial leaders,
youth recreation leagues, church groups, and college coaches were to do
the legwork on these sorts of projects. From the start, then, the executive
branch program for fitness was advisory. Recommendations and pressure,
not resources or requirements, made up the goals of this first Eisenhower
administration fitness plan.[37]

Even without a fear of Communism or big government, or Nixon's
hands-off approach, shaping the direction that school fitness policy took,
generations of American education politics had already substantially limited the policy options available. Schooling in the United States had been
managed primarily at the state and local levels since the nineteenth century,
and administrators assumed this decentralized control would remain the
standard even when the federal government introduced new goals and
plans like this fitness programming.[38] While funding often came in blocks
from the federal government, and schools around the country legally had
to comply with Supreme Court rulings like the necessity for desegregation
under *Brown v. Board*, state and local school boards maintained control
over decisions like whether or not, and how, physical fitness might be
incorporated into curricula.[39] Even the 1953 creation of the Department of
Health, Education, and Welfare did not overhaul the long-standing structure of this relationship.

The luncheon group then planned a conference on the subject of American fitness. Organizers invited over a hundred representatives of different
groups, the kinds of groups that would be exhorted to assist with the project
in the near future. The majority of invitees came from youth organizations,
civic groups, and nonprofits that already had a history of concerns about
physical fitness. The organizers wanted them to invest in the project from
the beginning. Chief of the Children's Bureau, Martha Eliot, and Marion
Folsom of the Department of Health, Education, and Welfare represented
agencies with longtime investment in child weight and fitness, such as the
Baby Weeks and Children's Year of the late 1910s. Heads of the voluntary
organizations that had long made some of those advisory body projects
possible, including the Boys and Girls Club, the Camp Fire Girls, 4-H, the
Girl Scouts, and the YMCA, were invited. The American Medical Association was there, representing the progression of child measurement and

height-weight into the realm of the professional and medical. National
security concerns tied to physique were also represented, with Surgeon
General of the United States Army Silas B. Hays in attendance.[40] The
remaining attendees—about one-third of the conference, by organizers'
estimates—"would include outstanding, serious-minded sports figures."[41]
These included golfer Robert T. Jones, boxer Gene Tunney, and "Mr. Basketball" himself, George L. Mikan. Their inclusion hinted at the important
role that celebrity culture would play in postwar fitness programs, as well as
in the postwar project of modeling ideal masculinities for youth to emulate.

The conference shared the luncheon group's investment in advisory
state methods, but it also welcomed a substantial mass media presence,
including CBS, NBC, ABC, and MBS (the Mutual Broadcasting System—a
major radio network). The President's Conference invited one writer and
one broadcaster from each major news station. Representatives from the
United Press Association, the Associated Press, and the International News
Service were also invited.[42] While previous national body projects had
included nonprofit and educational partners, mass media in the 1950s was
a much more important cultural touchstone than it had been before. As a
result, the conference catered directly to reporters in a way previous governmental body projects had not done. These reporters were not invited
simply to cover the conference, but to participate in it. In the postwar age
of mass media and mass consumption, it seemed possible that a major news
outlet might be just as useful an advisory state tool as a major nonprofit
organization.[43]

In addition to individual networks, the conference launched a partnership between the Advertising Council and federal fitness advocates. Theodore Repplier became the primary contact between the groups. Repplier
rose in the advertising industry by preparing ads for Packard, *Time*, and
General Foods, but began to work on public service announcements supporting the federal government during World War II. He became executive
director of the War Advertising Council in 1943, preparing campaigns
aimed at using women, retirees, and individuals with disabilities on the
home front. When the War Advertising Council was reincarnated simply as
the Advertising Council in 1946, Repplier served as its first president.[44]

Executives imagined that a public project of free "advertising in the public
interest" would clean up the dark image of the advertiser and help the industry avoid federal regulation and taxes that seemed to loom on the horizon.[45]
Eisenhower described the Ad Council as "one of the most important agencies

in the country."[46] Advertising was the ultimate symbol of open markets, free choice, and the pursuit of individual desires. Folding advertising into government projects helped develop the contrast between American and Soviet federal state–citizen relationships. Public service announcements and other social advertisements used what Eisenhower called "free cooperation . . . toward common purposes."[47] He explained that "so long as individuals do cooperate to get things done, freely instead of under coercion, our kind of society retains its elasticity and dynamism." The praise did not end there. Eisenhower appeared to have understood advertising as a critical component of helping Americans be good Americans. The Ad Council's origins in selling service to the nation during wartime helped feed this understanding.[48] "Once appreciating a need, the American people are quick to act," Eisenhower wrote. "But public education and communication are difficult. Through the advertising council complex, people are made aware of the programs in which they can cooperate. . . . You have demonstrated the possibility of public response in witness of a free society in action, at its best."[34] The administration understood the public-private mission of the Ad Council as a perfect fit with the overall message they wanted to convey. It also reflected how Eisenhower personally conceptualized Americans' relationship to the state. Media would not merely be a tool in these early Cold War fitness campaigns, then, but would also have a seat at the executive table.

The conference established American fitness as a site for modest federal intervention. Attendees focused on sounding the alarms of American unfitness, and were especially interested in reforming physical education in schools. But nothing concrete came out of the meeting. It was above all else meant to vocalize that the United States needed to remain a strong (in every sense of the word) power. Eisenhower, Nixon, and their assemblage of fitness experts moved forward cautiously. Nixon convened another conference the next year, 1956, at a site from which participants would be constantly reminded of the national security concerns that foregrounded the president's fitness project: the United States Military Academy at West Point. He began the conference by reading a statement from Eisenhower that would set the tone for the rest of the event. Echoing concerns over the relationship between national security and fitness, Eisenhower explained that all politics, all national and international policies, were "no more than words" if the American people were not physically and mentally fit.[49] Federal-level attention to fitness was necessary, he insisted. And monitoring citizen fitness fell within the purview of the federal government to the extent that it was necessary for ensuring such a government remained strong. With these words, he justified organized, large-scale intervention into the physique of American civilians.

The new attention to the government's role in physical fitness came with a firm insistence that it would be advisory, not directive. Eisenhower introduced Executive Order 10673 on the fitness of American youth. This order, signed in July 1956, established a President's Council on Youth Fitness (PCYF). The council would not, according to Eisenhower, create "an overriding Federal program."[50] Instead, it would be more like "a public relations firm for the notion of fitness."[51] Eisenhower explained that the PCYF would be staffed with members of his cabinet, who would coordinate the activities of thirty-five federal agencies invested in projects even tangentially related to physical fitness. Eisenhower imagined the government would arouse "in the American people a new awareness of the importance of physical and recreation activity." Eisenhower intended to use mass media outlets, and the assistance of the Ad Council, in developing this powerful public-private alliance.

Eisenhower appointed Shane MacCarthy, a man who had worked in both media and government positions, as the executive director of the council.[52] MacCarthy, working under Nixon, became the mouthpiece of the federal fitness project. As such, he explained that the new President's Council on Youth Fitness "*does not dictate fitness programs*" and "*does not give money for fitness*" (his emphasis). "Fitness can't be superimposed by mandate or money," MacCarthy said.[53] Instead, American educators and organization leaders would voluntarily accept federal fitness advice. Even knowing there was no financial incentive for their participation, groups like schools and camps completely restructured their physical education programming based on federal recommendations. This adoption of PCYF advice signaled patriotism, a genuine concern about American unfitness, and, at least in part, a desire to keep up with the fitness programming everyone else seemed to be offering. Many nonprofits and schools demonstrated their trust and respect for the federal government, but, at the same time, few wanted an explicit expansion of the council's powers, budget, or bureaucracy.[54] Through the early 1960s, the council maintained an office with four full-time staff members and a small clerical staff to assist them. The annual budget was a relatively meager $315,000, but this was sufficient.[55] The PCYF had social capital to spend.

Voluntary organizations quickly aligned with the PCYF, with the stated caveat that the council remain advisory and not overstep those boundaries.

The Boy Scouts of America was one of those voluntary organizations. Oscar Alverson, a regional director for the Boy Scouts of America, was explicit about not wanting to encourage the expansion of federal bureaucracy even as he assisted the new PCYF. He stated that "we will never have a physical development program superimposed and supervised by our federal government." Instead of such a program, which "would be abhorrent to Americans," Alverson suggested "a voluntary 'fitness' program to include the full use of mass educational media and salesmanship; television and news."[56] Alverson's statement so neatly summarized the mission of the early PCYF that the council included it in the pitch materials for a television program. While the show "Sport Rama" was never produced, the selection of Alverson's words illuminated what both the council and some of its backers were seeking from the young federal agency.[57]

In addition to voluntary groups joining in, a handful of local and state level governments built and funded their own programs based on the attention brought to American fitness by Eisenhower's PCYF. Washington, Nebraska, and New Mexico all held statewide fitness promotions including fitness weeks and conferences. City governments, including those of Philadelphia and Miami, prepared local programs and initiatives meant to draw attention to the perceived failure of American physiques.[58] The President's Council encouraged these activities but did not provide many resources. Its leadership stated that it was "neither the prerogative nor the responsibility" of the President's Council to assist financially with such programming, but it would contribute intellectually. MacCarthy explained that "the council is in a sense a catalyst, a stimulator, an idea-dropper, and a direction-pointer. Its major responsibility is stimulation of the initiative of the home, and of the community with its multiplicity of youth-serving organizations and resources, including the local units of national, public and private agencies."[59] MacCarthy repeated these words regularly during his tenure with the council. He had "no funds to dole," he remarked in various venues, and "no blueprinted activities, plans, or stereotyped fitness formulae to try to lower on the people."[60] MacCarthy's articulation of the agency's agenda reflected commonly held understandings of the proper limits of state expansion in postwar America, at least as far as it involved expansion into the purportedly private realm of the body.

The PCYF hoped to get a stronger and clearer message across not only by relying on voluntary organizations but also by using its mass media connections. In early 1957, White House Assistant Press Secretary Murray

Snyder wrote to Clarence Francis, recently retired chair of the Board of Directors at General Foods. During World War II Francis had become involved with U.S. military defense, and when he retired in 1954 he began devoting all his energies to government service. Snyder hoped that Francis's private-sector connections could make the federal fitness message widespread and relatable. The man from General Foods might "be able to make a great contribution to the 'youth fitness' effort in which the President is playing a leading part," Snyder proposed. He explained that Eisenhower had recently looked over some of the President's Council's plans, and decided that if the council could get its program endorsed by a celebrity it would give the plan much more popular appeal, especially for youth. Eisenhower, inspired by his grandchildren's fascination with television heroes, thought American kids would find such an endorsement especially exciting. In an early memo titled "The President's Ideas," Eisenhower expressed confidence in advertising-based advisory work. "Have [kids] see how to become a *HERO* by the *example* of someone on TV," he explained. "We need *slogans*—advertising power."[61] This message resonated. "If—by demonstration—these muscular actors would inspire youngsters to become experts at push-ups, chinning the bar and alike, the value of that example might be incalculable," an aid paraphrased. The President's Council would be most effective, Eisenhower thought, were it handled more like a corporate advertising campaign and less like a Washington agency.

Eisenhower's PCYF pursued, but never truly succeeded at, recruiting celebrities and developing television programs that might provide an advisory approach to the American body. Snyder suggested that Roy Rogers could endorse the President's Council on Youth Fitness while discussing the nutritional value of the products during advertisements or during the show. The General Foods executive, who regularly used Rogers to sell Jell-O Instant Pudding, Toasties, and Sugar Crisp Cereal, argued that the Ad Council's message would become dated in the syndication of a show like that. The executive instead recommended endorsements in live programming, and passed the information along to the current General Foods vice president for advertising.[62] This earliest attempt was not a resounding success, but it paved the way for other market-oriented advisory state efforts.

Eisenhower orchestrated a relationship between the President's Council and the Ad Council early in his administration, but only by the very end of his time in office did the partnership take off. Shane MacCarthy pushed Eisenhower to help the process along by making more media appearances.

Figure 9. This comic was part of a larger 1963 project using the Popeye cartoon as a means to encourage youth physical fitness and promote the President's Council on Physical Fitness. The campaign was run by King Features Syndicate-TV in the name of the PCPF, a typical approach for the celebrity-oriented, corporate-driven program. King Features encouraged twenty-two of their stations to run programming based on a man in a Popeye costume leading a physical fitness challenge. The insistence on using celebrity culture and television to get the President's Council message across was an innovation of the Eisenhower years but was more successfully executed under Kennedy. General Records of the Department of Health, Education, and Welfare, entry 35, box 34, folder: Re Popeye Physical Fitness Campaign, National Archives at College Park, College Park, MD.

He agreed only in 1960, and gave a fifteen-minute television and radio appearance on fitness to kick off the first night of his Youth Physical Fitness Week.[63] MacCarthy insisted that the President's Council under Eisenhower had been a success. He said it had "galvanized scores of recognized agencies . . . and commercial enterprises of impressive size and variety into reward-ing action."[64] The council had laid the groundwork for a market-oriented, advisory approach to repairing the perceived weaknesses of the American citizen. The president had established a relationship between his fitness agency and the Ad Council that would grow substantially during the next president's tenure.

Kennedy, Soft Americans, and the Media-Savvy Council of the 1960s

President John F. Kennedy embraced a popular fitness message even more aggressively than his predecessor had, and as a result his President's Council was successful at using media for advisory state purposes. The Eisenhower-era President's Council had put the perceived unfitness of Americans on the national radar. It had made unfitness such a concern, in fact, that Kennedy addressed it in a public forum during his first full month in office. He published a *Sports Illustrated* article on what he saw as the continuing prob-lem of "the soft American." To the Kennedy administration, individual unfitness—especially male softness of the physical, moral, and sexual sorts—was a national security issue. Kennedy wrote that, "in a very real and immediate sense, our growing softness, our increasing lack of physical fitness, is a menace to our security."[65] This problem, Kennedy explained in a twist on the popular Cold War concern over a "missile gap," constituted a "muscle gap."[66] This so-called muscle gap needed to be bridged through some form of federal intervention. Unlike the missile gap, which required epic defense spending, the muscle gap would be plugged primarily with advisory state tactics. Kennedy himself was focused on masculinity and courage, concerns historian K. A. Cuordileone attributes in part to Ken-nedy's long history of medical crises.[67] Whatever the root cause of his inter-est in the topic, President Kennedy was able to get across the fitness message in a way that garnered popular appeal.[68]

Kennedy had concerns about the physical fitness of American bodies, especially those of American children. While he also had concerns about adult male fitness, that was a politically intractable problem by the early 1960s, one that had been debated forward and backward in earlier conversations over Universal Military Training. The monitoring of children, children's submission to exercise programs, public service announcements, and even fitness advice was less politically fraught than any postwar attempt to manage adult men, who had more immediate ties with the U.S. military and military training. A more approachable problem, and a pressing one given the growing sense that the Cold War world order was the new normal, was the management of children's bodies. These bodies would be the soldiers and workers of tomorrow, and they could be molded now to make that tomorrow possible.

In Kennedy's eyes, children were as unfit in 1960 as they had been in the 1950s, despite the initial efforts of the President's Council on Youth Fitness. His PCYF would build on the work of the Eisenhower administration, but also try to escalate it. The timing for the growth of Kennedy's children's program was adroit as well. In 1961 the council announced that half of a 200,000 student pilot program failed its basic fitness test.[69] Simon McNeely, a physical education teacher and an adviser to the Kennedy administration, argued that Americans were not simply failing to keep pace with Soviet fitness, but were in fact becoming less fit all the time. Referencing a study of college freshmen, McNeely said that 60 percent of young men passed a fitness test in 1948, but in 1961 only 35 percent of men passed.[70] Meanwhile, the Selective Service chief Lewis Hershey continued making the connection between youth unfitness and national insecurity into the Kennedy years. "Young Americans must be made fit—to serve our nation in its hour of need," he explained in 1962. These youth must be "fit to face the future with confidence and strength," he continued.[71] Such statements and the accompanying fitness statistics circulating in the popular press were inconsistent. Some claimed that one out of six young men were unfit, others claimed one out of four, still others one out of two—it was not the reality of the numbers but the continuing anxiety that came with them that made physical fitness as pressing an issue as it was.[72] Kennedy himself called the numbers "frightening."

Kennedy trusted the numbers too much, as many Americans did when quantification lent legitimacy to even unreasonable fears.[73] These studies and test results confirmed what he already believed, and as a result spurred him on to more aggressive rhetoric. Kennedy argued that "it is paradoxical that the very economic progress, the technological advance and scientific breakthroughs which have, in part, been the result of our national vigor have also contributed to the draining of that vigor." He continued on, blaming automation, transportation, and sedentary entertainment options for this lack of vigor. This leisure and luxury, he explained, could be "the instruments of the decline of our national vitality" and prevent continued national progress.[74] The imagined consequences of American unfitness loomed large for the president.

From the start, the Kennedy-era PCYF focused on the use of mass media to promote its advisory message. While there has been contemporary attention to the use of "awareness" advertising instead of messaging with a clear plan forward, this was not a neoliberal innovation.[75] Rather, it has long been part of the advisory state agenda. From the start, Kennedy's council made developing awareness of unfitness a top priority, and threw itself even more into advertising projects than Eisenhower's council had done. The council changed its name from the president's council on "youth" to the president's council on "physical fitness," broadening its appeal.[76] In 1961 the council hired Oklahoma football coach Bud Wilkinson as their first celebrity spokesman. Wilkinson neatly fit into Kennedy's imagination for the program, right down to his insistence that the "continued leadership and vigor of our nation depend upon our possessing superior energy, strength and stamina."[77] The updated council quickly began advertising, including a 1961 series of one-minute TV spots by astronauts (market research, now transformed into a tool for policy making, had shown that Cold War American kids *loved* astronauts). A New York City firm handled the ads pro bono, and networks like ABC provided free airtime.[78]

Kennedy's renamed President's Council on Physical Fitness (PCPF) succeeded especially in its use of this modernized advisory state. The Ad Council and the PCPF united to promote fitness with a series of print and radio ads, advice books and booklets, and music and film specials. The Ad Council's large collection of designers and writers and its extensive network of media contacts made it simple for an agency like the President's Council to run countless ads and get plenty of free airtime. By 1961 the Ad Council had fully embraced the agency, dramatically expanding the reach of the organization. It would now help the Kennedy administration sell physical fitness to American citizens through regular advertising. "We cannot *force* youth to become fit," explained one bureaucrat, "we must motivate them to *want* to do the things that will *make* them fit."[79] Comparing the job of the PCYF with that of the breakfast cereal companies he was more used to

Figure 10. This 1965 advertisement focuses on the Cold War need for strong boys and men, with an emphasis on the space race. It links living a vigorous life with meeting one's potential, especially one's professional potential. The PCPF and Ad Council published a related advertisement in 1968, which featured a boy alongside astronaut Captain James A. Lovell with a caption that read, "Any kid who wants my job will have to be in pretty good shape." Records of Temporary Committees, Commissions, and Boards, President's Council on Physical Fitness and Sports, A1 34125A, box 4, folder: Publicity #11, National Archives at College Park, College Park, MD.

working with, one Ad Council representative explained the importance of making physical fitness "palatable" and "popular" if they were going to make people "pant to buy our product."[80] The sales effort would also need to be backed up with a merchandising program, he explained. That was advertising speak for how involved parents and teachers were expected to become if the fitness message were to be translated into voluntary programming.

In the first year of the active PCPF and Ad Council partnership, they placed ads with over 600 newspapers, 650 television stations, and 3,500 radio stations. These spots were designed and placed by the Ad Council, especially relying on the advertising firm Young and Rubicam.[81] In 1963 the President's Council reported that it had used 15 million dollars of advertising "at no cost to taxpayers."[82] With the help of the organizational support of the Ad Council and the financial support of the Equitable Life Insurance Company, the President's Council even released a film. *Youth Physical Fitness: A Report to the Nation* included appearances by Gene Kelly, Bob Hope, Alan Shepard, and, of course, John F. Kennedy.[83] The film reached an audience of more than 84,000 citizens who saw it on the big screen, and another three million who saw it during one of the film's ninety television screenings.[84]

In addition to films, PCPF advertising memorably included the calisthenics song "Chicken Fat," written by Meredith Wilson (better known for composing *The Music Man*) and sung by Robert Preston (better known for starring in *The Music Man, Mame,* and other Broadway productions and films). "Chicken Fat" sold 115,000 records in its first year of release.[85] Bing Crosby's son sang what the *New York Times* referred to as a "labored" version of the song on a 1962 television special.[86] Dinah Shore sang a reportedly less labored version on the Dinah Shore Chevy Show.[87]

Despite its crossover appeal, the intended audience for "Chicken Fat" was actually primary schools. Teachers played the records in the classroom (or over the school's intercom first thing in the morning). The song exhorted its listeners to exercise "every morning," and "not just now and then." Through toe touches, push-ups, and marching in place, the calisthenics record encouraged basic exercises to a catchy tune. The PCPF-commissioned song lasted just under six-and-a-half minutes (the long version), which hardly made for a lengthy sweat session. "Chicken Fat" was more messaging than programming. Like other PCPF campaigns, the song reminded youth of the importance of a hard (not soft) body and of vigor as a component of good citizenship. As the song phrased it, "nuts to the flabby guys!" Its lyrics insisted instead that kids "give that chicken fat back to the chicken, and don't be chicken again."[88] With the relationship between fat and cowardice (being "chicken") established, the song exhorted all the students to sing the final refrain aloud to really hammer it in: "go, you chicken fat, go!" The song, with its comments about "flabby guys" and "chicken fat," centered on concerns about failed wartime masculinities, especially linking the soft body with cowardice. While the song referenced school girls' participation as well (while reifying their status as an afterthought, with lyrics like "Alright girls, you're in this too!"), the overriding anxieties about crafting a martial, heterosexual masculinity colored the performance.

Alongside media campaigns, Kennedy's PCPF continued to rely on schools. In addition to incitements to exercise and the "Chicken Fat" song, new school programs increasingly proposed fitness testing in schools. While the Eisenhower-era PCYF promoted general movement, play, and activity (what they called "total fitness"), Kennedy-era advertisers opted to include specific guidelines and parameters for what that fitness should look like.[89] Kennedy himself agreed, desiring what has been called "a utilitarian, systemized approach based on measurable performance standards."[90] In August 1961, Bud Wilkinson offered a five-point program for youth fitness in the American Medical Association publication *Today's Health*. He advocated fitness screening for children and exercise programs for students who failed fitness tests.[91] The programming suggestion was perfectly in line with the small government ideology/big government aims of the council, and it turned Wilkinson's ideas (which had been developed with oversight from medical and educational organizations) into a 112-page book. Alongside its partnership with the American Medical Association to spread and support Wilkinson's message, obtaining voluntary participation from schools remained a part of the President's Council's mission.

The next year, Wilkinson pressed harder for fitness testing and group calisthenics by urging schools and school boards to initiate programs based on PCPF booklets.[92] At multiple points in one speech, Kennedy emphasized just how voluntary such programming was. "The Council does not desire to prescribe specific activities or tests. However, it strongly encourages every school to adopt the basic philosophy of Wilkinson's program." As a starting point, the president recommended that interested parties send forty cents to the U.S. Government Printing Office for a copy.[93] Such campaign-based programming further distanced the council from those it was theoretically designed to serve. Still, the program was working when measured against President's Council goals: almost 28,000 schools had requested programming information from the federal agency by 1964.[94]

The push toward physical testing and calisthenics slowly transformed physical fitness programming in schools. According to the council's published statistics, fewer than 18 million school children had participated in physical education programs in 1961, while about 27 million had by 1964. Sixty percent of those students had a physical education program of some sort at least three times a week. At the encouragement of the council, schools elected to conduct fitness tests on about 55 percent of school-age children.[95] Some of these fitness initiatives even got to the point of political and legislative interests at the state and local levels. By 1963 thirteen states had formally strengthened their physical education requirements, and thirty-one states had some sort of state level fitness commission.[96] By 1964 twelve states had toughened their requirements for school accreditation in health and physical education.[97]

Especially in its school programming, and in the early 1960s in physical fitness campaigns, the President's Council also began to specifically promote fitness for girls. As with "Chicken Fat," the language was still of girls as afterthoughts, but it is notable that the council now made even that effort. "Physical fitness is for everybody," one radio ad prepared for the council explained, "girls, too."[98] Like the promotions aimed at boys, the council also framed its advertising for girls around potential career paths with the tagline "the future is for the fit." Bud Wilkinson explained how the PCPF might apply to girls. "What do you want to be when you grow up?" he asked all the children. "A doctor or an engineer? A scientist or a technician?" Then he added that, "if you are a girl, you may plan to combine a career in teaching, business, or some other field with being a housewife and mother."[99] The vision of what the future might hold for fit young women (usually, though not exclusively, assumed to be white and middle class) was certainly not the same as the image of a fit young man's future. As one television spot explained: "girls, besides helping you shape the *future*, physical fitness does pretty nice things for your *own* shape, too!"[100] While the program language highlighted the limited career opportunities for girls, the inclusion of a physical fitness component for girls was a reflection of changing economic realities. The council did not seek to undermine its heavy interest in the heterosexual family unit by overemphasizing extrafamilial work for women, but it did want to optimize the bodies of those women who would join the nation's paid workforce.

The PCPF focused most of its energies on youth fitness, where the most malleable bodies and greatest political access was possible, but in the late Kennedy years the council also started to take up the cause of adult fitness. Council projects aimed at adult physical fitness were always intensely voluntary, and since they could not use the existing public school infrastructure, they never gained the traction that youth fitness programming did. Still, by 1963, the council published a new document, its *Official U.S. Physical Fitness Program*.[101] The program was aimed at adults and children, and was built on the idea that American unfitness could be corrected not only in future generations but also in current generations.

The PCPF shifted to include girls and adults of both sexes in its fitness project as a result of increasing attention to the economics of unfitness. While a military impetus for fitness programming and filling muscle gaps remained strong, a discourse about the necessity of fitness for economic reasons was gaining in importance as well. Campaigns for adults considered how the physically unfit adult, however intelligent, was not living up to his or her potential. Poor physical fitness was imagined to contribute to inadequate work performance. Critics voiced concern that American civilians were too weak to hold down jobs, especially the unknowable jobs of the future. Absenteeism and industrial accidents were attributed almost entirely to employee unfitness, and, according to one federal statistic, a full 1.25 million people were absent from work every day because of this.[102] Adult unfitness was expensive, American business research suggested.

The employability of men relied as much on their metaphorical strength as their physical strength, especially as increasing numbers of middle-class jobs became sedentary. Even though men did not need physical strength to perform many jobs in the changing economy, broad fears of "softness" among American men spoke to more than muscular strength. In the early 1950s, State Department and Veterans Administration purges of gay men as security risks firmly linked sexuality and employability.[103] Additionally, the policy interest in reaffirming the heteronormative family unit during the Cold War also pushed this broad definition of fitness to encompass normative sexuality as well as musculature. Especially after the perceived excesses of wartime sexuality, policy makers sought ways to reduce the threats of both homosexuality and nonmarital sexuality they imagined as other drains on the nation's manly strength.[104]

The growing role of white, middle-class women in the remunerated economy reinforced the idea that the American family unit was under threat. In the 1950s 29 percent more women entered the workforce. In the 1960s that figure grew by 39 percent.[105] Many women temporarily entered the workplace in World War II, and typically those women who could afford to do so then left or were forced out at the end of the war.[106] In the postwar boom, though, new jobs in clerical work, retail, nursing, and teaching required white-collar female workers. At the same time, higher marriage rates and earlier weddings meant there were fewer unmarried women available in the pool of workers, resulting in pink-collar professions increasingly opening up to married women with children. Additionally, there was plenty to consume in the postwar period. This further encouraged some middle-class families to consider sending the woman into the paid workplace in order to conform to a trend of rising consumption. By 1960, 40 percent of women over sixteen had participated regularly in the paid workforce.

In the wake of so many women entering the paid economy by the mid-1950s and early 1960s, the female employee's physique increasingly drew new attention. This was particularly true as the class composition of working women also adjusted. While women have always worked for wages, these women were usually young, unmarried, and childless middle-class women who worked temporarily, and of course low-income, immigrant, and black women. But by the early 1960s, white women with college degrees were entering the workforce and staying there. The bodies of women of all classes were now imagined to be at risk for failing at productive work, not just the reproductive work that had been historically emphasized. Men's bodies were then rendered even more vulnerable as they experienced threats from both a sedentary lifestyle and emasculating female coworkers.

As the position of women in the economy changed, so did their relationship with the state. Alice Kessler-Harris has argued that "economic citizenship" is a critical component of access to national citizenship that political theorists have long overlooked. For women, economic citizenship has been largely unattainable, not by choice but because the idea that women were not economic citizens was unthinkingly written into legislation on such things as taxes and social security throughout the twentieth century.[107] The closer women came to becoming economically important, perhaps even economically independent, the closer they came to being citizens in the eyes of the state. In a liberal economy, political and social citizenship are impossible without economic citizenship.

It is in this context that the physical fitness and physique of women really came to the fore. Women's bodies, especially the middle-class bodies on which many assessed the future, mattered as workers. While women's physique had been heavily monitored before this period for its reproductive capacity, an increased attention to the physique of women in the mid-1950s and 1960s was most directly a result of their changing position in the productive economy.

Female workers in a modern economy, however, needed physical monitoring. They were at risk of what Bud Wilkinson considered the double threat of "stenographer's spread" and "chauffeur's spread." Stenographer's spread was the ever-widening backside attributable to sitting in a chair and typing all day, while chauffeur's spread was the same ailment owing instead to expressing excessive mothering through constantly driving ones children to and fro. Even worse in Wilkinson's analysis was that these stenographers were gaining access to electric typewriters. The lighter keys and easier typing meant lower calorie burn, in an amount that he fastidiously calculated would cause a woman to gain an extra ten pounds a year.[108] Technological improvement, Wilkinson explained, "has made more secretaries fat than the two-hour lunch."[109] Modern working women not only suffered from jobs that were not physically demanding enough, according to critics like Wilkinson, but their poor physiques also threatened employers when those spreading rears did not show up to work or exert the necessary energy or stamina for their jobs.

PCPF/Ad Council campaigns began special efforts to appeal to women and girls, and they did so with a pointed focus on women as workers. One advertisement told mothers to "fit your daughter with a better looking future," alluding both to the understanding that women would pursue body shaping for looks more than health or strength, as well as the actual future plans of these girls beyond homemaking. The copy continued:

Mention physical fitness and most girls think about the boy they know who plans to be a jet pilot, or the one who wants to be a Navy frog man. . . . These are the ones, they feel, who must be physically fit. They couldn't be more wrong. Physical fitness is for everyone . . . including your daughter. Vivaciousness and grace in social situations . . . energy and stamina to see a job through cheerfully and efficiently: That's physical fitness . . . a simple matter of looking, feeling and working your best. A homemaker, a mother, a nurse, a secretary, an airline stewardess . . . they will all be happier, more efficient, and successful if they are looking, feeling, and working their best. There is a job like one of those in your daughter's future. She'll do better at it if she remembers that the future belongs to the fit, and she prepares for it.[110]

While the advertisement, of course, emphasized the fact that many women would be homemakers and mothers for at least part of their lives, it also underscored the other economic choices they might make, and the importance of their body to those potential futures. Other aspects of the President's Council's program also put great weight on women's place in the paid workforce, especially in newer jobs that signaled their exciting future role within the economy. It was a discussion of fitness absolutely saturated with the demands of capitalism: energy, "stamina to see a job through cheerfully," efficiency, and success. This was a body project that valued looking thin and pretty but that also equated women's bodies with their economic contributions.

Wilkinson proved a particularly strong advocate for this link between the economic future and the physical body. In a speech drawing on the same themes and language of the council, he said, "Whatever you want to be, your dreams are more likely to come true if you are physically fit." The problem was that "when your muscles are not used enough, they become flabby and soft and cannot do all of the jobs they are supposed to do. Then, if you try to . . . work hard, you quickly become weak [and tired]."[111] Whether for women or, more commonly, for men, Kennedy-era advisory campaigns increasingly considered the relationship between fitness and employment. The President's Council even sent out form letters with Adult Physical Fitness pamphlets to the thousand largest companies in the nation, with the message that employers could use them to inspire their executives—and, in time, all their employees—to higher levels of fitness. One of the five stated goals of the council by the early 1960s was to spread private and government employee fitness programs.[112] In a nation where the rights and opportunities of citizenship were based on male employment, any theoretical threat to one's ability to do one's job was a political threat.[113] Now, though, there was a government agency designed to undo the damage. As with schools and churches, the council actively encouraged companies to promote fitness through programs and incentives, allowing workplace regulation to carry the burden of forceful programming.

The most invested employers, and the ones most able to direct the personal habits of their employees, were federal agencies. They were spurred

Figure 11. This 1965 advertisement illustrates a growing interest in the weight and fitness of young girls. It aimed to encourage mothers to address their daughters' bodies, emphasized gender-normative careers like teacher, nurse, and homemaker, with a nod toward a much less normative path (scientist). The newer interest in women's and girls' weights, like the longer-term interest in men's and boys' weights, was tied closely to middle-class career choices and productive citizenship. Records of Temporary Committees, Commissions, and Boards, President's Council on Physical Fitness and Sports, A1 34125A, box 4, folder: Publicity #10, National Archives at College Park, College Park, MD.

toward action by these fitness initiatives, starting with the Federal Aviation Agency's development of voluntary employee fitness programs. The President's Council used the Federal Aviation Agency's program as a shining example, reporting success as weight loss: in the first six months, men lost an average of seven pounds and women an average of eighteen.[114] Soon after, the program was introduced to employees at the National Aeronautics and Space Administration (NASA) and the Department of Health, Education, and Welfare (HEW). While federal agencies became the first to institute voluntary employee fitness programs, mirroring some of the work the PCPF had done in schools, they did not spark much in the way of a broader trend. The PCPF had neither the interest nor the authority to make demands of private-sector American businesses or their employees.

Youth advertising, in a similar vein, used the language of "pioneering," which united issues of economic success, the future, and masculine independence, and proved popular in explaining the goals of a physical fitness program. Youth in poor physical shape supposedly had a worse attitude toward schoolwork, earned lower grades, and skipped more classes than their fit peers.[115] The numbers used to support these assertions were questionable, and the differentiation between the grades of the fit and unfit was insignificant. Even dramatic differences, however, would only prove a correlation rather than a causal relationship. Nevertheless, the idea of a threat to productivity from poor fitness spread. How would postwar economic growth continue with weak bodies and weak wills? Voluntary fitness programming appeared the only feasible postwar answer, though at times it left fitness experts and politicians alike frustrated by slow progress.

At the 1960 Democratic National Convention, Kennedy declared that the nation needed "leadership, not salesmanship." Through his work with the President's Council, though, the two were entangled. The actual message of the program was complicated, as Eisenhower had focused mostly on fitness as a necessity of national security, while Kennedy kept that message but also mixed in one of an individualistic rather than communal purpose to physical fitness.

In the 1950s and 1960s, the President's Council used advisory state techniques to encourage national fitness. This was not simply the result of limited financial and bureaucratic resources. Anti-Communism and antistatism led the President's Council to remain small. Instead of delivering programming, drafting regulations, or funding local level innovation, the council focused above all on public service announcements and the publication of supplementary materials. This approach had inherent problems. As Bud Wilkinson once described, "nobody's really against us or this program, but nobody's really for it, or if they are they only pay lip service to it."[116] For the President's Council, the possibility that no one would take the fitness program seriously was still preferable to an expansion of state power or bureaucracy. Ironically, the tools that had been singled out as weakening America were selected for use in physically strengthening America. As public intellectuals and even Kennedy himself blamed affluence for weakening America, advertising campaigns became one of the few politically acceptable ways of trying to physically strengthen citizens.

The council grew in size after Kennedy, but it remained consistent with advisory state principles and programs. Under Lyndon B. Johnson, the fitness campaign grew even more focused on the individual. Americans became increasingly interested in this less democratic purpose to fitness, and increasingly pursued programs with an interest in private gains. While the PCPF and policy makers remained concerned about population level fitness, programming was often aimed at individual rather than democratic goals.

Johnson renamed the council once again, dubbing it the President's Council on Physical Fitness and Sports.[117] The emphasis on sports was meant in part to resist some of the rigidity of Kennedy-era calisthenics and fitness measurement, instead focusing a bit more on games and team sports.[118] While much of Johnson's work with the council, like so much of the work of his presidency, centered on continuing the legacy of Kennedy, Johnson still put some of his own agenda into the council. He recommended that large sums be allocated for fitness programs aimed at disadvantaged youth. This mattered a great deal, given the structure of the council, since the schools that generally adopted council programming tended to be those with the resources to do so—not the schools typically serving low-income youth. While Johnson recommended $195 million for a youth development act and another $53 million for a physical education act, the council's efforts were never truly aimed at poor youth.[119] Body projects aimed at low-income youth and adults in the same period proved more aggressive than the advisory efforts of the council. As we will see, after the discovery of and political response to the emaciated body in the 1960s, the reach of the state in postwar American body projects depended decidedly on socioeconomics, gender, and race.

CHAPTER 5

Wasted Bodies: Emaciation and the War on Poverty

In 1965 an article in the journal *Nutrition Reviews* proclaimed the end of hunger in America. Encouraging nutritionists to instead focus on obesity, the author explained how "nutritional deficiency diseases . . . have almost disappeared."[1] She was not alone. Most Americans seemed sure that "nobody starves in America," as one news article later reflected.[2] Americans' dogged instance on this point reflected optimism around postwar abundance and apparently limitless economic growth.[3] It was against this backdrop that the President's Council on Physical Fitness pushed Americans to avoid "softness," and not let national abundance reshape their waistlines. For several years, hunger was converted into a foreign policy issue for Americans, something they related to nations in turmoil. It was not a domestic issue in the American imagination.

Just three years later, discussion of domestic hunger was inescapable. Now *Nutrition Reviews* reported that "there is considerable malnutrition in our country."[4] There was no need to hunt down a nutrition journal for debate over hunger in 1968, though. The Field Foundation released a heavily publicized report on malnutrition. A group of nonprofit leaders founded a pressure group, the Citizens' Board of Inquiry into Hunger and Malnutrition in the United States. Nearly every major paper ran stories on the subject, and network television programing splashed hungry children on screens across the country. By 1968 Americans had "discovered" domestic hunger, and the attention to the issue shaped domestic policy—and certain citizens' bodies—in the years that followed.

In the late 1960s, hunger politics and racial politics collided in what became a debate over how body politics apply to different Americans. The advisory state tactics at the heart of managing body weight and physique typically assumed a rational client (like the teachers and middle-class parents of the President's Council), or at least a client who could learn to be rational through quantification (like the mothers influenced by the Children's Bureau health programs). When policy makers in the late 1960s sought to address the emaciated bodies of poor Americans, often women and children of color, both the political Left and Right were wary of applying advisory techniques to manage those who had so long been characterized as irrational citizens.

The image of the emaciated child suggested a need for federal intervention, especially with the imagined single-income family of the 1930s still at the center of social welfare planning.[5] Interventions ranging from the Food Stamp Program to the Civil Rights Act all suggested there was a place for an activist program. The original left-liberal proposal was a plan to increase food access for low-income Americans—essentially to improve existing food welfare programs. This was not a proposal made up of nutrition regulations or restrictions. Such restrictions were unnecessary if one imagined the problem to be one of access—simply make food accessible, and people would be fine. In a sense, this was to be the anti-advisory state—hands-on, tangible benefits without the moralizing that sometimes came with health advice or with social welfare programs like Aid to Families with Dependent Children.

While this model provided the most freedom for welfare clients, it was actually grounded in a problematic understanding of them—especially of female and nonwhite clients—as docile and helpless. This was especially telling since it coincided with the height of the organized welfare rights movement in the United States, a moment when reality quickly countered any claims of meekness. When the emaciated body provided evidence of the legitimately hungry body, it encouraged a move to food stamps without purchase requirements, and with few restrictions on purchases.

On the other end of the political spectrum, however, some Southern Democrats tried to counter these claims for intervention and benefits by invoking the overweight black body. Depending on who deployed the language and imagery of the overweight black southerner, it typically conveyed both that low-income Americans had access to enough food and that, if they needed any state intervention at all, they needed intervention in how to use their money. In most cases, the image of the overweight black American was meant to bolster the idea that the American state should get out of the food welfare business. Unintentionally, though, it actually convinced many that *greater* federal intervention was needed in the form of advisory state programming. Rather than countering claims that black, rural southerners lacked food, in the longer term the obsession over the weight of welfare clients and the desire for visual evidence of their suffering (or nonsuffering) created a demand for increasing control over client consumption and physique.

The rediscovery of hunger came as the U.S. poverty rate had been declining and federal food aid programs, like the 1964 Food Stamp Program, had been improving. These changes in fortune, however, were experienced unequally. In retaliation for the successes of the Civil Rights Movement, some social welfare offices reportedly held back food aid from black clients, especially if those clients had registered to vote.[6] The lack of aid was both a way of keeping social hierarchies in order, and more practically a way of ensuring cheap, desperate laborers who would be available for seasonal agricultural labor.[7] The growing expectation that hunger should be a thing of the past in this affluent nation, however, was challenged by the mid-1960s media attention to inequalities in food access.

Popular Senator Robert F. Kennedy went to observe the rural hunger in Mississippi during the spring of 1967 and news crews followed.[8] Prompted by Michael Harrington's bestseller on poverty, *The Other America*, Kennedy was neither the first nor the only member of Congress concerned about hunger in that moment.[9] Still, the Kennedy celebrity brought critical media attention to malnutrition. The fact that television crews went down to Mississippi when Kennedy did was part of the visualization central to the rediscovery of hunger. In the late 1960s, the black body became a standard image of American want.[10] As a result, the story of hunger in those years became a story centered on the black body. For Democrats like Kennedy, the thin, bony body of a black child, sometimes with a belly bloated from starvation, symbolized the epidemic. This emaciated body seemed proof of a lack of access to food, and indicated large-scale economic inequalities. The images became omnipresent in contemporary news coverage, books, and documentaries on hunger. They provided an image of hunger that was more difficult to contest than words alone, and for those in favor of expanded social welfare programs, the images provided justification for action. Liberals primarily communicated about the social harms of hunger through images of emaciated black bodies.

Critics on the right, mostly Southern Democrats, also adopted the black body as a symbol of domestic poverty in this period, albeit to tell a diametrically opposed story. To these critics, the malnourished body was physical evidence that black Americans made bad choices about food. Indeed, looking at the same images of malnourished Americans of color, some on the left declared the subjects dangerously thin while some further to the right declared them problematically fat. For Southern Democratic critics of food welfare, the physical appearance and approximated weights of malnourished clients functioned as evidence of the clients' own missteps. These critics looked south and saw not underweight black children, but—likely influenced by antiwelfare iconography—large black families. These were not blameless bodies, the critics argued, but rather the bodies of irresponsible parents and lazy workers.[11]

There was ample cultural and historical baggage around the idea of the black body, especially the black female body, and its consumption habits, which made it such a powerful political symbol. Political observers situated hunger within a number of stereotypes that surrounded black consumption, including the idea that black Americans had lowbrow culinary tastes, and thus needed less aid.[12] Southern Democrats' stereotypes about black consumption and black physique reached back even further, though, back to shifting ideas of the "mammy" figure. During American slavery, the fat mammy figure served as an overabundant maternal figure. Her love for her white charges was so genuine, and so extensive, that white slaveholders did not need to feel guilty for exploiting this maternal labor.[13] While the mammy remained in the American imagination long after the end of slavery, by the 1960s that image of abundant black womanhood was contrasted with another image—that of the black welfare mother. Eventually branded the welfare queen, she was portrayed as having as much excess flesh as the mammy. The media portrayed her as a failed mammy who was the cause of her own and her children's poverty.[14] Her fat signaled a lack of a work ethic rather than an abundance of motherliness.

As the black welfare mother stereotype suggested, the Democratic mainstream argued that body size and weight were attributable primarily to individual choices. The solution was not more food aid; it was more nutrition education and purchasing advice. While Lyndon Johnson and Orville Freeman, secretary of the Department of Agriculture, had been enlarging the American social welfare state for years, their decisions about hunger were based on popular narratives blaming black welfare mothers for their poverty. These decisions shaped the trajectory of American food welfare programs.

Embodying Hunger

"If you will go look," the left-leaning Citizens Board of Inquiry into Hunger and Malnutrition wrote in 1968, "you will find America a shocking place."[15] The emaciation narrative took over discussions of poverty in America that year, replacing most general discussion of poor living conditions with a specific, embodied idea of poverty. Southern black children had "hollow eyes," were "thin," and lacked "much energy," observers noted.[16] The Citizens Board wrote that they had "found evidence overwhelming their worst preconceptions," and that "shocked their educated and carefully briefed sensibilities."[17] These advocates suggested that hunger was a widespread social problem, not an individual problem. The coupling of poverty and emaciation seemed useful evidence that direct intervention was necessary.

Senators Robert Kennedy and Joseph Clark asked to see evidence of this problem themselves. The spark that engaged Kennedy, and in turn got the cameras down to Mississippi, was simply a Senate hearing. The Subcommittee on Employment, Manpower, and Poverty was surveying American poverty in early 1967. A number of organizations were mobilizing independently on the issue, part of a larger push toward economic justice within the civil rights movement.[18] Senators Kennedy and Clark heard NAACP lawyer Marian Wright testify to the extent of hunger in the Mississippi Delta. Wright explained that many Mississippians understood the hunger in the Delta as "part of an overall State policy to not respond . . . in order to force these Negroes out."[19] "They are starving. They are starving," Wright continued. "Starvation is a major, major problem now." Clark wanted to "have the opportunity to see some things by eye as opposed to just by ear."[20] Wright agreed, and shepherded the senators through the Mississippi Delta in early April 1967.

The Kennedy and Clark trip—broadcast widely—amped up national interest in hunger. Video footage and photography from this trip captures the men seeing "by eye," and reproduced those visuals on a national scale. A *New York Times* article described a Mississippi child with "a distended stomach" with some umbilical cord still attached.[21] Kennedy himself

Figure 12. Senator Bobby Kennedy visits the Mississippi Delta in 1967, following NAACP lawyer Marian Wright's testimony that black Mississippians were being kept from federal antihunger programs and were starving. James Lucas Estate.

reportedly described what he had seen to his own children, telling them over dinner about Mississippi children who "are covered with sores and their tummies stick out because they have no food."[22] The formal report did not shake up the general public very much, but this was some of the first footage to get the discussion started. Another senator had been to Mississippi and observed the same hunger back in 1966. No one much cared. When Robert Kennedy was moved almost to tears, his celebrity encouraged others to take an interest.[23] Upon his return to Washington, Kennedy committed to fighting hunger. His assistant Peter Edelman described Mississippi hunger as a "national emergency," and the two men angled to get President Johnson to declare it as one.[24]

Johnson's administration was less easily convinced. Some people reflecting on the period have attributed this to the miserable relationship between Robert Kennedy and Lyndon B. Johnson. Johnson was hardly eager to embrace Kennedy's pet project.[25] The tension was as likely political as personal, though. The Food Stamp Program had first seen light on his brother John F. Kennedy's watch, but it was Johnson who signed the legislation making it permanent. The 1964 Food Stamp Act developed a system

Figure 13. Bobby Kennedy committed to fighting hunger when he returned from the Delta. While he was not the first U.S. senator to "discover" the problem of American hunger, his celebrity status meant that the images of his trip and his findings garnered public interest. Here, Kennedy and Kenneth Dean, the executive director of the Mississippi Council on Human Relations, visit a family as part of the Delta trip. James Lucas Estate.

of food coupons, meant to increase low-income Americans' access to food. While the program's transition to permanence was slow, and the problems with administering food stamps real, Johnson was proud of the program, calling it "one of our most valuable weapons for the war on poverty."[26] Secretary Freeman said that 470,000 people were receiving agriculture-based welfare in Mississippi, making it the state with the largest distribution in the nation—hardly the place where hunger should be most dire.[27] When Robert Kennedy and his allies pointed out the limitations of food stamps, they seemed to challenge all of Johnson's war on poverty policies.

Johnson needed further convincing to accept both that his food stamp plan was not adequately reaching Mississippians, and that this publicity blitz was more than just Bobby Kennedy trying to undermine him. Johnson's Department of Agriculture, headed by Orville Freeman, was responsible for food stamps and related food programs, and also distrusted the

Kennedy and Clark appearances. Just days after Kennedy and Clark returned from the Delta, in April of 1967, Freeman sent two of his own men to investigate.[28] Those men, Howard P. Davis and William Seabron, came home and begrudgingly backed the senators' stories.[29] "We saw a young baby in her house whose stomach and navel was extended, possibly from malnutrition or hunger," they reported.[30] Behind closed doors, the Department of Agriculture representatives were less impressed. One of the men confided in a superior that he believed he was "given a conducted tour" and that the scenes of hunger were "rigged."[31] That superior, explaining the exchange to Freeman, said: "right or wrong the people in Washington believe that people are starving in Mississippi. . . . I am sure somebody can find one Negro person down there that is hungry, and if we whitewash it this person will be produced and we will look silly."[32] With reluctance, Kennedy and Freeman aligned on both the need for food stamp reform and increased program oversight. What those reforms might look like, though, they could not agree on.

The Food Stamp Program became permanent in 1964, and the program quickly grew. Still, as with much of the War on Poverty, it spread unevenly as it rolled around the nation, and was unavailable in many counties for the whole of the decade. The Food Stamp Program originated in the late 1930s and early 1940s as a means of distributing surplus commodities to the poor through the "normal channels" of shops and grocery stores.[33] The program was dismantled during World War II, and was not brought back until 1961.

Even where it was available, however, the Food Stamp Program was often unpopular with clients. When simply given a choice between a federal program that doled out surplus goods, and a federal program that provided vouchers to be used to purchase goods in stores, most Americans below the poverty line preferred the voucher method. Johnson often showed off statistics to this effect. Food stamps were not such simple vouchers, though. In the 1930s, and again in the 1960s, low-income Americans were sold the stamps rather than being given them. Food stamps required an up-front payment, based on the number of family members to be fed. Clients then received coupons with a face value of about twice their outlay. Most low-income families reported that they could not produce so much money all at one time, making the Food Stamp Program difficult to use. The growth of "food deserts," wherein mass supermarkets avoided areas with low-income consumers, added problems in spending the stamps.[34] Moreover, localities were not allowed to support both a surplus commodities program and a Food Stamp Program. When a town or county switched to food stamps, the surplus commodities which had once been freely distributed were suddenly unavailable.

Here is where Kennedy and Clark parted ways with the administration. Kennedy and Clark wanted food stamps distributed for free, without an up-front buy-in—at least for the poorest of the poor. Freeman disagreed, believing that free stamps undermined the role of the USDA in the program. If food stamps were free, Freeman reasoned, the program was simply a welfare program, not an agriculture purchasing program. It would do nothing to increase food spending, which was a key rationale for the Food Stamp Program.

Democratic support for farmers, especially for large northern farmers, had been part of the backbone of the New Deal coalition.[35] This relationship continued through the 1950s and 1960s, and Freeman—the former governor of Minnesota—sought to uphold this relationship once appointed Secretary of Agriculture. In the 1960s, however, Freeman's attempts to preserve this partnership increasingly seemed a desperate clinging to the past. As the number of farmers in the United States shrank dramatically, Freeman found the emphasis on the USDA as a consumer agency rather than simply a farm agency to be a useful rebranding. If commodity spending was not just about helping a minority of large farms, but instead about feeding low-income Americans, the incredible amount spent each year on commodity supports looked much more reasonable.[36] This relationship was precarious too, though—Southern Democrats were suspicious of food aid that went to black Americans, and of the possibility that commodity supports helped northern farmers more than their southern counterparts.[37] Meanwhile, farm-oriented northern Democrats like Freeman were uncomfortable with food aid programs that evolved to help low-income Americans more than farmers. Freeman especially hated his adversarial relationship with antihunger activist groups, whom he believed were unfairly portraying USDA efforts around poverty.[38]

Even beyond his agricultural commitments, Freeman remained skeptical that there were Americans who could not afford food stamps. "How would they exist?" he reportedly asked.[39] Democrats in the Department of Agriculture surmised that "low-income families place less value on food than we think," as a way of explaining the lack of food stamp purchases.[40] Kennedy and Clark vehemently disagreed. Senator Clark accused Freeman of being unable to adjust to addressing hunger needs rather than only farmers' needs.[41] The Department of Agriculture was stalling, Clark argued.[42] A couple of months after the original trips to Mississippi, there had been much talk but no policy change.[43]

Instead, the Johnson administration arranged for a stop-gap antihunger measure. By late 1967, the Department of Health, Education, and Welfare (HEW) and the Office of Economic Opportunity (OEO) agreed to split the costs of a four-month stop-gap measure. Freeman insisted that the Department of Agriculture was not able to give out free food stamps. Instead, HEW and OEO were to provide low-income Americans who could not afford food stamps with funds to buy in to the Food Stamp Program.[44] The USDA, in the meantime, was meant to sort out its regulations. HEW and OEO made it clear that they would not take on the program long term. The clunky stop-gap measure was unsustainable. The Senate's Subcommittee on Employment, Manpower, and Poverty, which included Joseph Clark and Robert Kennedy, composed a letter to President Johnson. The subcommittee emphasized the need for action once again through the visual of emaciation. "Some of the [Mississippi] children could not go to school . . . and had distended stomachs . . . and were extremely lethargic—all of which are the tragic evidence of serious malnutrition," the subcommittee's letter explained.[45] Johnson reportedly refused to accept the letter at first, although he ultimately relented. The Food Stamp Program was not designed to fix problems like distended stomachs, but merely to supplement existing diets while improving crop prices. Even though some politicians acknowledged the limits of this system of supplementing food to fight hunger, they had put that system in place through extended, sometimes ugly, political compromises. It was hard to imagine going back to the drawing board on food assistance.

The discussion about hunger, especially talk of the emaciated black body, grew both in and outside of Washington. The Field Foundation followed the trend of sending cameras and writers down to Mississippi to capture black poverty. From mid-1967 through early 1968, the foundation sent doctors to conduct interviews, observe medical facilities, and collect data.[46] The first report they issued, *Children in Mississippi*, lent medical authority to those concerned about domestic hunger. Describing the "nutritional and medical condition" of Delta children as "shocking," the doctors' report chided the quibbling over whether there was "malnutrition," "hunger," or "starvation"—three words with very different weights, all applied to the Mississippi situation. The Field Foundation doctors reported "obvious evidence of severe malnutrition, with injury to the body's tissues—its muscles, bones, and skin." The emphasis on the physical damage caused by want, using the language of nutrition science, buttressed the case for immediate federal intervention. They saw bodies consuming their own protein tissues, they explained, and the wasting of muscles. They saw, the doctors continued, "the presence of abdominal edema (so-called 'swollen' or 'bloated' belly)." Ultimately, they rejected the more medical language of "malnutrition," instead opting for the more powerful vocabulary of starvation: "They are suffering from hunger and disease and directly or indirectly they are dying from them—which is exactly what 'starvation' means. We found it hard to believe we were examining American children of the twentieth-century." Senator Clark quickly embraced the Field Foundation report, and let the medical description stand beside the Kennedy photographs—both were undeniable evidence of starvation, he noted.[47]

Around the same time, the Citizens' Board of Inquiry into Hunger and Malnutrition made headlines with a 1968 report, *Hunger, U.S.A.,* featuring an introduction by Kennedy.[48] All these pressure groups were interconnected. The Board of Inquiry, which included the executive director of the Field Foundation, took on the American food welfare system with full force. Kennedy's introduction explained that "we must change our Food Stamp Program." He further drew lines in the sand, noting the United States must "reform the policies of the Agriculture Department, which have at times hindered the efforts to feed the poor."[49] The main text portrayed the battle over hunger as one between the Johnson administration and the Kennedy team. The report, just shy of a hundred pages, was nearly half photography. The photographs emphasized children and adults who were small, underweight, and often dirty. In the tradition of Progressive Era muckrakers, the report used photography to tug at heart strings. They also showed other aspects of poverty—especially poor housing conditions—meant to accentuate the images of hunger. The Citizens' Board report did not simply point out malnutrition, but again adopted the imagery of emaciation and starvation. The report described one-year-olds who weighed less than their birth weights, and five year olds weighing just twenty pounds.[50] Press coverage of the report described the "pathetic, near-dead babies" of the South.[51] "Hunger," said Kennedy in the introduction, "was a scar across an affluent nation."[52] Activists consistently tried to frame hunger as something visceral. This was complicated, however, as it continued to reify the idea that the physique of low-income Americans could evidence their deservingness.

Explaining the Starved Body

At the end of the Citizens Board of Inquiry report on hunger, a map identified American counties with hunger problems, and those with more pressing "emergency hunger." Half of Mississippi was shown in black, meant to signal the omnipresence of that hunger.[53] The high emergency-hunger statistics and mapping were a lob at the Johnson administration, especially at Secretary of Agriculture Orville Freeman. The USDA's antihunger efforts, the report emphasized, were not working.

Freeman was incensed. He first tried to head off the problem with a note to one of the founders of the Citizens' Board. The secretary of agriculture explained that he hoped the report's "dramatizing the need" would end up being constructive.[54] He attached a *Washington Post* article critiquing the report to his letter. "I hope we don't muff [this window of opportunity] in an orgy of emotionalism," Freeman wrote.[55] This approach led to further division. Within the Department of Agriculture, employees were split as to how to address the charges from the Citizens' Board. An agricultural nutritionist told Freeman the report overestimated American hunger, but that hunger did still seem to be a real problem requiring intervention.[56] Outside the USDA, bureaucratic opinion was also split. The surgeon general declared that "there is obvious malnutrition."[57] Freeman, though, remained defensive. The "emotionalism" he critiqued, though, would soon be much more widespread.

A little over a year after Kennedy and Clark's trip to the Mississippi Delta, *Hunger in America* aired on primetime network television. This Peabody Award–winning documentary, produced and written by Martin Carr and Peter Davis, was supposedly inspired by Kennedy, who had pitched the idea to a CBS producer during a cocktail party in 1967, according to various stories.[58] While Kennedy had no involvement with the documentary after that, the program was consistent with his and Clark's representation of domestic hunger.

The one-hour documentary used both emaciation imagery and a critique of existing Department of Agriculture programs to garner extensive attention. Beginning with a close-up of a dramatically underweight baby, the voice-over explained that "hunger is easy to recognize when it looks like this. This baby is dying from starvation."[59] The infant's death was captured on film. The narrator then segued to a discussion of how that is *not* the typical look of hunger—instead, it was hunger that was more felt than seen. "When we begin to see hunger in the faces of people," a priest working in a low-income part of San Antonio told the audience, "it is because it is no longer felt."[60] In other words, it only garners attention when it is (as with the dying-on-camera infant) too late. The film surveyed four groups of hungry Americans—white, black, American Indian (Navajo), and Mexican American.[61] Viewers learned that many were undernourished, and most were underweight. A Navajo doctor told the camera that the American Indian children living on reservations were "shorter than they should be" and "thinner than they should be."[62] The issue of domestic hunger came alive through the use of television, especially the discussion of underweight children and the evocation of sympathy.[63] In this instance, the racial composition of the groups in this story was notably more complicated than a simple invocation of the black emaciated body and all the history bound up in that image. Additionally, the bodies of the American Indian and Mexican American children were described somewhat differently. Often they were described as soft or malnourished as a result of the limited government foods available to them, while the narrative about southern black bodies was more commonly about a total lack of access. Although the racial diversity in this film indicates the complexity of lived hunger in the United States, for most policy making and advocacy this diversity was collapsed into the singular emaciation narrative in which babies and sharecroppers "were shown crippled and dying from malnutrition."[64]

Since the documentary suggested that Freeman and the USDA were those most immediately responsible for American hunger, angry letters quickly filled the department's mailroom. Freeman, who felt personally attacked and misrepresented, unintentionally strengthened the perception that he was responsible for hunger when he demanded equal time to go on CBS and explain his side. Neither the initial documentary nor Freeman's rebuttal won him support from his critics. "I kept repeating over and over that what was being portrayed just could not be true," one man wrote, emphasizing his emotional connection to the social issue came via the emaciation images. "But with the vision of child after child showing the scars of malnutrition," he continued, "it seemed to me that your department has some explaining to do." He critiqued surplus commodities, saying that provided food should have more protein, and describing the commodity products as "bland" and "white."[65] Another viewer got right to the point: "I saw you on the idiot box (T.V.) last night," he told Freeman. "You fit the role."[66]

In general, Secretary Freeman was overwhelmed by the responses he received to the Emmy Award–winning hour of television.[67] Liberals hated him, as in the letter calling him an idiot. More surprising to Freeman, though, was how many people on the right praised him for denying there was hunger in America—which was not his position. Enacting the politics of the "silent majority" that would become so critical in the election just a few months later, critics complained about the presentation of hunger and starvation in the CBS special. "These pictures were undoubtedly taken by liberals," one wrote.[68] "The people he showed looked well and healthy to me," wrote another, "It was the worst faked show I have ever looked at."[69] While the emaciation narrative seemed like incontrovertible evidence of a hunger problem to Kennedy, Clark, and the Citizens Board of Inquiry, these critics disagreed about the use of this film evidence. They were not entirely wrong, either, as the dying baby focused on in the first scene was revealed later to have died for reasons wholly unrelated to hunger (or poverty—it was the baby of a middle-class black couple).[70] Critics embraced the revealing of CBS's mistakes and manipulation, extrapolating from them that hunger itself was also a lie. One woman described the whole situation as the "poverty hoax," arguing that "if the tax-payer is gullible enough to swallow such nonsense that 10 million people is on starvation in this country, then it is tragic."[71] "The people he showed looked well and healthy to me," another wrote.[72] Freeman *did* believe there was poverty in America, though. He had been bringing this up for years, he insisted. He wanted to defend his own reputation for *fighting* that hunger, not disavow its existence. When letter writers praised Freeman for protecting the nation from the supposedly "Socialistic goals" of CBS, for instance, Freeman was taken aback.[73] Nonetheless, his office labeled most of these letters as approval for Freeman, perhaps indicating just how much he was hurting for allies at the moment.

While some critics believed *Hunger in America* was lying to them with the camera, others argued that the emaciated bodies in the documentary were perhaps real, but not representative of a larger problem. The documentary "showed a hospital that had a few starved babies," one woman wrote. "But they were neglected children from lazy and not very bright mothers."[74] Even while looking directly at images of emaciated children, the responders could dismiss them as outliers. Although the documentary featured four racial groups, these letter writers seemed to associate poverty and welfare only with black Americans. They associated black women with fatness, which they also correlated with laziness and dependence.[75] This conflation of excessive black flesh has a long history within the U.S. context, and critics of food assistance could find examples of it whenever they needed to.[76] Herein lies the core problem with the attempt to demonstrate hunger through emaciation.

Letter writers regularly based their ideas about the legitimacy or illegitimacy of hunger using low-income bodies as their evidence. "Mr. Freeman you know those would be poor in Washington are not starving," a disgruntled citizen wrote. Instead, she explained, "if they were any fatter they would burst."[77] Around the same time, Mississippi's governor refuted the claim of starvation by pointing at black women's bodies. He explained: "Nobody is starving in Mississippi. The nigra women I see are so fat they shine."[78] Another wrote that "it would be hard for me to believe those fat cheeked roly poly youngsters and their fat parents are on starvation." As with the other letter writers, this woman linked welfare mothers with laziness, and that laziness with body problems. "The mothers will not cook, they just buy light bread, bologna, pepsi cola, and peanuts and candy and junk of that kind, so whose fault is it that the children are undernourished," she asked.[79] Another letter writer complained not about welfare mothers but about the liberal priest who appeared in the documentary and supported these hunger claims. "CBS had a big fat Catholic priest" discussing hunger, the writer explained. "When one man . . . is overweight and then he tries to preach of the poor to me it doesn't make sense."[80] Emaciated bodies were suspect, as they might be fakes or frauds. Nonemaciated bodies were also suspect, however, as they undermined concerns about whether the poor really had access to food. Even the bodies of those trying to support the hungry became suspect in this telling—if they cared so much, they would have bodies that somehow reflected this.

Most frequently, conservative Southern Democrats interpreted the attention to black southern hunger as part of the threat of an expanding welfare state. In response, such critics emphasized bodies both too small and too large as evidence of poor decision making. The issue was not one of access to food, but one of making bad choices about consumption. These

Americans opposed expansions of food welfare as they would expansions of any welfare program. "Please oppose any expanded food or welfare programs in order to cut the deficit and save our dollars and to avoid socialism," one man told Freeman.[81] Another complained of the "giveaways" by the "soft headed do-gooders" of liberal politics.[82] These citizens linked fat bodies with laziness and a reliance on social welfare. One doctor writing earlier to the House Committee on Agriculture explained that "I know a great many people . . . who are . . . monstrously obese from a lifetime on 'commodities' which tend to be pretty heavy on the starch and fat content." While the authors of *Hunger USA* and *Hunger in America* made similar points to argue for the reform of commodities, this man interpreted his evidence differently. High-calorie commodities were an appropriate foodstuff, he explained, "as it enables a man to put in a good hard twelve hours in the sun on a handle of a hoe or shovel."[83] It is the lack of laboring (he is "just sitting around waiting for his next welfare check") rather than the distributed foods that were to blame. Laziness, poverty, and body problems were quickly rolled into one. The coded discussion of all these problems rested on the idea of personal economic responsibility.

Meanwhile, Freeman's confusing stance on hunger further deteriorated what was left of the Johnson administration's credibility with the Left. Freeman explained that he had increased the value of commodities by more than five dollars per person per month since he began as secretary of agriculture.[84] He explained that a welfare problem was not the same as a farm problem, arguing that food welfare should be handled by a different federal department.[85] Freeman told CBS their piece was "bluntly and simply . . . a travesty on objective reporting.[86] He had become secretary of agriculture specifically to address the hunger problem, he stated, and called it "ironic" that he was now understood to be denying hunger. He privately described the response to *Hunger in America* as his being "impaled on this wild shaft fired by CBS."[87] Freeman's old friends even wrote him angry notes. One woman, a friend of Freeman's from his days in the Minnesota Democratic Farmers–Labor Party, compared Freeman to liberals Hubert Humphrey and Walter Mondale. "You are fast becoming an empty man, a hollow man," she wrote, "I grieve for what has become of [you]."[88] Freeman dashed off a note of annoyance—"I didn't think I'd see the day when you would take Time magazine as a basis for criticizing your old friend." The secretary of agriculture was seriously upset about the backlash against his programs, and unable to understand the criticisms aimed at him.[89]

While Freeman was lost in all the backlash, there was more room for conservative Southern Democrats to take charge of this newly public problem. Jamie Whitten of Mississippi sat on the House Appropriations Committee, and W. R. Poage of Texas chaired the Committee on Agriculture. Whitten reportedly had great private sway over Lyndon Johnson. Poage, on the other hand, took his critique of *Hunger in America* public. Representative Poage mailed letters to public health representatives around the country, especially those in what had recently been dubbed "hunger counties." Poage asked these representatives for "any personal knowledge of any actual starvation in your county."[90] As his phrasing implied, Poage began from the idea that this discovery of hunger was bunk, and set out to discredit those trying to raise social welfare funding.

These Southern Democrats staked out a more conservative position than Freeman ever did, emphasizing parental ignorance and neglect rather than a lack of resources. The resulting House Committee on Agriculture publication was a compilation of the responses to Poage's question about "actual starvation." The report emphasized the personal responsibility of low-income women for their own suffering. Poage blamed a "wave of emotionalism" for all the attention to hunger, and concluded that "the basic solution to the nutritional problem in this country is to be found through education and a sharpened sense of family responsibility."[91] The press release Poage issued with the report was more provocative, advocating incentivized birth control for low-income women, and more restrictions on food welfare. Freeman was distressed that the press release misrepresented the story. A Department of Agriculture assistant summarized: "the committee overstated their 'findings' almost as badly as Hunger/USA."[92] In a more casual note affixed to the press release, the same administrator was blunter: "This is a tragic bit of farce."[93]

Poage and the conservative House Committee on Agriculture twisted the groups' claims about what the emaciated body represented. Both overweight and underweight children could be the result of maternal irresponsibility. "The basic problem is one of ignorance as to what constitutes a balanced diet, coupled with indifference by a great many persons who should and probably do know better," read Poage's report. Nixon would later adopt those words, blaming ignorance and inadvertence for American hunger at a 1969 conference. Poage's report was more sensationalist, and even blamed some malnutrition on "deliberate parental neglect." Starvation, the report explained, may have "been willfully brought on as a means of getting rid of an unwanted child."[94] The complaints about poor mothering were not subtle.

The more common explanation, though, was not a murderous mother but simply a lazy or stupid one. A southern board of health offered that "if there is a problem, it is one of education and of personal decision." The director of a North Carolina health department told Poage that "there are many indifferent and careless mothers who do not supervise the small children in their eating habits." A woman from Texas explained that her financially above-average neighbors know better but still give their children "a coke and pretzel or potato lunch."[95] Based on this observation, the woman reasoned that people "are not properly feeding their children," and that the availability of food had nothing to do with it.[96] Another Texan, a shop owner, explained that it made him ill to see people "purchase very little real food" and instead buy "popcorn, potato chips, candy bars, pop, cigarettes and many other snack items." A Mississippi relief worker complained that about one-third of low-income parents did not "bother" to pick up the available relief food. The problem was not a lack of access to food, they emphasized, no matter what photographs of Kennedy might have suggested.[97]

Poor black mothering became a regular refrain for prominent Southern Democrats, especially against the backdrop of the 1965 Moynihan Report, which cast black women as "matriarchs" helping to perpetuate their family's poverty.[98] The matriarch image and the welfare mother image overlapped in this telling, and both images suggested to welfare critics that black women did not need an expansion of benefits. Essentially, they suggested that nutrition education was necessary, but did not propose ways to provide or fund it. Some thought nutrition education would be an expansion of government and should be a private or state concern, while others argued that low-income women were basically beyond such help. Poage said that "in many cases relief clients are virtually uneducable." One Arkansas physician explained the root problem was "a poverty of mind, not matter." It was a "poverty of morals," he elaborated. In a letter published by Poage, a Georgia public health nurse explained that when she encountered hungry children, it was always "due to the parent's indifference and neglect, not to inability of the individual to buy food or receive public assistance."[99]

In the shadow of Moynihan, poor fathering, and absent fathers, also became explanations for hunger and malnutrition in Poage's report. Mothers were understood as the family shoppers, meal planners, and cooks.

Fathers, whatever the actual economic reality of the family, were the ones held responsible for bringing home a "breadwinning" wage. In the *Hunger in America* documentary, for instance, San Antonio's senior county commissioner (a villain in the documentary), explained that low-income fathers were to blame for hunger. If children were hungry, he said, it was because "their father won't work, and I mean *won't* work. . . . They won't work, do you expect the tax payer to raise all the kids 'cause the daddies won't work?" "Some men," he continued, "just ain't worth a dime."[100] Similarly, Poage's report attributed hunger to "fatherless households where numerous children are reported born and reared out of wedlock."[101] When the father was around, the Poage report also might find him to blame. Children were suffering, the report explained, because low-income fathers "spent disproportionately large sums on liquor and/or extramarital sexual relations."[102] An assortment of perceived moral failings were tied to inadequate providing.

This was the problem with the original emphasis on the low-income body as evidence of hunger, as popularized by *Hunger in America*, the Citizens Board of Inquiry into Malnutrition and Hunger, and politicians like Kennedy and Clark. In part, the nonemaciated body became proof of a *lack* of hunger to critics. Additionally, the emphasis on body weight allowed for questions about consumer choice rather than economic realities to dominate discussions about hunger. The physical body became critical evidence for proving the legitimacy and illegitimacy of hunger.

The Democratic Party had ruptured by the time of the 1968 election. Not only hunger issues, of course, but also issues of war and of economic inequality left the party rudderless. Robert Kennedy, one of the most vocal politicians on the hunger issue, was killed that summer. At the 1968 Democratic National Convention in Chicago, the party struggled with violence just outside the convention hall. Inside the hall, a centrist Democratic Party led by Hubert Humphrey adopted a platform that included expanding existing food welfare programs. While Humphrey supported these programs and some food welfare expansion, he also sidled up to the conservative stance that low-income women were creating nutrition problems for their families. Humphrey said that "mothers must make sound food investments," for instance.

Hunger proved an astonishingly divisive issue for Democrats, in turn making space for a moderate Republican co-opting of the issue. Earlier that summer, the Republican National Convention had added the hunger problem to its platform. "Recent studies indicate that many Americans suffer from malnutrition despite six separate federal food distribution programs," the platform read. "Here again, fragmentation of federal effort hinders accomplishment. We pledge a unified federal food distribution program, as well as active cooperation with the states and innovative private enterprise, to help provide the hungry poor sufficient food for a balanced diet."[103] The Republican plan borrowed the same complaints about existing food welfare that the Citizens Board of Inquiry had used, but reformulated them as attacks on bloat and wasteful spending in ways that resonated with more conservative citizens amid the late-1960s welfare backlash. That language would become even more important in the early 1970s. When a new food welfare program, the Special Supplemental Food Program for Women, Infants, and Children (WIC), was introduced, questions of both body weight and personal nutritional responsibility would be inextricable from program design. In that case, as we will see in the next chapter, the result was not an advisory food program but in fact a much more controlling food program, which took to heart many of the complaints about poor women's spending in the late 1960s.

CHAPTER 6

Poor Choices: Weight, Welfare, and WIC in the 1970s

"Out of wedlock child admitted to WIC [Women, Infants, and Children] program," read a 1975 clinic report. The nine-month-old child had a white mother, recorded as being "excessively involved in drugs," and a black father with a "local police and prison record."[1] Employees at the child nutrition clinic wrote that the young child consumed a "diet of coffee, beer, occasional meal."[2] WIC advocates later read this description into congressional testimony, hoping to convey the necessity of the program. The child in question had recently been cut from a local WIC program due to budget and caseload limitations. Nonetheless, the clinic advocates emphasized—in explaining his diet and his race—that the child needed WIC. The WIC program provided access to formula and certain foods, which certainly might help the youngster. Perhaps more importantly, the WIC program used food, surveillance, and nutrition education to guide child feeding. This combination could protect an innocent child from bad mothering, which WIC literature suggested was a low-income child's principal problem. This meant that cuts to WIC might put the child in danger, at risk of having nothing stand between itself and its mother.

WIC clinicians then added a contrasting case history to the testimony. Here, a premature white female infant stood in for all the good that a well-funded WIC program, paired with a supposedly good mother, could do. "Mother was and is very interested in nutrition education," these case notes explained. The mother "takes every opportunity to obtain nutrition counseling." This model of WIC success included not only a mother who used the (at that time optional) education components of the program, but also one who fully embraced the language of nutritional optimization. The "mother has been very interested and excited in the positive changes in her child's anthropometric measurements," clinicians recorded with pride.[3] Crafting good mothers and shaming bad ones was at the heart of WIC nutrition policy.

The origins of the WIC program lay in the hunger policy of the late 1960s. Then, politicians thinking through food stamps and surplus commodities argued over whether hungry Americans needed nutrition education or simply nutrition, over whether antihunger policy should center on the direct distribution of food or on an advisory state project to educate Americans on food consumption and diet. While most antihunger activists of the late 1960s centered their campaigns on images of the "blameless poor," especially those of the emaciated child, the plans that came out of that activism had limits. Increasingly, the "excessive" black female body, the one deemed overweight, symbolized women using social services in general and WIC mothers in particular. The fat black female body signified a lack of control, a lack of rational decision making, and more generally an unfit citizen. Against that backdrop, northern and southern Democrats remained deeply divided on social welfare issues, especially when those issues included both raw racial politics and contentious agricultural concerns. When the new Republican administration set out to address the specter of American hunger, these policy makers increasingly portrayed the problem as one of individual poor choices rather than systemic failures.

As a result of this thinking, policy makers introduced an advisory state plan to educate low-income women on food consumption as a solution. By the late 1970s, WIC added advisory programming as a prerequisite to material benefits. In the body projects of the 1920s and 1950s, the advisory state had functioned as a "soft touch" of government meant to keep a supposedly large state out of the way of average Americans. The advisory state addition of 1970s food policy did the opposite. With the recipients of welfare benefits limited to only low-income women, there was less concern that programming—advisory or hands on—would interfere with their rights or freedoms. The earlier anxiety that advisory state measures could only be applied to rational (middle-class) citizens was belied by the decision to combine advisory and hands-on body projects for WIC mothers in the 1970s. As a consequence, WIC used both advisory and more aggressive programming to correct and control the nutritional behavior of low-income Americans.

Through a combination of WIC clients being portrayed as fat (irresponsible) and on welfare (also increasingly read as evidence of irresponsibility), an unusually aggressive approach was employed. This also owes, in part, to the idea that these women's choices directly imperiled fetuses and young children. When women were conceptualized as nutritional delivery services rather than individuals, federal involvement in the female body could become notably harsher than it could with other weight-oriented body projects. While the tension of individual rights and fetal personhood discussed in nutritional guidelines does not reach the heights of other discussions of fetal rights—such as cases where women are imprisoned for using drugs during pregnancy—the subtler, daily coercions of these nutrition guidelines are useful when exploring the relationship between citizen physique and intervention. In short, at first through the provision of food and advice, and later through the development of mandatory nutrition education focused on body weight, the rules that kept state interventions advisory did not apply to these women or this program. As the first federal food welfare program to define pregnant women as a special eligible class, WIC defined mothers as deserving of aid only so long as their child was nutritionally dependent on them. It also implicitly defined low-income mothers as risks to their children, best demonstrated through the program's strict (and sometimes arbitrary) nutrition guidelines.

Making WIC

The WIC program emerged out of a White House nutrition conference. After a couple of years of energetic hunger activism shaping the food welfare agenda, the exiting Democratic administration and incoming Republican administration both argued that they needed a scientific, evidence-based agenda. A White House Fellow complained that despite all the "emotional concern about hunger," there was "no reliable scientific knowledge" on the subject.[4] Food programs "cannot proceed rationally," he warned, without further information.[5] Both centrist Democrats and the Nixon administration argued for more research. Nixon's first secretary of agriculture called for a 1969 White House Conference on Food and Nutrition, designed to emphasize the role of the private sector in nutrition management.[6] Nixon then appointed nutrition professor Dr. Jean Mayer—someone the outgoing secretary of agriculture, Orville Freeman, had fought with publicly—to head the conference.[7]

Many deemed the conference a waste of time and money. The total conference cost was expected to exceed $850,000. Others distrusted the experts brought in. Nixon and Mayer requested that the conference be underwritten by a number of large foundations, and ultimately received $300,000 from the Ford Foundation and $100,000 from the Rockefeller Foundation. More questionably, the administration also solicited and accepted a $100,000 donation from the W. K. Kellogg Foundation (of Kellogg's cereals).[8] All the donated money was funneled through a nondescript nonprofit organization, Food, Nutrition, and Health, Inc. Federal funds were also used, and came through the Department of Health, Education, and Welfare and the Department of Agriculture. The National Welfare Rights Organization protested the event, with slogans like "let them eat conferences" and "White House conferences are part of the problem, YOU can be part of the solution."[9] The conference was decidedly not designed to increase food welfare benefits, and seemed a distraction or stalling technique to activists.

The 1969 White House conference had at least one critical implication, though. It included several panels on prenatal and infant nutrition. Following the conference, the USDA privately considered the importance of prenatal nutrition. Patrick Moynihan, then a counselor to the president, asked Secretary of Agriculture Clifford M. Hardin to research the connection between prenatal nutrition and developmental delays. At the time, Hardin emphasized the uncertainty of all the research. "There is no good evidence to substantiate or refute" the idea that poor prenatal nutrition can cause "mental retardation," he explained.[10] Hardin wrote up a memo saying he believed most malnutrition in the United States was not extreme enough to cause brain damage, but that it was likely to make children struggle in school later.[11] Scientists increasingly spoke of the time in utero as a crucial period for brain development. They cited studies from Holland, Mexico, and Canada, all arguing that enhanced in utero nutrition improved the prospects of the fetus.[12] While certainly not the only version of nutrition concerns that the conference addressed, it pointed to the growing interest both professionally and politically in fetal and prenatal nutrition.

Political concerns about fetal nutrition, especially when tied to the easy-to-understand problem of low birth weights, grew. Doris L. Thornton, a government nutritionist, went so far as to say that poverty is "probably providing a chain of undernourished mothers bearing physically and even mentally handicapped babies."[13] Robert Dole, then one of a few Republicans willing to work with Democrat George McGovern on hunger and nutrition issues, took a related stance. "To deny an impoverished pregnant woman proper nutrition," Dole said in the Senate, "is to greatly enhance the risk that her child will suffer malnourishment, or even brain damage."[14] House Democrat George Miller took the economic stance. "It's damned well to be sure that that [low-income] child is going to be part of the caseload the next fiscal year," he argued, "if they don't do something about that pregnant woman this year."[15] McGovern explained that ten dollars' worth of food would help an infant more than ten dollars' worth of care would "help a slow learner, or rehabilitate a dropout, or teach a mentally retarded child—all problems that stem from malnutrition."[16] Doctors like William McGanity, chairman of the American College of Obstetrics and Gynecology's nutrition committee, pushed the economic benefits of a prenatal feeding program as well, saying that good in utero nutrition could save the nation in costs for premature infants.[17] Whether the real benefit was in public health or in saving money, the idea was really set to bloom by the early 1970s. McGovern, always prolific on this topic, proclaimed that "any attempt to break the cycle of poverty" must include a nutrition element, or else this wastage of human life will continue unabated."[18] The idea of who the "innocent" victim of malnutrition was shifted slightly, from the underweight child to the underweight infant.

The underweight infant was increasingly understood as a victim of unfortunate maternal choices. Thus, the "obese welfare client" and the "low-birth weight infant," which appear on the surface to be unrelated issues, built upon one another. The low-income mother was presumed to be making bad dietary choices for both herself and her fetus or young child. As concerns over both issues, but especially those over fetal weight, rose to the fore, so also arose a call for greater federal intervention into managing these clients' bodies.

As with other twentieth-century dietary projects, both WIC proponents and critics found nutrition inseparable from their conceptions of the physical bodies of those they monitored. The previous chapter showed how, in the late 1960s, the emaciated child's body became the public symbol of extreme poverty. Politicos debated what that underweight, bony child—usually black, southern, and rural—meant in terms of federal responsibility, but its centrality to discussions of need was clear. By the 1970s, however, a different figure sat at the center of debates around hunger and poverty.

Increasingly, the dominant depiction of hungry Americans was not the underweight child, but the overweight mother. Although underweight children, especially newborns, remained a medical concern, policy makers increasingly placed the woman rather than the child at the center of their planning. Fatness was the new malnutrition, report after report claimed.[19]

The emphasis on the overweight mother told a very different tale than discussions of underweight children did. The overweight body was used to suggest poor decision making and an improper use of ones' resources. While an underweight child of the 1960s was depicted as blameless, the overweight mother of the 1970s was anything but. In the case of children, especially newborns, the fault of hunger lay with the adults around them and the women carrying them in utero. Individuals from all over the political spectrum turned to consider how they might intervene in this conceptualization of hunger—in the idea that low-income women needed not *access* to food, but rather *guidance* in their consumption of that food.

The overweight or fat body, especially when tied to low-income mothers, implied irresponsibility. The fat body, once a sign of prosperity, had symbolized laziness and a lack of self-control and self-discipline for much of the twentieth century.[20] These were already qualities many associated with women on public assistance.[21] Additionally, fatness suggested that malnourishment was an issue of individual, not societal, failings.[22] If a woman had enough access to food to become obese, welfare critics argued, then surely she had access enough to avoid issues like anemia. In place of concern over systemic poverty, an emphasis on individual poor choices became central to the 1970s food welfare discourse.

In its earliest years, from trial runs in the early 1970s up through 1978, the WIC program advised clients on what to consume at the same time it provided them vouchers that could only be used for foods deemed acceptable. The formal pilot of the Women, Infants, and Children Special Supplemental Food Program was started in 1972. Hubert Humphrey sponsored the legislation, which created WIC through an amendment to the Child Nutrition Act of 1966, a law on school lunches. The program was supposed to be a two-year pilot, and was labeled as a "supplemental food program," rather than a "supplemental nutrition program," as it would be rebranded later.[23] Modeled after a Johns Hopkins University experiment of "prescription foods," or vouchers meant to deliver foods that were medically indicated, the pilot program was aimed at helping people defined as "nutritional risks."[24] These risks were often caused by poverty, but the legislation was careful to avoid the language that would imply it was welfare. The original target population group was pregnant women, postpartum women up to six weeks, lactating women up to one year after delivery, infants under one year of age, and children under four years of age. These individuals were only eligible once a physician, nurse, dietician, or health official designated them as in need of supplemental food for both health and income reasons.[25] The prescribed foods reinforced the idea that WIC was a health, not a welfare, program. WIC foods were theoretically selected based on their high-quality protein, iron, calcium, vitamin A, and vitamin C.[26] It provided foods like iron-fortified infant formulas, infant cereal high in iron, fruit juice high in vitamin C, milk fortified with vitamin D, and regular cereals with iron added.[27] The limited food list and vouchers helped emphasize that the program was a medical, not a social, welfare program.[28]

The medical or public health claims of the program added an extra element of coercion. They detailed what could be bought, and usually many specifics about individual items—the food's size, weight, brand name, color (brown versus white eggs), and composition (white versus whole wheat pasta). These limits do not mean the program was unhelpful. Mothers and clinic workers often sang the praises of the food vouchers they received. At the same time, WIC, according to an early critic, was a very "in-kind, highly constrained form of income assistance."[29] It was more coercive and controlling than any previous nutrition advice program designed to shape the bodies of Americans. The language of mother blame and the medical language around fetal health both suggested the same response to 1970s policy makers (Democrat and Republican alike): a sterner approach to low-income women's diets was necessary. They would find this in the development of WIC.

There were some major practical problems in the public health approach, problems that almost killed the early program. Above all else, the Department of Agriculture was uneasy about its own relationship to food welfare. While Nixon's administration proudly proclaimed concerns about nutrition at their 1969 White House conference, when it came time to fund fifteen state agencies in a trial program in 1972–73 they were less enthused.[30] The roots of food welfare were in finding ways to get rid of agricultural surplus, which is why the WIC program was under USDA jurisdiction. For several reasons, though, the idea that food welfare could help the USDA stopped making sense in the 1960s. Although, certainly, some surplus was still distributed domestically—especially to schools, camps, and Indian reservations—there was simply less surplus available for distribution. The food welfare program, like the Food Stamp Program, expanded slowly over the course of the 1960s and early 1970s, and surplus distribution continued in locations where the Food Stamp Program was not yet active. These surplus programs were fading into the background, though, as programs that brought welfare clients through the normal channels of the grocery store appealed to merchants, clients, and social workers. The actual amount of surplus food available domestically declined, the USDA replaced price supports with price targets, and a growing livestock industry meant that when surpluses of crops like corn emerged, human food could be repurposed as cheap animal feed.[31] Nixon's second secretary of agriculture, Earl Butz, explained that "commodity procurement has become relatively more costly" and that "on some commodities (like cheese) we can get no bids at all."[32] The Department of Agriculture thus found itself tied to food surplus programs with no surplus, and responsible for food welfare programs due more to precedent than organic interest.

The emphasis on WIC as a public health good meant the Department of Agriculture leadership had little to gain from a serious or speedy implementation of the program. The small trial size, which reached only those original fifteen state agencies, drew George McGovern's ire. McGovern, who notably had just lost his 1972 presidential bid to Richard Nixon, argued that the Nixon USDA was intentionally dragging its feet with the implementation of WIC. Several welfare rights organizations shared this opinion, and sued the secretary of agriculture for not setting up the WIC program in a timely manner. In the 1973 lawsuit, *Dotson v. Butz*, the court ruled for McGovern and the welfare rights groups. Earl Butz and his Department of Agriculture were pushed to seriously expand the WIC pilot.[33]

As 1973 went on, though, the Department of Agriculture insisted it could not manage a large health program. The assistant secretary of agriculture, Clayton Yeutter, explained to one critical senator that the USDA did try to implement WIC quickly, but "the role of medical evaluation, and then difficulty getting a medical contractor, was the problem."[34] McGovern leaked a document in which Yeutter argued that the USDA should stop procuring food commodities. McGovern raised the emotional stakes of the memo, explaining that the end of food commodities would harm "schools, orphanages, and disaster victims."[35] Publicly, an irritated Earl Butz argued that commodity support and social welfare programs "need to be kept separate."[36] Privately, he ranted that his critics "never bat an eye when you throw $6 billion down a rathole in food distribution programs. What a wonderful world!"[37] The response was just as McGovern hoped—a swarm of angry letters to Butz. One woman told Butz that "he was an extremely cruel man!!!!"[38] Another simply said, against the backdrop of Watergate, "Birds of a feather flock together. No wonder President Nixon selected you for this post."[39] While McGovern's committee and the secretary's office fought over the implementation of WIC, the battles masked the larger issues with the medicalization of food welfare.

Following the *Dotson v. Butz* lawsuit, the WIC program grew rapidly. In early 1974, the first WIC site was opened. By late 1974, forty-five states had a WIC program somewhere. Programs were typically run at the county level, so this figure by no means indicates that the majority of low-income women had access to WIC, just that the program was steadily expanding. Then, after six years of talk, three years of pilot programming, and one year of actually funding pilot programming, Congress made the WIC program permanent in 1975. Instead of the $20 million allocated in 1972, $100 million was allocated to the program for the 1975 fiscal year.[40] Once the USDA released funds, the program grew quickly. That same year, there were 1,200 WIC clinics, handling a monthly caseload of 402,000 people.[41]

WIC Weigh-Ins

Public Law 94–105 transferred WIC from pilot status to permanent program status. It also expanded eligibility to children up to five years old (in the pilot program, only children up to four were included, but the gap between WIC coverage and children's access to the school lunch program around age six was later amended). The revised and now-permanent program also included women for a full six months after they had given birth. The pilot program had only included postpartum women so long as they were breastfeeding, but this was also a point of contention. The low-income mothers using WIC, often teenagers, were themselves at serious nutritional risk, advocates argued. The idea that these women were of child-bearing age and needed to remain healthy for future pregnancies was a powerful argument.

The incredible growth of the program, despite the animosity of Butz and President Gerald Ford, was not a straightforward victory for social welfare. The program seemed perpetually under threat of defunding. While

Figure 14. A WIC nutrition class in Pineville, Kentucky, in January 1974. An emphasis on improving pregnant women's and young children's bodies was central to WIC programming. By 1978 nutrition counseling and nutrition classes like this one were mandatory components of the program. United States Department of Agriculture, Office of Communications, 1974, 20120105-OC-AMW-0057, National Archives and Records Administration.

the argument that made WIC possible was focused on the nutritional needs of pregnant women and young children, the establishment of the program in the language of public health meant that there would be different reasons to keep the program running. To justify continued funding, WIC data was now expected to prove the medical value of the program.

In turn, WIC looked to emphasize its public health benefits. Detailed medical evaluations, however, required experts and expensive equipment like centrifuges.[42] As a result, supporters emphasized pregnant women's weight gain as a benefit of the program. While the newly established program was meant to improve nutritional status and, more generally, health, the simplest shorthand for health was once again body weight.

Participants agreed to office weigh-ins as a condition of continued aid. A smaller number had to consent to hemoglobin tests, but the effort was

too costly to be a primary program metric. The measurements were supposed to give an approximation of how WIC was aiding the health of clients, especially through increased iron and vitamin intake. The use of
anthropometric shortcuts to assess health, though, was meant as a practical
measure.

In 1976, when the program was once again struggling to maintain its
funding, attention to client weights as evidence of the program's success
became more critical. Although weight data was supposed to have been
collected since the start of the program, program administers had actually
only collected rather uneven data. McGovern, who argued the lack of data
reflected the slowness of program expansion, attacked the USDA. "I wish it
wasn't necessary for the Nutrition Committee to keep looking over USDA's
shoulder," McGovern snipped.[43] Hubert Humphrey backed McGovern,
saying that WIC "has truly been an unwanted orphan on the doorstep of
the Department of Agriculture."[44]

Secretary of Agriculture Earl Butz explained the medical nature of the
program meant it was difficult to expand WIC. There "must be evidence
that the program is achieving the goals for which it was established," the
assistant secretary of agriculture chimed in.[45] Beginning in 1976, then, the
WIC program developed an Advisory Committee. This nutrition-oriented
committee was meant to think through the foods allowed by WIC. Most
importantly, though, the Advisory Committee was meant to calm the
USDA's complaints that it had no business managing a public health program. The experts in this committee included representatives from the
American Dietetic Association, the American Public Health Association,
the Department of Health, Education, and Welfare, and the Centers for
Disease Control and Prevention.[46] The committee, which held its first meetings in fall 1976, sought a way to balance public health with the immediate
interests of McGovern and Humphrey in getting WIC to run widely.

The erratic collection of health statistics in the first years of WIC concerned Advisory Committee members, especially those from a public health
background. The Advisory Committee decided it needed a better set of
medical data, and that it needed it in about a year's time. Committee members painstakingly set out to rank the anthropometric data they needed,
and to assess the reasonableness of asking clinics to produce that data. The
most important measurement to track, the committee decided, would be
children's heights. Next to that would be the weights of WIC clients of all
ages.

While the Advisory Committee preferred measurements of hemoglobin or hematocrit levels, they acknowledged that large-scale blood tests were relatively impractical. The advisors agreed these were the most important numbers to analyze regarding WIC and health "since iron deficiency was the single finding of significant frequency in previous surveys."[47] When clinics had the means to do blood tests, this approach would be helpful. After all, anemia was the number one problem of adult WIC clients, and was in no way assessable through height and weight. The committee, however, could not expect most of its clinics to draw or test blood. Blood tests cost more than simpler measures, training was required, and data did not come back instantly—which was of particular concern to the committee who decided reappropriations required hard health data in at most sixteen months.

Measurement shortcuts, namely, a focus on height-weight measurements, would have to do. Height measurements, the Advisory Committee decided, could be a "measure of caloric adequacy of diet during [an] active growth period."[48] Weight was a critical, but somewhat messier, data proposition. Weight could be a "measure of caloric intake in . . . undernutrition [and] excess in overnutrition." WIC analysts needed to monitor body weight in both directions, since there were some critics insisting that a large number of children in the WIC program had "excess weight for height."[49] The Advisory Committee compared client weights with the 1976 weight charts of the National Center for Health Statistics.[50] We "should encourage or even request" that WIC clinics assess clients using weight grids, the committee decided.[51]

Weight and Morality

While client weight was not central in the first couple of years of WIC experiments, by the late 1970s there had been few discussions of WIC that did not mention overweight or obese clients at some point. Anthropometrics were designed to measure the program—was it working, were pregnant clients gaining (the appropriate amount of) weight? Were they healthier in some way that could be correlated with their WIC packages? The discussion of the data was quietly transformed. Rather than serving solely as an assessment of program success, though, those weights were increasingly used as an assessment of the women's and children's value.

A government-sponsored study of WIC's medical success used a "nutritional index" to determine the success of the program. The index, though, was simply a formula based on height and weight.[52] By 1976 this nutritional index had eliminated the category of underweight. The woman who would have been called underweight or undernourished in 1966 was relabeled in 1976 as a much less concerning "thin."[53] Now, a woman's physical body was only evidence of poor nutrition if she was overweight. The idea of the blameless underweight poor was long gone.

In its place, with weight still the primary way WIC quantified nutrition, the program paid increasing attention to the relationship between WIC foods and weight gain. WIC opponents critiqued the lack of nutrition education in the social program, and its proponents emphasized the presence of such education. The casual correlation between WIC users (low-income mothers and children) and overweight morphed into a truth for program opponents. With the program metrics firmly fastened to height and weight data, low-income women's improper weights—which now meant their status as overweight—went from the very reason clients needed WIC (to encourage pregnancy weight gain and high birth weights) to the reason clients should not be allowed access to the program.

The concern about client weight, especially the weights of black mothers, was closely related to the growing trope of the so-called welfare queen. This trope of the irresponsible mother, especially the irresponsible mother of color, reflected growing American anxieties about nonwhite women's access to social welfare, as well as about welfare clients' supposed opting out of the paid economy when an increasing number of middle-class women were economically driven to opt in. At a time of economic turmoil and growing American conservatism, critics and media outlets often portrayed black women's mere access to the social welfare system as their abuse of it. This imagined abuse was then written on women's bodies, as the matriarch of the Moynihan Report and the welfare queen of popular imagination were both overweight figures.[54]

By the early 1970s, policy debates were regularly describing women using welfare programs as fat and lazy.[55] When welfare rights activists protested in Las Vegas in 1971, opponents shouted at the women to "get off your fat asses."[56] As the public increasingly imagined social welfare programs benefiting black women, they simultaneously imagined those beneficiaries were overweight.[57] To critics, that weight suggested that food access was not an issue, while poor food choices were. In that same period, some women on assistance tried to own the insults, hoping to sever the idea of fatness from accusations of laziness. In 1972 welfare rights activist Johnnie Tillmon famously described herself as black, fat, poor, and on welfare, explaining that "in this country, if you're any one of those things you count less as a human being. If you're all those things, you don't count at all."[58] Her statement was powerful, but went unheard by most. During the 1970s, alongside the development of the WIC program, the American middle class often managed its own economic trouble by resenting and blaming low-income mothers and their fat bodies.

In 1978 when appropriations for the WIC program were up for debate, political opponents targeted those same women's choices. In one hearing, Republican Senator Henry Bellmon, of Oklahoma, grilled the WIC director. "Suppose a woman prefers to drink beer to milk, what do you do then?," he asked. "You aren't going to have us wake up in Congress with . . . a column saying that the women come in wearing their minks and driving their Cadillacs and carrying off WIC packages?," he continued.[59] Referencing the 1970 hit "Welfare Cadillac," Bellmon suggested both that low-income women did not actually need the food resources made available through WIC, and that they would not properly use the resources anyhow—"preferring," as he suggested, beer to milk. Women on WIC, Bellmon emphasized, were not to be trusted.

By way of a response, WIC supporters trotted out both clients and social workers to explain just how educationally valuable the program was. In other words, they reframed the program as one of educating the welfare client, rather than simply feeding her. Client Anita O'Malley argued that "there's no nutritional education available on Earth that is superior to having the milk and other foods delivered." O'Malley did not buy cheese or orange juice until WIC, she explained, but now these nutritious foods were in her regular rotation.[60] WIC nutrition education lessons suggested disgusting food combinations, like stirring iron-fortified infant cereals into family stews, and mixing surplus infant formula into chicken gravy.[61] The emphasis was both on fortified foods and on instruction. A WIC administrator from Jamaica Plains, Massachusetts, insisted that "we are not just handing out food to people, but are also giving them a nutritional assessment and ongoing nutritional counseling if they need it."[62] The emphasis on nutrition education and weight management made it possible to reframe the program as advisory, even as it had more power and sway (and material goods and benefits to distribute) than other advisory programs.

The growing attention to nutrition education also assumed that, without instruction and supervision, low-income women would make poor choices. One WIC administrator, the director of a Kentucky health clinic, argued that "parents seem to have no idea. . . . They have no concept of what iron rich foods are. Many believe that a fat baby is a healthy baby."[63] The ideas that low income Americans were especially overweight, especially bad at budgeting, and especially ill equipped to manage their children's health all had currency. The late 1970s marked a shift toward a more general political interest in obesity. The claim that low-income women knew little about child nutrition was actually an accusation leveled against women of all classes as anxieties about American diets grew. WIC clients, though, who relied on federal services for their material well-being, could be made the subjects of nutrition education and intervention in a way most populations could not.

The 1978 reappropriation for WIC came with a bold pronouncement—mandatory nutrition education for all WIC clients. There would now be "individual or group sessions" and materials meant "to improve health status" and "achieve positive change in dietary habits."[64] The 1978 changes to the WIC program included the development of required nutrition education, rules for supplemental foods (that they be relatively low in salt, fat, and sugar), and a mandate that other social services like counseling, family planning, and immunizations be available at WIC sites. Nutrition education materials had to be made available in languages other than English when there were many non-English-speaking low-income families in an area, and both women using the program and parents of children using the program were meant to engage in nutrition education.[65] States were required to evaluate local nutrition education programs annually.[66] These 1978 additions to WIC, especially the nutrition education and food rules, reshaped low-income Americans. Program head Carol Tucker Foreman told one critic that "we certainly agree with you that persons may be obese because of improper eating habits. . . . This is one of the reasons that the Congress mandated nutrition education in WIC legislation."[67] Nutrition education and WIC might improve the bodies of low-income Americans.

WIC, with the addition of nutrition education and food rules, was not "just a free food program," Foreman explained.[68] Rather, it was a program to help clients "maximize their well-being."[69] In this language of optimization, the implied purpose became monitoring and directing welfare clients'

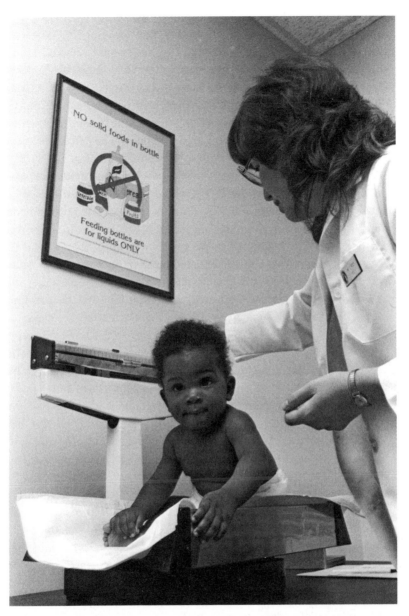

Figure 15. An infant in North Carolina is weighed as part of the WIC program in August 1983. The program weighed WIC clients, including both children and pregnant women, as a way of monitoring their weight gain and thus their success with the program. WIC aimed to improve health outcomes through improved nutrition but did not trust low-income women to reach these nutrition goals without some structure like weighing, vouchers, and nutrition education. United States Department of Agriculture, Office of Communications, 1983, 20120105-OC-AMW-0057, National Archives and Records Administration.

consumption. Prior to this decision, nutrition education had been optional in the program.[70] On average, 10 percent of WIC administrative budgets were spent on nutrition education. This was not a huge amount, and did not lead to many resources for clients. There was some individual counseling, but most programs were aimed at larger groups. Political scientists polling WIC clients in the mid-1970s found that nearly 90 percent of clients said that the nutrition education did not affect their thinking.[71]

The introduction of mandatory nutrition education in 1978 allocated more money to that component of the program—up to 20 percent of administrative costs. It also centralized some of the work of nutrition education. Now the question would become just what nutrition education WIC clients needed. Should it prioritize the pregnant woman, the fetus, or the young child? Would it emphasize prepared foods or home cooking? Would it recommend foods high in fat, calories, or sugar, or push for a diet specifically low in those items? How would it account for ethnic and regional differences in tastes? Nothing about nutrition education was low stakes.

One way for the USDA to sidestep these complexities was by directing clinics to free, but nongovernmental, literature. Although there was no directive on what would be taught in WIC nutrition education programs, there was plenty of advice on the subject given out. With only modest nutrition education budgets, many small programs that had not offered nutrition education prior to the mandate turned to the USDA for help preparing their programs. The USDA referred WIC nutritionists to a number of places already producing free pamphlets of nutrition advice. They recommended the nutritionists turn to trade organizations such as the Cereal Institute, the National Dairy Council, the National Livestock and Meat Board, and the Egg Board. They also recommended materials from commercial companies such as food companies, film companies, and supermarket chains, so long as there was not "excessive promotion of a commercial product or other bias."[72] WIC nutritionists, then, were encouraged to use private industry as an advisory tool. The pamphlets in this case were not coming directly from the government, but the nutrition advice still was presented to clients through WIC.

WIC nutritionists did not all rely on corporate materials. Many localities produced their own brochures, with some state and federal guidance. Some of this guidance was focused on vitamins, and some on calories. Overwhelmingly, though, foods were simply labeled as good or bad. Their goodness or badness was tied to how they might impact body weight. It is unclear why WIC materials focused on dieting and abstinence when meant for an audience who needed assistance simply acquiring food. Perhaps clients suggested a desire for it to clinic staff (unlikely), or perhaps clients themselves made comments about their weight that led the nutritionists to *believe* weight loss was a priority. The nutritionists themselves likely reflected the middle-class obsession with slenderness that spread in the 1970s. The clients may have been influenced by the same media, and left balancing contradictory messages: gain weight while pregnant, but not too much, make sure your baby gains enough weight, do not let your baby become fat.

Once nutrition education was mandatory, WIC nutrition resources reinforced this troubled relationship between women using welfare and food. Programs included films, posters, pamphlets, and slide shows while women sat in the waiting room. One manual recommended that "catchy slogans" be worked into WIC nutrition education. Suggestions included clichés like "a moment on the lips, forever on the hips," "overeating is like a credit card—splurge now, pay later," and "what you eat today is what you wear tomorrow."[73] Other advice to WIC educators included a suggestion that they motivate clients to make food choices with the goal of "improved appearance," and that educators should "emphasize [the] appearance benefits of losing weight."[74] Nutrition education that was ostensibly about avoiding anemia and birth defects grew increasingly obsessed with the physique of both adult and child clients.

The idea that WIC clients had a public responsibility in how they used their vouchers was made clear in the educational materials. "What you eat in private, shows in public," one manual recommended telling clients.[75] Teaching nutrition to WIC mothers was both "enormously difficult" and a "fulfilling challenge" for young social workers.[76] The language of nutrition education, far from neutral, judged low-income women as poor consumers. WIC clients' unruly bodies were taken not just as evidence of laziness but as noncompliance.[77]

The initial WIC aim of feeding children and pregnant women was increasingly replaced with the disciplining of WIC nutrition education.[78] One WIC employee praised the program in 1978, while advocating for the nutrition education her clinic provided to become the national approach. She described the material assistance provided by WIC as a supplement to the nutrition education, rather than the other way around. "Instead of saying 'Eat less sugar; eat more whole wheat; eat more fruits and vegetables,'" she explained that she could tell clients to "'give your child orange juice, which we provide, instead of Kool Aid; use the WIC cheese and cereal for snacks; give crackers instead of cookies.'"[79] Explaining that "pregnant women and mothers of young children are very teachable," this Massachusetts clinic WIC employee was much less hostile (albeit still condescending) toward her clients.[80] Another public health nurse wrote a similar story: "to offer nutrition education to a mother that does not have funds to buy food," she wrote, "is a futile and heartbreaking experience."[81] What she really was explaining, though, was that the WIC program made it possible to tell, not just teach, low-income women what to eat and what to feed their children.

Most accepted the idea of low-income women's personal responsibility in their nutrition choices, so the idea of nutrition education as a solution to malnutrition made sense. Nutrition education programs had a bad reputation among welfare rights activists, who argued that education on proper foods was often patronizing and sometimes racist.[82] Nutrition education for WIC emphasized some extremely simple recipes, such as freezing WIC orange juice to make popsicles and adding WIC cheese to plain grits. At the other extreme, recipes put out by some clinics focused on foods for less common situations, such as recipes for camping, and foods that required equipment like blenders.[83]

As both fatness and medicalized obesity became hotter topics outside the government, they further influenced the use of WIC energies. Some dieticians argued that "generous provision" of milk, cheese, and eggs under WIC was a nutrition problem. As low-fat, low-cholesterol food was increasingly equated with health in American nutrition circles, critics eyed the full-fat WIC rations and worried that "future generations could have good reason to accuse us of 'dumping' these unwanted surplus foods on the underprivileged."[84] Some worried that WIC might be contributing to high rates of obesity, diabetes, and heart disease among low-income Americans. "I'm sure we will just go on having fat mothers producing fat babies who become fat mothers who produce fat babies with the resulting health problems," wrote one doctor, complaining about the WIC infant feeding schedule.[85] Likewise, at hearings over the 1978 revamping of WIC, one WIC opponent argued that providing postpartum, nonnursing women with food assistance was "possibly a nutritional hazard, with respect to developing obesity in the female."[86] Instead of free access to food, the nonnursing mother "needs to have some caloric restrictions," he explained. Again, nutrition education and behavioral changes were recommended, rather than food assistance. "She certainly does not need to add further pounds," he concluded.[87] Any discussion of WIC was now saturated with weight management and anti-obesity rhetoric. When a conservative critic writing in the early 1990s looked back on the history of WIC, he argued that WIC was failing because its clients' problems were behavioral, not nutritional. "Nutritional programs like WIC have 'succeeded' only in contributing to the alarming prevalence of morbid obesity among the poor, especially among Native Americans," he insisted.[88]

This anxiety about the obesity of WIC clients was unfounded. Even prior to the 1978 introduction of mandatory nutrition education, WIC clients' weights were recorded as more or less matching desired weight curves. Janet Berkenfield, the WIC director for the Massachusetts Public Health Department, argued that "WIC infants have better growth curves" than their non-WIC siblings, including less obesity and greater heights.[89] Ann M. Byrne, who was working on low-income nutrition for Detroit's Wayne County Health Department, argued that "WIC will be reducing the incidence of obesity in the long-run, rather than contributing to it."[90] Carol Tucker Foreman cited data from one WIC test location to argue that "fifty-six percent of the children who had been obese no longer suffered from this condition and 49 percent of the children who previously were at high risk to be stunted had been raised to normal heights after a year."[91] Weight is a consistently poor indicator of nutritional health, but one that has been used time and time again by an advisory state eager to supervise large populations in a rapid fashion. According to weights, the indicators of health some WIC researchers were using, WIC clients were growing healthier even before mandatory nutrition education was instituted.

The attention to fatness and obesity, rather than to the specific health problems that were the original rationale for WIC, made maternal weight and size highly political. Critics of WIC blamed the mothers using the program. The weight of WIC mothers became contentious. A group of public health nurses in Jonesburg, Arkansas, wrote about their dislike of WIC, saying the problem was not lack of food (a social welfare problem) but simply lack of knowledge about food (an education problem). The nurses explained that "when you see the 200 and 300 pound parents you know they have funds to purchase food."[92] The last thing these parents needed, the women went on, was extra money for extra food. Others assumed WIC clients had the nutritional knowledge to make good food choices, but opted not to do so (a behavioral problem). The Arkansas nurses, who could not decide if the problem with WIC was client education or client behavior, explained that the WIC program was "encouraging parents to be lazy and dishonest."[93] This association between the welfare client and fraud and criminality was part and parcel of the larger emerging discourse about the welfare queen.[94] While discussed as a social welfare program emerging from concerns about American hunger, by the 1970s the focus on nutrition education had become part of a growing emphasis on physiological optimization.[95] While WIC nutrition was at first all about serious medical concerns—low birth weights, developmental delays—the 1978 emphasis on nutrition education represented a shift to attaining optimal health rather than avoiding the major dangers of nutritional deficiencies. Nutrition education and WIC program metrics used weight as a stand-in for more complex questions of health.

Nothing about nutrition education was apolitical. By the late 1970s, the obsession with a limited, middle-class definition of health was now transferred wholesale to welfare clients receiving WIC assistance. Notably, this took place at a moment when multiple Senate hearings had questioned *all* Americans' consumption of sugar, saturated fat, and salt. George McGovern had begun crusading on this point in the late 1960s, and, to his credit, he wanted to change the diets of all Americans, not simply those of welfare clients. McGovern's Committee (as it was nicknamed) held hearings on sugar, salt, meat, and artificial sweeteners. His committee's 1977 report on American health, *Dietary Goals for the United States*, recommended food labeling, rules for food advertising, and financial support for national nutrition education.[96] They also, infamously, suggested that Americans eat less or decrease consumption of certain foods.[97]

In the process, McGovern learned that it was much more difficult to challenge the diets of middle-class Americans than the diets of low-income Americans. Pressure groups got loud. The Salt Institute said that recommendations to decrease salt intake might "very well work against the committee's aim of getting people to eat good diets . . . since it may leave those foods less palatable."[98] Instead, Americans should just be encouraged to "exercise reasonable prudence in salt consumption." The International Sugar Research Foundation (the sugar industry's lobbying group at the time), the National Dairy Council, and the National Canners Association all made similar statements. The meat lobbyists hit back hardest on the recommendation that Americans eat less meat. As a result, the committee rewrote its guidelines to say that Americans should "choose meat, poultry and fish which will reduce saturated fat intake."[99] Revisions hardly mattered, though, since, by then, the ten-year-old McGovern Committee had already been disassembled. As part of larger committee reorganization, the committee shrank dramatically and was transformed into an agricultural subcommittee. In this new position, it would not be able to cause so much trouble for food industry lobbyists. *Dietary Goals* prompted a national conversation on nutrition, disease, and the role of the state in these matters. It did not, however, lead to the nutrition education, food labeling, or advertising regulations it had set out to tackle. Not only could middle-class food consumption and weight not be regulated in the 1970s, even advisory material from the federal government would be fought tooth and nail.

The fight over *Dietary Goals* was evidence that there would be an uneven application of nutrition education in the nation. WIC provided a venue where more aggressive and controlling tactics could be used without fears of violating personal freedoms—few worried about the consumer freedoms of low-income mothers. This included those on the right, who blamed low-income women for their consumption of improper foods *and* those on the left, who blamed corporations for pushing such foods. For instance, at the WIC hearings over sugary cereal in 1978, Vermont Democrat Senator Patrick Leahy complained about recent advertising he had seen for a sugary cereal "called Count Chocula, or something like this."[100] Leahy said that it was "not much more than chocolate bars disguised as something good for breakfast" and that "General Foods and a number of the other large companies . . . should be sued . . . for even suggesting that these are good things for people's breakfasts."[101] No one was going to actually sue General Foods, though. Those lessons had been learned by the McGovern Committee the year before. So, for those on the political left and those on the political right who wanted some level of control over consumerism, low-income clients provided the only space for implementing restrictions.

Against a backdrop of increasing anxieties about sugar, body weight, and health, WIC became a venue for directive public policy changes on the issue. By 1978 the women collecting WIC benefits were being weighed and measured. They were also being counseled on nutritional choices for themselves and their fetuses and young children. The advice, coming from a hodgepodge of sources, often touted weight maintenance and weight loss as nutritional goals. It did all this as if the nutrition education it provided was voluntary, rather than coercive—as if it were designed to help clients rather than discipline them or eliminate benefits because of their unworthiness. The requirement that women sit in the clinic space and listen to or participate in such education to receive (circumscribed) material benefits, though, undercut the idea that this was an advisory program. A mandatory advisory program, itself a contradiction-packed statement, hid the coercive power of WIC. WIC made it possible to tell, not just teach, low-income women how to eat and how to feed their children. It did so, moreover, while defining weight as the central characteristic of nutritional health.

Governing American Bodies

The first issue of *Captain America*, published in 1941, featured a thin, weak young man named Steve Rogers. Ashamed of his physique, he held his head in his hand as authority figures surveyed his body. One of these men, a military scientist who planned to subject Rogers's wiry frame to a secret experiment, provides narration. "Observe this young man closely. . . . Today he volunteered for Army service, and was refused because of his unfit condition! His chance to serve his country seemed gone!" Rogers failed the U.S. Army's physical examination, presumably owing to his weight or musculature. The military scientist aimed to repair this failed body, and in doing so, the failed masculinity of Rogers, whose inability to serve suggested he was an inadequate man, a failed "citizen-soldier." The scientist injected Rogers with a strengthening serum. "He's changing!," an observing bureaucrat exclaimed. Change he did. The serum transformed the scrawny Rogers into a superhuman figure, twice his original size and all muscle. The scientist dubbed the changed man "Captain America."

The popular Captain America story is, at its core, a parable of the physiological transformation of the citizen in the name of the state. While Rogers submits to the state willingly, his submission is part of the process of sharpening and asserting his masculinity. This moment is presented as a science-fiction anomaly, not some prescription for how all male citizens should interact with the state, but even its existence was due to the exigencies of wartime. For that brief moment, national emergency made assertive federal intervention into the white, male, middle-class body politically and socially acceptable. During most of the twentieth century, however, federal body projects aimed at that demographic would be presented more subtly and with an emphasis on their voluntary nature.

As Americans today grapple with the politics of our collective size and shape, and try to understand soda taxes and trans-fat bans, we do so in the shadow of more than a hundred years of debate over how physique should be managed. In the twentieth century, state projects to manage the shape, size, weight, and physique of American citizens were handled through advisory techniques except in cases of total war and mass mobilization. Through research, education, advertisement, advice, publications, and standardization, the state shaped the American body in ways that could not be directly legislated. In unusual circumstances such as war, more directive programs were possible. In general, though, the state instituted these body projects in ways that strongly encouraged, rather than mandated, that citizens monitor their bodies according to federal interests. After about 1965, the nature of these body projects split. Rather than navigate the difficult terrain of regulating American bodies as a whole, new dietary regulations zeroed in on the bodies of those relying on social welfare.

The advisory state, then, has played a critical role in facilitating federal investment in the weights and bodies of American citizens. Occasionally, this interest has moved into the realm of other aspects of physique, including musculature, fitness, and nutrition, but at its core these body projects have all focused on the *aesthetics* of the body over its internal functioning, and on the belief that objective measurements of the body could reveal information about a citizen's worthiness in the eyes of the state.

Since both federal interest in citizens' bodies and federal tactics for managing bodies have changed over the last hundred years, it is impossible to pinpoint precisely where the boundaries between public and private lie. In fact, the story of American weight politics suggests that, while there has long been an investment in maintaining these boundaries, they have shifted constantly. As recent scholars of reproductive rights in the United States have demonstrated, efforts to separate the public from the private and to maintain American citizens' autonomy from the state have only applied to certain Americans. The advisory state has served as an effective mechanism for managing those citizens privileged enough to be able avoid the coercive side of state policy. Advisory state policy has been more commonly applied to the white and middle class, those whose bodies *and* whose political opinions have historically mattered to the state. Citizens' experiences with social welfare programs—including the Civilian Conservation Corps and Women, Infants, and Children—demonstrate that more overt and aggressive state interventions are made possible by the social position of the targeted citizen.

As a historically grounded theoretical concept, the advisory state can seem messy, but its messiness is the very element that makes the concept useful. It is one of many modes through which the state manages and interacts with citizenry. It is almost certainly not the most common or the most effective mode of this interaction, though it is likely the most banal.[1] As the diverse federal programs and political moments discussed in this book demonstrate, no single idea of how the state manages citizen weight will do. Additionally, while patterns abound, the arc of these interactions is not a simple one of increasing government or growing American anxiety over state growth. The ebb and flow of the advisory state, instead, is about the mechanisms through which citizen interactions with the state are made invisible and visible.

The advisory state concept opens up a new way of approaching smaller and subtler state projects as serious sites for state and citizen building. Future inquiry into the advisory state will most likely find this mechanism of governance strongest in areas that walk the line between the public and private. These might include food safety and recalls, national nutrition and vitamin guidelines, and prenatal recommendations. When more aggressive regulation wins out over an advisory approach, such as in the case of mandatory vaccinations, antismoking regulations, or seat-belt laws, it would be valuable to consider the historical context that made it possible. When federal agencies opt for less aggressive approaches and programs, though, we must take them seriously. Those pamphlets and tables are as much political history as legislation and court decisions are, and in some cases they even do a better job at showing ordinary citizen interactions with the state.

While body projects differ, many Western countries are grappling today with a so-called obesity crisis. This anxiety about citizens' bodies is a continuation (and sometimes an escalation) of a century of state investment in those bodies. Citizen bodies are more important than ever to the state, with citizens as laborers, as soldiers, and, increasingly, as clients of Medicare, Medicaid, and subsidies from the Affordable Care Act. Male bodies garnered the most attention in body projects of the twentieth century, primarily because of the historically sexist structure of paid labor and the military. Today, in an awkward victory of sorts, the federal government has a more even stake in male and female bodies. Just as the range of citizens being monitored has increased, so, too, has the intensity of such monitoring. Anxieties over obesity have led to martial metaphors, like the war on obesity. The weights of adults and children have been of concern. Yet, as all this anxiety about the body has intensified, even when fears of the obesity epidemic seemed inescapable in the late 2000s, the federal response has been heavily advisory.

Between about 2000 and 2010, critics of American weight and physique fueled a number of approaches to address the issue. Some, including the Obama administration, argued that an increased role for the federal government was necessary. Others argued that the federal government must get out of all food and nutrition programming. They claimed that federal interventions have historically been bad news—exemplified by a confusing food pyramid, lenient height-weight standards, or agricultural policy choices that value profit over health.[2] This opposition was shaped by increasingly directive body projects like soda taxes, trans-fat bans, and mandatory nutrition labels.[3] While taxes have only been used at the local and state levels, federal regulations put in place in 2015 required the slow removal of trans fats from the national food supply. While that decision more directly hit food companies, American consumers still expressed "slippery slope" fears that this ban was the first of many.[4] An expansion of such measures, including federal level regulation, is still regularly debated. It is unclear just how directive or advisory future state body projects will be.

At present, some Americans continue to imagine raids by the so-called french fry police, or more realistically, soda taxes and vending-machine regulation. Political interest in weight ebbs and flows as other issues take over, but even at moments when there is little discussion of federal body projects, many citizens express anxiety not about the actual programs the state might implement but about the specter of state power any political interest in the body suggests. The fear of the "french fry police" collapses easily into a larger fear of the "nanny state," or the idea of the overbearing and undermining government. The tension between what the state can do, how it can do it, and to whom it can do it, are tensions of the present as much as the past.

Whatever steps are taken next, they will be part of a long history of federal attempts to manage the American citizen body without provoking citizen anxiety. This history is important. When Michelle Obama promoted programs to shape children's weights, she was unconsciously drawing on the same techniques and strategies that the Children's Bureau used in the 1920s. The history of federal weighing projects built on the voluntary labor of mothers and teachers has slowly normalized both the idea that this is mothers' work and the idea that the scale holds objective truth about health. It is only in the absence of the history of American body politics and the advisory state that Americans can erroneously imagine the numbers on the bathroom scale and the curve on a height-weight chart are private, apolitical concerns.

NOTES

Introduction

1. Let's Move, About, 2010, http://www.letsmove.gov/about.

2. *Hannity*, September 14, 2010, cited in Shauna Theel, "Right-Wing Media Attack Michelle Obama for Fighting Childhood Obesity," *Media Matters*, September 17, 2010, http://mediamatters.org/research/2010/09/17/right-wing-media-attack-michelle-obama-for-figh/170761.

3. *Glenn Beck*, September 14, 2010, in Theel, "Right-Wing Media Attack." For similar comments Beck made earlier in the week, see Jeremy Holden, "Beck Attacks Michelle Obama for Trying to Raise Awareness of and Combat Childhood Obesity," *Media Matters*, February 12, 2010, http://mediamatters.org/blog/2010/02/12/beck-attacks-michelle-obama-for-trying-to-raise/160422.

4. Jonathan Weisman and Jess Bravin, "Obama's Regulatory Czar Likely to Set a New Tone," *Wall Street Journal* (January 8, 2009), http://online.wsj.com/article/SB12313805168 2263203.html.

5. Richard H. Thaler and Cass R. Sunstein, *Nudge: Improving Decisions About Health, Wealth, and Happiness* (New Haven, CT: Yale University Press, 2008); Cass R. Sunstein, "It's for Your Own Good!," *New York Review of Books* (March 7, 2013), http://www.nybooks.com/articles/archives/2013/mar/07/its-your-own-good/.

6. Ariel Edwards-Levy, "Cass Sunstein Received Death Threats, He Says in New Book," *Huffington Post* (March 22, 2013), http://www.huffingtonpost.com/2013/03/22/cass-sunstein-death-threats_n_2931871.html; Tory Newmyer, "Meet Cass Sunstein: Obama's Superego," *Fortune* (February 22, 2013), http://features.blogs.fortune.cnn.com/2013/02/22/cass-sunstein-simpler/; Dan Froomkin, "Cass Sunstein's Resignation Encourages Advocates of Health and Safety," *Huffington Post* (August 4, 2012), http://www.huffingtonpost.com/2012/08/04/cass-sunsteins-resignation_n_1738438.html

7. To be as clear as possible, I am not actually uniformly for or against regulations around weight. When I explain the book project, audiences sometimes assume that I am either fiercely opposed to federal overreach into the private realm or, conversely, that I am some anti-obesity warrior who is anxious about an epidemic of fat children. Neither is true. Instead, in this book I aim to question the false, ahistorical premises on which both sides make such arguments. Federal involvement in the body is not new, and has often been organized in specific ways so as not to be deemed overreach. This is where the advisory state comes in. It has long been alright for the state to encourage mothers and teachers to monitor children's body weights in peacetime, just as it has been alright for the military to raise concerns about

men's bodies in wartime. The problem of federal involvement instead rests with the way we discuss many of these body issues. Part of making the body easier to regulate and debate has been a strong emphasis on quantification as the premier way to know the body. Quantified weights and weight tables have allowed nonexperts to seemingly take control of managing their and their children's bodies. At the same time, these often arbitrary numbers make it possible to label certain bodies as too large or too small—as outside the normal range. Such labels have had material consequences ranging from military rejection to welfare office lectures. This also means that the broad, amorphous category of health has often been simplified into something quantifiable. Sometimes this is blood pressure or cholesterol level (problematic enough by themselves), but most often it is body weight that we use as a synonym for health. Whether in a contest for infant health or part of the criteria for earning a presidential fitness badge, the conflation of health with weight underlies a whole array of political interventions into the body. These underlying assumptions and their implications are my primary concern here.

8. Joan Jacobs Brumberg, *The Body Project: An Intimate History of American Girls* (New York: Random House, 1997).

9. Persuasion, as Sarah Igo has argued, is critical to knowledge production. It is also, I would argue, critical to knowledge consumption, especially through advisory state methods. Sarah E. Igo, "Subjects of Persuasion: Survey Research as a Solicitous Science; or, the Public Relations of the Polls," in *Social Knowledge in the Making*, ed. Charles Camic, Neil Gross, and Michele Lamont (Chicago: University of Chicago Press, 2011), 285–305.

10. Katharina Vester, "Regime Change: Gender, Class, and the Invention of Dieting in Post-Bellum America," *Journal of Social History* 44, no. 1 (Fall 2010): 39.

11. Gary Taubes, *Calories In, Calories Out: Fats, Carbs, and the Controversial Science of Dieting and Health* (New York: Anchor Books, 2008), ix–x.

12. Louise Foxcraft, *Calories and Corsets: A History of Dieting over 2,000 Years* (London: Profile, 2011); Laura Fraser, *Losing It: America's Obsession with Weight and the Industry That Feeds on It* (Hialeah, FL: Dutton Press, 1997).

13. Charles Dana Gibson, *The Gibson Girl and Her America* (New York: Dover Press, 1969).

14. Tamara D. Fangman, Jennifer P. Ogle, Marianne C. Bickle, and Donna Rouner, "Promoting Female Weight Management in 1920s Print Media: An Analysis of *Ladies Home Journal* and *Vogue* Magazines," *Family and Consumer Sciences Research Journal* 32, no. 3 (2004): 213–253.

15. Margaret A. Lowe, *Looking Good: College Women and Body Image, 1875–1930* (Baltimore: Johns Hopkins University Press, 2003), 143–144; Susan Yager, *The Hundred Year Diet: America's Appetite for Losing Weight* (New York: Rodale, 2010).

16. Hillel Schwartz, *Never Satisfied: A Cultural History of Diets, Fantasy, and Fat* (New York: Free Press, 1986); Peter Stearns, *Fat History: Bodies and Beauty in the Modern West* (New York: New York University Press, 1997). Warren Belasco discusses an emerging dieting culture of the 1960s as in part a project of avoiding the burdens and "weight" of a bourgeois existence, for instance, in *Appetite for Change: How the Counterculture Took on the Food Industry* (Ithaca, NY: Cornell University Press, 2006), 225. Judith Sealander analyzes the Progressive Era playground movement and the development of school lunches for the underweight as a sign of children's physical health becoming a political project in *The Failed Century of the Child:*

Governing America's Youth in the Twentieth-Century (New York: Cambridge University Press, 2003), 293.

17. For rationing, see Amy Bentley, *Eating for Victory: Food Rationing and the Politics of Domesticity* (Urbana: University of Illinois Press, 1998). For the rise of vitamins, see Rima Apple, *Vitamania: Vitamins in American Culture* (New Brunswick, NJ: Rutgers University Press, 1996). For the pure food and drug movement, see Lorine Swainston Goodwin, *The Pure Food, Drink, and Drug Crusaders, 1879–1914* (Jefferson, NC: McFarland, 2006); and Philip J. Hilts, *Protecting America's Health: The FDA, Business, and One Hundred Years of Regulation* (New York: Alfred A. Knopf, 2003).

18. Brian Balogh, *The Associational State: American Governance in the Twentieth Century* (Philadelphia: University of Pennsylvania Press, 2015); Brian Balogh, *A Government Out of Sight: The Mystery of National Authority in Nineteenth-Century America* (Cambridge: Cambridge University Press, 2009); Suzanne Mettler, *The Submerged State: How Invisible Government Policies Undermine American Democracy* (Chicago: University of Chicago Press, 2011); Christopher Howard, *The Hidden Welfare State: Tax Expenditures and Social Policy in the United States* (Princeton, NJ: Princeton University Press, 1997); Christopher Howard, *The Welfare State Nobody Knows: Debunking Myths About U.S. Social Policy* (Princeton, NJ: Princeton University Press, 2008); James T. Sparrow, William J. Novak, and Stephen W. Sawyer, eds., *Boundaries of the State in U.S. History* (Chicago: University of Chicago Press, 2015); William J. Novak, "The Myth of the Weak American State," *American Historical Review* 113, no. 3 (June 2008): 752–772. See also the responses to Novak, and then his defense, in the June 2010 issue of the *American Historical Review*.

The growing literature on federalism also complicates our understanding of how citizens experience the state. For instance, Adam Sheingate argues that the design of American government, in which power and resources are concentrated at the local and state levels rather than the federal level, has helped "hide" the state. The state is not hidden, he says, it is in plain sight—we simply do not read local employees like police officers and teachers as part of the "government." Adam Sheingate, "Why Can't Americans See the State?," *Forum* 7, no. 4 (2009): 1–14. See also Karen M. Tani, *States of Dependency: Welfare, Rights, and American Governance* (Cambridge: Cambridge University Press, 2016); and Brent Cebul, Karen Tani, and Mason B. Williams, "Clio and the Compound Republic," *Publius: The Journal of Federalism* 47, no. 2 (April 2017): 235–259.

19. On the voluntary state, see Christopher Capozzola, *Uncle Sam Wants You: World War I and the Making of the Modern American Citizen* (Oxford: Oxford University Press, 2010); Elizabeth S. Clemens and Doug Guthrie, eds., *Politics and Partnerships: The Role of Voluntary Associations in America's Past and Present* (Chicago: University of Chicago Press, 2010); and Andrew J. F. Morris, *The Limits of Volunteerism: Charity and Welfare from the New Deal through the Great Society* (Cambridge: Cambridge University Press, 2009). On the public-private state, see H. Brinton Milward and Keith G. Provan, "Governing the Hollow State," *Journal of Public Administration Research and Theory* 10, no. 2 (2000): 359; H. Brinton Milward, "Symposium on the Hollow State: Capacity, Control, and Performance in Organizational Settings," *Journal of Public Administration Research and Theory* 6, no. 3 (April 1996): 193–196; Jennifer Klein, *For All These Rights: Business, Labor, and the Shaping of America's Public-Private Welfare State* (Princeton, NJ: Princeton University Press, 2003), 8; and Jacob S. Hacker, *The Divided Welfare State: The Battle over Public and Private Social Benefits in the*

United States (Cambridge: Cambridge University Press, 2002). On the improvisational state, see Gary Gerstle, *Liberty and Coercion: The Paradox of American Government from the Founding to the Present* (Princeton, NJ: Princeton University Press, 2015).

20. Balogh, *The Associational State*, 8.

21. Sarah Igo, *The Averaged American: Surveys, Citizens, and the Making of a Mass Public* (Cambridge, MA: Harvard University Press, 2008); Alice O'Connor, *Poverty Knowledge: Social Science, Social Policy, and the Poor in Twentieth-Century U.S. History* (Princeton, NJ: Princeton University Press, 2002); Richard Rottenburg, Sally Engle Merry, Sung-Joon Park, and Johanna Mugler, *The World of Indicators: The Making of Governmental Knowledge Through Quantification* (Cambridge: Cambridge University Press, 2015).

22. Theodore M. Porter, *Trust in Numbers: The Pursuit of Objectivity in Science and Public Life* (Princeton, NJ: Princeton University Press, 1995), 11, 73–78.

23. Geoffrey C. Bowker and Susan Leigh Star, *Sorting Things Out: Classification and Its Consequences* (Cambridge, MA: MIT Press, 2000), 53; Martha Lampland and Susan Leigh Star, eds., *Standards and Their Stories: How Quantifying, Classifying, and Formalizing Practices Shape Everyday Life* (Ithaca, NY: Cornell University Press, 2009); Theodore M. Porter, *Trust in Numbers: The Pursuit of Objectivity in Science and Public Life* (Princeton, NJ: Princeton University Press, 1995); Theodore M. Porter, *The Rise of Statistical Thinking, 1820–1900* (Princeton, NJ: Princeton University Press, 1988); Ian Hacking, *The Taming of Chance* (Cambridge: Cambridge University Press, 1990); Ian Hacking, *The Emergence of Probability: A Philosophical Study of Early Ideas About Probability, Induction, and Statistical Inference*, 2nd ed. (Cambridge: Cambridge University Press, 2006); Stephen M. Stigler, *The History of Statistics: The Measurement of Uncertainty Before 1900* (Cambridge, MA: Belknap Press, 1990), 169–174; Frank H. Hankins, "Adolphe Quetelet as Statistician" (PhD diss., Columbia University, 1908).

24. Kathryn Kish Sklar, *Florence Kelley and the Nation's Work: The Rise of Women's Political Culture, 1830–1900* (New Haven, CT: Yale University Press, 1997); Robyn Muncy, *Creating a Dominion in American Reform, 1880–1935* (Oxford: Oxford University Press, 1994); Molly Ladd-Taylor, "Toward Defining Maternalism in US History," *Journal of Women's History* 5, no. 2 (Fall 1993): 110–113; Nancy F. Cott, *The Grounding of Modern Feminism* (New Haven, CT: Yale University Press, 1987); Ellen Fitzpatrick, *Endless Crusade: Women Social Scientists and Progressive Reform* (New York: Oxford University Press, 1990); Kathryn Kish Sklar, "Hull House in the 1890s: A Community of Reformers," *Signs* 10 (Summer 1985): 658–677; Seth Koven and Sonya Michel, "Womanly Duties: Maternalist Politics and the Origins of Welfare States in Germany, Britain, France, and the United States, 1880–1920," *American Historical Review* 95, no. 4 (1990): 1076–1108.

25. Capozzola, *Uncle Sam Wants You*, 87.

26. A major exception, of course, is literature on managing reproduction. In this arena, weight could occasionally become a concern, as with fears that white women over-dieting in the 1920s would damage their reproductive potential. This concern never became a state body project, though, so, outside the realm of reproduction, women's bodies often seemed peripheral to state concerns. On reproductive rights, see Jeanne Flavin, *Our Bodies, Our Crimes: The Policing of Women's Reproduction in America* (New York: New York University Press, 2010); Linda Gordon, *The Moral Property of Women: A History of Birth Control Politics in America* (Urbana: University of Illinois Press, 2002); Leslie J. Reagan, *When Abortion Was a Crime: Women, Medicine, and Law in the United States, 1867–1973* (Berkeley: University of California

Press, 1998); Dorothy Roberts, *Killing the Black Body: Race, Reproduction, and the Meaning of Liberty* (New York: Vintage Books, 1998); and Johanna Schoen, *Choice and Coercion: Birth Control, Sterilization, and Abortion in Public Health and Welfare* (Chapel Hill: University of North Carolina Press, 2005). On women and the body, see Susan Bordo, *Unbearable Weight: Feminism, Western Culture, and the Body* (Berkeley: University of California Press, 1993); Naomi Wolf, *The Beauty Myth: How Images of Beauty Are Used Against Women* (New York: William Morrow, 1991); Susie Orbach, *Fat Is a Feminist Issue* (London: Paddington Press, 1978); and Susie Orbach, *Bodies* (New York: Picador, 2009).

27. Michael Kimmel, *Manhood in America: A Cultural History* (New York: Free Press, 1996), 13.

28. E. Anthony Rotundo, *American Manhood: Transformations in Masculinity from the Revolution to the Modern Era* (New York: Basic Books, 1993), 218; Gail Bederman, *Manliness and Civilization: A Cultural History of Gender and Race in the United States, 1880–1917* (Chicago: University of Chicago Press, 1995).

29. Lisa Duggan, "Queering the State," *Social Text* 39 (Summer 1994): 9; Nancy F. Cott, *Public Vows: A History of Marriage and the Nation* (Cambridge, MA: Harvard University Press, 2002), 219.

30. The obsession with maintaining heteronormativity often has the unintended effect of showcasing all the limits of supposedly normative sexuality, as scholars like Duggan, "Queering the State," and Licia Fiol-Matta, *A Queer Mother for the Nation: The State and Gabriela Mistral* (Minneapolis: University of Minnesota Press, 2002), have pointed out.

31. Amy Rutenberg, "Drafting for Domesticity: American Deferment Policy During the Cold War, 1948–1965," *Cold War History* 13, no. 1 (2013): 1–20; Michael Sherry, *In the Shadow of War: The United States Since the 1930s* (New Haven, CT: Yale University Press, 1995).

32. Audra Jennings, "Engendering and Regendering Disability: Gender and Disability Activism in Postwar America," in *Disability Histories*, ed. Susan Burch and Michael Rembis (Urbana: University of Illinois Press, 2014); John Williams-Searle, "Cold Charity: Manhood, Brotherhood, and the Transformation of Disability, 1870–1900," in *The New Disability History: American Perspectives*, ed. Paul K. Longmore and Lauri Umansky (New York: New York University Press, 2001).

33. Greg Eghigian, *Making Security Social: Disability, Insurance, and the Birth of the Social Entitlement State in Germany* (Ann Arbor: University of Michigan Press, 2000).

34. Kim E. Nielsen, *A Disability History of the United States* (Boston: Beacon Press, 2012); Susan M. Schweik, *The Ugly Laws: Disability in Public* (New York: New York University Press, 2009).

35. Russell Shuttleworth, Nikki Wedgwood, and Nathan J. Wilson, "The Dilemma of Disabled Masculinity," *Men and Masculinities* 15, no. 2 (June 2012): 174–194; Thomas J. Gerschick and Adam S. Miller, "Coming to Terms: Masculinity and Physical Disability," in *Men's Health and Illness: Gender, Power, and the Body*, ed. Donald Sabo and David Frederick Gordon (Thousand Oaks, CA: Sage, 1995).

36. As a result of these kinds of advisory state body projects, even when the state is encouraging citizens to care for their own minds and bodies in specific ways, citizens do so not because their government is demanding it but rather because they believe they want to do it for personal reasons. Citizens opt into body projects because it is moral, normal, and responsible. Advisory projects, then, are typically aimed at "good," middle-class citizens. More

aggressive body projects, those outside the realm of the advisory state, are more often aimed at low-income citizens who seemingly have not internalized what it takes to be a "responsible" member of society. This approach also helps us make sense of what we cannot easily measure, in this case how subtle, advisory state projects alter the mentality of citizens. Although citizens who are exposed to both subtle and aggressive policies are shaping their bodies to meet political and social standards, individuals will feel and behave as though they are doing so out of free will. Only through such an analysis can we understand how policies and projects of the advisory state are not peripheral but central to modern governance.

Chapter 1

1. Wilbur Olin Atwater, "The Chemistry of Foods and Nutrition V: The Pecuniary Economy of Food," *Century* 35, no. 3 (January 1888): 438.

2. Cybelle Fox, *Three Worlds of Relief: Race, Immigration, and the American Welfare State* (Princeton, NJ: Princeton University Press, 2012), 29–30; John Whiteclay Chambers II, *The Tyranny of Change: America in the Progressive Era, 1890–1920* (New Brunswick, NJ: Rutgers University Press, 2000), 26.

3. Robert H. Wiebe, *The Search for Order, 1877–1920* (New York: Hill and Wang, 1996), 166; Steven J. Diner, *A Very Different Age: Americans of the Progressive Era* (New York: Hill and Wang, 1998), 6.

4. Nell Irvin Painter, *Standing at Armageddon: A Grassroots History of the Progressive Era* (New York: Norton, 2008); Alan Dawley, *Changing the World: American Progressives in War and Revolution* (Princeton, NJ: Princeton University Press, 2003).

5. James Harvey Young, *Pure Food: Securing the Federal Food and Drugs Act of 1906*, (Princeton, NJ: Princeton University Press, 1989); Philip J. Hilts, *Protecting America's Health: The FDA, Business, and One Hundred Years of Regulation* (New York: Alfred A. Knopf, 2003); Lorine Swainston Goodwin, *The Pure Food, Drink, and Drug Crusaders, 1879–1914* (Jefferson, NC: McFarland, 1999); Courtney I. P. Thomas, *In Food We Trust: The Politics of Purity in American Food Regulation* (Lincoln: University of Nebraska Press, 2014).

6. While food safety and purity have long been understood as a key project of Progressive reform, the growth of scientific nutrition in this moment has been less discussed until recently. Harvey A. Levenstein's *Revolution at the Table: The Transformation of the American Diet* (New York: Oxford University Press, 1988) is foundational. Scholars like Charlotte Biltekoff and Helen Zoe Veit have begun to put nutrition—and, in turn, female scientists—at the center of some of these reform narratives. Charlotte Biltekoff, *Eating Right in America: The Cultural Politics of Food and Health* (Durham, NC: Duke University Press, 2013); Helen Zoe Veit, *Modern Food, Moral Food: Self-Control, Science, and the Rise of Modern American Eating in the Early Twentieth Century* (Chapel Hill: University of North Carolina Press, 2013).

7. Gerald F. Combs, "Celebration of the Past: Nutrition at USDA," *Journal of Nutrition* 124, no. 9 (September 1994): 1729S; Andrew R. Ruis, *Eating to Learn, Learning to Eat: The Origins of School Lunch in the United States* (New Brunswick, NJ: Rutgers University Press, 2017).

8. Wilbur Olin Atwater, *Methods and Results on the Investigations of Chemistry and Economy of Food* (Washington, DC: Government Printing Office, 1895), 10.

9. Kenneth J. Carpenter, "The Life and Times of W. O. Atwater," *Journal of Nutrition* 124, no. 9 (September 1994): 1708S; Wallace E. Huffman and Robert E. Evenson, *Science for Agriculture: A Long Term Perspective*, 2nd ed. (Ames, IA: Blackwell, 2006), 17–18. On the

broader international exchange of social policy, see Daniel T. Rodgers, *Atlantic Crossings: Social Politics in a Progressive Age* (Cambridge, MA: Harvard University Press, 1998), 4.

10. Judy McBride, "Wilbur O. Atwater: Father of American Nutrition Science," *Agricultural Research* 41, no. 6 (June 1993): 7.

11. Carpenter, "Life and Times of W. O. Atwater," 1708S.

12. Carolyn Thomas de la Peña, *The Body Electric: How Strange Machines Built the Modern American* (New York: New York University Press, 2003), 23–25.

13. Wilbur O. Atwater and Edward B. Rosa, *Description of a New Respiration Calorimeter and Experiments on the Conservation of Energy in the Human Body*, U.S. Department of Agriculture, Bulletin No. 63 (Washington, DC: Government Printing Office, 1899), National Agricultural Library, Beltsville, MD, Special Collections, Wilbur Olin Atwater Papers, coll. no. 261, box 1, series 2, folder 5; Levenstein, *Revolution at the Table*, 73–74.

14. Anson Rabinbach, *The Human Motor: Energy, Fatigue, and the Origins of Modernity* (Berkeley: University of California Press, 1990), 127–130; Nick Cullather, "The Foreign Policy of the Calorie," *American Historical Review* 112, no. 2 (April 2007): 337–364; A. Hunter Dupree, *Science in the Federal Government: A History of Policies and Activities*, rev. ed. (Baltimore: Johns Hopkins University Press, 1986).

15. James C. Scott, *Seeing Like a State: How Certain Schemes to Improve the Human Condition Have Failed* (New Haven, CT: Yale University Press, 1998), 36.

16. Jessica J. Mudry, *Measured Meals: Nutrition in America* (Albany: State University of New York Press, 2009), 36.

17. Atwater, "Chemistry of Foods and Nutrition V," 442.

18. Atwater, "Chemistry of Foods and Nutrition V," 443.

19. Atwater, "Chemistry of Foods and Nutrition V," 444.

20. Tracey Deutsch, *Building a Housewife's Paradise: Gender, Politics, and American Grocery Stores in the Twentieth Century* (Chapel Hill: University of North Carolina Press, 2010), 13–16.

21. Carolyn M. Goldstein, *Creating Consumers: Home Economists in Twentieth-Century America* (Chapel Hill: University of North Carolina Press, 2012), 39.

22. Wilbur Olin Atwater, *Principles of Nutrition and Nutritive Value of Food*, Farmers Bulletin No. 142 (Washington, DC: Government Printing Office, 1902), 33–34.

23. Atwater, *Principles of Nutrition and Nutritive Value of Food*, 33–34.

24. Jacqueline L. Dupont, "Research in the Agricultural Research Service/USDA: Introduction and Early History," *Journal of Nutrition* 139, no. 1 (January 2009): 171–172.

25. Levenstein, *Revolution at the Table*, 74–75.

26. Atwater, "The Chemistry of Foods and Nutrition III," 404; Levenstein, *Revolution at the Table*, 47.

27. Ellen H. Richards, "Domestic Science as a Synthetic Study for Girls," in *National Education Association Journal of Proceedings and Addresses of the Thirty-Seventh Annual Meeting* (Chicago: University of Chicago Press, 1898), 773.

28. Wilbur Olin Atwater, "Food: Nutritive Value and Cost," Farmers Bulletin No. 23, U.S. Department of Agriculture (Washington, DC: Government Printing Office, 1894), 3, 7, box 2, Wilbur O. Atwater Papers, Division of Rare Books and Manuscripts, Cornell University, Ithaca, NY.

29. Atwater, *Principles of Nutrition and Nutritive Value of Food*, 44–45.

30. Wilbur O. Atwater and A. P. Bryant, *The Chemical Composition of American Food Materials*, U.S. Department of Agriculture, Bulletin No. 28 (Washington DC: Government Printing Office, 1894 original print, 1906 revision), National Agricultural Library, Beltsville, MD, Special Collections, Wilbur Olin Atwater Papers, coll. no. 261, box 1, series 1, folder 1.

31. Carl Vrooman to D. F. Houston, May 14, 1915, 54, National Archives at College Park, College Park, Maryland (hereafter cited as NACP), Record Group 16, Records of the Secretary of Agriculture, entry 15, vol. 5; B. T. Galloway to Sen. Morris Sheppard, April 8, 1914, 44, NACP, RG 16, Records of the Secretary of Agriculture, entry 15, vol. 4; D. F. Houston to Sec. of War, May 9, 1914, 76, NACP, RG 16, Records of the Secretary of Agriculture, entry 15, vol. 4.

32. Nancy Duran, "Farmers' Bulletins Advice to Women on Diet, Food, and Cooking," *Journal of Agricultural and Food Information* 6, no. 1 (2004): 52.

33. Robyn Muncy, *Creating a Dominion in American Reform, 1880–1935* (Oxford: Oxford University Press, 1994); Megan J. Elias, *Stir It Up: Home Economics in American Culture* (Philadelphia: University of Pennsylvania Press, 2008).

34. "Explanation of the Work of the Office of Home Economics, made at a meeting of the Division of Medical Sciences, National Research Council, January 19, 1921, to consider the work of the Washington Evening Clinic for Women," NACP, RG 176, Records of the Bureau of Human Nutrition and Home Economics, entry 5, Subject Correspondence of the Chief of the Bureau of Home Economics and Its Predecessors, 1917–30, box 594, folder: Mss.

35. Kathryn Kish Sklar, "The Historical Foundation of Women's Power in the Creation of the American Welfare State, 1830–1930," in *Mothers of a New World: Maternalist Politics and the Origins of Welfare States*, ed. Seth Koven and Sonya Michel (New York: Routledge, 1993), 43–93.

36. Rima D. Apple, *Perfect Motherhood: Science and Childrearing in America* (New Brunswick, NJ: Rutgers University Press, 2006); Rima D. Apple, *Mothers and Medicine: A Social History of Infant Feeding, 1890–1950* (Madison: University of Wisconsin Press, 1987).

37. While teachers and nurses were paid to do their work, of course, managing child weights was not a typical duty of teachers, and still not always a duty of nurses. When I describe their labor as "voluntary" I refer to the additional, unpaid labor of learning, adopting, and explaining height-weight measures—typically a "volunteered" service.

38. Quoted in Eleanor Taylor, *On Behalf of Mothers and Children: The Story of the Children's Bureau* (Washington, DC: National League of Women Voters, 1930), 45.

39. George W. Coleman, "Address," in *American Association for Study and Prevention of Infant Mortality: Transactions of the Fifth Annual Meeting* (Baltimore: Franklin Printing Company, 1915), 266.

40. Rep. Frank Barlett Willis speaking on Department of Labor Appropriations, April 16, 1914, to the House, 63rd Cong., 2nd Sess., *Congressional Record*, 6809–6810; Julia Lathrop, "The Children's Bureau," *American Journal of Sociology* 18, no. 3 (November 1912): 322.

41. Alice Boardman Smuts, *Science in the Service of Children, 1893–1935* (New Haven, CT: Yale University Press, 2006), 88–89.

42. For analysis of the broader successes and limitations of the Children's Bureau, see Richard A. Meckel, *Save the Babies: American Public Health Reform and the Prevention of Infant Mortality, 1850–1929* (Baltimore: Johns Hopkins University Press, 1990); and Alisa Klaus, *Every Child a Lion: The Origins of Maternal and Infant Health Policy in the United States and France, 1890–1920* (Ithaca, NY: Cornell University Press, 1993).

43. Alice O'Connor, *Poverty Knowledge: Social Science, Social Policy and the Poor in Twentieth-Century U.S. History* (Princeton, NJ: Princeton University Press, 2002), 3.

44. John Duffy, *The Sanitarians: A History of American Public Health* (Urbana: University of Illinois Press, 1990); Nancy Tomes, *The Gospel of Germs: Men, Women, and the Microbe in American Life* (Cambridge, MA: Harvard University Press, 1998); George Rosen, *A History of Public Health*, revised and expanded edition (Baltimore: Johns Hopkins University Press, 2015).

45. C. M. Kelley, "A 'Nutrition' and Intelligence Quotient Slide Rule," *Journal of the American Medical Association* 80, no. 6 (February 10, 1923): 397–398.

46. Robert Woodbury to Miss Steever, May 14, 1925, NACP, RG 102, Records of the Children's Bureau, entry 3, Central File 1914–1920, box 277, folder 4-11-4-5.

47. Amanda M. Czerniawski, "From Average to Ideal: The Evolution of the Height and Weight Table in the United States, 1836–1943," *Social Science History* 31, no. 2 (2007): 273–296.

48. Robert Woodbury to Blanche Haines, August 2, 1922, box 197, folder 4-11-4-5; Anna Rude to Phillip K. Brown, September 29, 1921, box 197, folder 4-11-4-5; Theodore C. Merrill to Anna Rude, August 11, 1920, box 197, folder 4-11-4-5; Robert Woodbury to Emmett Holt, June 29, 1922, box 197, folder 4-11-4-5; Association for Improving the Condition of the Poor to Robert Woodbury, November 19, 1923, box 197, folder 4-11-4-5; Emmett Holt to Anna Rude, April 26, 1923, box 197, folder 4-11-4-5; Ella Oppenheimer to Ethel Thompson, April 4, 1931, box 378, folder 4-5-11-0; all in NACP, RG 102, Records of the Children's Bureau, entry 3, Central File 1914–1920.

49. The Children's Bureau, *April and May Weighing a Measuring Test, Part 3: Follow-Up Work*, Bureau Publication No. 38 (Washington, DC: Government Printing Office, 1918), 4.

50. Giorgio Bedogni, "Body Mass Index: From Quételet to Evidence-Based Medicine," in *Body Mass Index: New Research*, ed. Linda A. Ferrera (New York: Nova Science, 2005), 2.

51. Taliaferro Clark, Edgar Sydenstricker, Selwyn D. Collins, "Weight and Height as an Index of Nutrition," *Public Health Reports* 38, no. 2 (January 12, 1923): 53.

52. Bird T. Baldwin, "The Use and Abuse of Weight-Height-Age Tables as Indexes of Health and Nutrition," *Journal of the American Medical Association* 82, no. 1 (January 5, 1924): 1–4.

53. *Official Proceedings of the White House Conference on Child Health and Protection*, Supplement to the United States Daily 5, no. 288 (November 1930), 7, box 57, folder 6, New York State College of Home Economics Records, 1875–1917, Cornell University Division of Rare Books and Manuscript Collections, Ithaca, NY.

54. Hillel Schwartz, *Never Satisfied: A Cultural History of Diets, Fantasy, and Fat* (New York: Free Press, 1986).

55. Judith Sealander, "Perpetually Malnourished? Diet, Health, and America's Young in the Twentieth Century," in *Children's Health Issues in Historical Perspective*, ed. Cheryl Krasnick Warsh and Veronica Strong-Boag (Waterloo, ON: Wilfrid Laurier University Press, 2005), 184n43; Laura L. Lovett, *Conceiving the Future: Pronatalism, Reproduction, and the Family in the United States, 1890–1938* (Chapel Hill: University of North Carolina Press, 2007), 148–149.

56. "American Baby Health Contest Association Suggestions for Organizing and Carrying on Baby Health Contests," n.d. (between 1914 and 1920), NACP, RG 102, Records of the Children's Bureau, entry 3, Central File 1914–1920, box 37, folder 4-14-2-3-0.

57. Gabriel N. Rosenberg, *The 4-H Harvest: Sexuality and the State in Rural America* (Philadelphia: University of Pennsylvania Press, 2015), 7–8.

58. Alexandra Minna Stern, *Eugenic Nation: Faults and Frontiers of Better Breeding in Modern America*, 2nd ed. (Oakland: University of California Press, 2016), 85–86; Wendy Kline, *Building a Better Race: Gender, Sexuality, and Eugenics from the Turn of the Century to the Baby Boom* (Berkeley: University of California Press, 2001), 29–30.

59. Edward J. Larson, *Sex, Race, and Science: Eugenics in the Deep South* (Baltimore: Johns Hopkins University Press, 1995), 93.

60. Annette K. Vance Dorey, *Better Baby Contests: The Scientific Quest for Perfect Childhood Health in the Early Twentieth Century* (Jefferson, NC: McFarland, 1999), 6.

61. Lovett, *Conceiving the Future*, 15.

62. Examples of the adoption of standards include publications like the Kansas State Board of Health Score Card and baby health contests like the one put on by the Iowa branch of the National Mothers Congress, which suggest the quick dissemination of the idea. See NACP, RG 102, Records of the Children's Bureau, entry 3, Central File 1914–1920, box 37, folder 4-14-2-3-2.

63. American Medical Association, 1916 revised pamphlet, NACP, RG 102, Records of the Children's Bureau, entry 3, Central File 1914–1920, box 37, folder 4-14-2-4-0.

64. Larson, *Sex, Race, and Science*, 20–22; Rebecca M. Kluchin, *Fit to Be Tied: Sterilization and Reproductive Rights in America, 1950–1980* (New Brunswick, NJ: Rutgers University Press, 2009).

65. It is critical to understand the differences between eugenic movements. Much of the eugenic activism of the early twentieth century came through subtle methods. This does not mean they were any less racist or ethnocentric—their projects were those of remaking immigrant and nonwhite Americans in an idealized white, native "American" fashion, in arenas as diverse as health, nutrition, parenting, and lifestyle.

66. Indianapolis Baby Week, October 3–9, 1915, 12, NACP, RG 102, Records of the Children's Bureau, entry 3, Central File 1914–1920, box 36, folder 4-14-2-2-4.

67. Michele Mitchell, *Righteous Propagation: African Americans and the Politics of Racial Destiny After Reconstruction* (Chapel Hill: University of North Carolina Press, 2004), 96, 98.

68. Dorey, *Better Baby Contests*, 35.

69. Quoted in Dorey, *Better Baby Contests*, 27.

70. Grace Abbott, Lathrop's sucessor, echoed Lathrop's stance. Grace Abbott to M. V. O'Shea, November 18, 1921, box 194, folder 4-11-0-5-1; Julia C. Lathrop to M. Russell Perkins, February 13, 1915, box 37, folder 4-14-2-3-0; Julia C. Lathrop to Dr. Frederick R. Green, September 18, 1914, box 37, folder 4-14-2-3-0; Woman's Home Companion Editor to Julia Lathrop, 26 June 1913, box 37, folder 4-14-2-3-0; Agnes Ditson to Mary Watts, November 25, 1912, box 37, folder 4-14-2-3-0; all in NACP, RG 102, Records of the Children's Bureau, entry 3, Central File 1914–1920.

71. Alexandra Minna Stern, "Making Better Babies: Public Health and Race Betterment in Indiana, 1920–1935," *American Journal of Public Health* 92, no. 5 (May 2002): 742–752.

72. Max West to Roscoe C. Main, August 18, 1915, NACP, RG 102, Records of the Children's Bureau, entry 3, Central File 1914–1920, box 37, folder 4-14-2-3-0.

73. Frank Spooner Churchill to Julia Lathrop, May 6, 1914, NACP, RG 102, Records of the Children's Bureau, entry 3, Central File 1914–1920, box 37, folder 4-14-2-3-3.

74. Quoted in Children's Bureau, *Baby-Week Campaigns: Suggestions for Communities of Various Sizes*, Bureau Publication No. 15 (Washington, DC: Government Printing Office, 1918), 54.

75. Kriste Lindenmeyer, *"A Right to Childhood": The U.S. Children's Bureau and Child Welfare, 1912–46* (Urbana: University of Illinois Press, 1997), 71.

76. David M. Kennedy, *Over Here: The First World War and American Society*, 25th Anniversary Edition (Oxford: Oxford University Press, 2004); Alan Axelrod, *Selling the Great War: The Making of American Propaganda* (New York: Palgrave Macmillan, 2009); Celia Malone Kingsbury, *For Home and Country: World War I Propaganda on the Home Front* (Lincoln: University of Nebraska Press, 2010).

77. In most cases, the overweight child was not understood as a problem until the 1950s. Individual children could certainly be deemed overweight, but there was not a systemic understanding of "overweight" equaling "unhealthy" in children at this point, since there was such a strong emphasis on children needing to gain weight in the shadow of malnutrition. The "overweight" equals "unhealthy" equation did apply to adults as early as the 1910s, but this was not a direct concern of the Children's Bureau.

78. Alexandra Minna Stern, "Making Better Babies."

79. Julia Lathrop and William B. Wilson, Letter of transmittal for *Infant Care* (Washington, DC: Government Printing Office, 1914), 7.

80. Julia Lathrop, *Third Annual Report of the Chief, Children's Bureau, to the Secretary of Labor* (Washington, DC: Government Printing Office, 1915), 11.

81. Barbara Ehrenreich and Deirdre English, *For Her Own Good: 150 Years of the Experts' Advice to Women* (New York: Doubleday, 1978); Julia Grant, *Raising Baby by the Book: The Education of American Mothers* (New Haven, CT: Yale University Press, 1998); Ann Hulbert, *Raising America: Experts, Parents, and a Century of Advice About Children* (New York: Vintage, 2003).

82. Welfare Administration, *The Story of Infant Care*, U.S. Department of Health, Education, and Welfare, Children's Bureau, 1965, 5; 10.

83. Welfare Administration, *Story of Infant Care*, 11.

84. Others followed her lead, as with the Red Cross nurses' queries into which specific brand of scale the Children's Bureau recommended. Red Cross Department of Nursing to Julia Lathrop, June 9, 1920; Julia Lathrop to Red Cross Department of Nursing, June 15, 1920; both in NACP, RG 102, Records of the Children's Bureau, entry 3, Central File 1914–1920, box 37, folder 4-14-2-4-0.

85. Quoted in Congress, Senate, 64th Cong., 2nd Sess., *Congressional Record* (January 19, 1917), 1678.

86. Children's Bureau, *Save 100,000 Babies: Get a Square Deal for Children*, Children's Year Leaflet 1, Bureau Publication 36 (Washington, DC: Government Printing Office, 1918), 2.

87. The war provided a number of opportunities for other aspects of the Children's Bureau, which had goals beyond child health. Those concerned with child labor, for instance, argued near the end of the war for stricter child labor laws. They used the premise that children were taking jobs that could go to returning soldiers. During the war, the argument against child labor was that soldiers abroad should not need to fret over their children's safety. War opened up new opportunities and dialogs, even in the seemingly unrelated realm of U.S. children's welfare. Ida Clyde Clarke, *American Women and the World War* (New York: D. Appleton, 1918), chap. 6.

88. United States War Department, *Mobilization Regulations, Prescribed by the President Under the Authority of the Selective Service Law, Act of May 18, 1917* (Washington, DC: Government Printing Office, 1917), 11.

89. Children's Bureau, *Save 100,000 Babies*, 4.

90. Jacqueline H. Wolf, *Don't Kill Your Baby: Public Health and the Decline of Breastfeeding in the 19th and 20th Centuries* (Columbus: Ohio State University Press, 2001), 119.

91. Children's Bureau, *Children's Year: A Brief Summary of Work Done and Suggestions for Follow-Up Work*, Bureau Publication No. 67 (Washington, DC: Government Printing Office, 1920), 9.

92. Children's Bureau, *April and May Weighing and Measuring Test, Part 1: Suggestions to Local Committees*, Bureau Publication No. 38 (Washington, DC: Government Printing Office, 1918), 3.

93. Children's Bureau, *April and May Weighing and Measuring Test, Part 1*, 7.

94. Children's Bureau, *April and May Weighing and Measuring Test, Part 2: Suggestions to Examiners*, Bureau Publication No. 38 (Washington, DC: Government Printing Office, 1918), 2–3.

95. Children's Bureau, *April and May Weighing and Measuring Test, Part 2*, 4.

96. Children's Bureau, *April and May Weighing and Measuring Test, Part 1*, 8.

97. Children's Bureau, *Our Children*, 1919, NACP, RG 102, Records of the Children's Bureau, Motion Pictures, Film Reel.

98. When asked directly by Red Cross nurses, Julia Lathrop said that a grocer's scale was fine for weighing infants (although she did not believe it was adequate for weighing older children). The inclusion of the grocer as another stop on the tour of unscientific motherhood in the film, though, emphasizes that the bureau belied the importance of expertise and the need for professional intervention into mothers' habits. Red Cross Department of Nursing to Julia Lathrop, June 9, 1920; Julia Lathrop to Red Cross Department of Nursing, June 15, 1920; both in NACP, RG 102, Records of the Children's Bureau, entry 3, Central File 1914–1920, box 37, folder 4-14-2-4-0.

99. Mary D. to Brown Sherbon, February 9, 1920; Anna Rude to Ruth Dodd, November 5, 1920; Mrs. C. P. Sembach to Children's Bureau, June 4, 1920; Frances E. Thorp to Children's Bureau, April 9, 1920; all in NACP, RG 102, Records of the Children's Bureau, entry 3, Central File 1914–1920, box 28, folder 4-4-9.

100. And a standard set for the regular questions the bureau received about child weight. Gladys Stockman to Children's Bureau, June 22, 1923, box, 28, folder 4-5-4-1; Robert Woodbury to Charles S. Prest, April 9, 1924, box 197, folder 4-11-4-5; Charles S. Prest to Robert Woodbury, April 15, 1924, box 197, folder 4-11-4-5; all in NACP, RG 102, Records of the Children's Bureau, entry 3, Central File 1914–1920.

101. Children's Bureau, *April and May Weighing and Measuring Test, Part 3*, 3.

102. Children's Bureau, *April and May Weighing and Measuring Test, Part 1*, 6.

103. Instead, the Bureau increasingly recommended that women take their children to doctors for proper weighing. Viola Russell to F. J. Reynolds, March 2, 1927, box 277, folder 4-11-4-5; Frances C. Robert to Mrs. Ed Redford, September 21, 1931, box 378, folder 4-5-12-6; Frances C. Robert to Mrs. Charles Zien, August 28, 1929, box 380, folder 4-6-3-1; all in NACP, RG 102, Records of the Children's Bureau, entry 3, Central File 1914–1920.

104. Children's Bureau, *April and May Weighing and Measuring Test, Part 3*, 4–5.

105. The medical specialty, alongside the idea that children's health needs were substantially different from adult health needs, was new but rapidly growing. The American Academy of Pediatrics (AAP) would not be founded until 1929—interestingly, the same year that the Sheppard-Towner Act would be defunded.

106. The act is appropriately portrayed as a welfare state and public health milestone. The overemphasis on Sheppard-Towner, however, means that it is easy to overlook a number of other critical moments in Children's Bureau work that actually had more staying power (if not as much funding or reach). On Sheppard-Towner, see Theda Skocpol, *Protecting Soldiers and Mothers: The Political Origins of Social Policy in the United States* (Cambridge, MA: Harvard University Press, 1992); Molly Ladd-Taylor, *Mother-Work: Women, Child Welfare, and the State, 1890–1930* (Urbana: University of Illinois Press, 1994); Sheila M. Rothman, "Women's Clinics or Doctor's Offices?: The Sheppard-Towner Act and the Promotion of Preventative Health Care," in *Social History and Social Policy* (New York: Academic Press, 1981); Milton Kotelchuck, "Safe Mothers, Healthy Babies: Reproductive Health in the Twentieth Century," in *Silent Victories: The History and Practice of Public Health in Twentieth Century America*, ed. John W. Ward and Christian Warren (New York: Oxford University Press, 2006), 112; Lindenmeyer, *"Right to Childhood,"* 76; Meckel, *Save the Babies*.

Chapter 2

1. James McEntee, *Now They Are Men: The Story of the C.C.C.* (Washington, DC: National Home Library Foundation, 1940), 58, National Archives at College Park, College Park, MD (hereafter cited as NACP), Record Group 35, Records of the Civilian Conservation Corps, entry 53, Division of Selection, Publications, 1939–42.

2. Wesley C. Cox, "The Morale of Good Health," in *The Spirit of the Civilian Conservation Corps*, ed. Alfred C. Oliver, Jr., and Harold M. Dudley (London: Longmans, Green, 1937), 44.

3. Domesticized and, perhaps ironically, militarized through almost the same discourses and practices.

4. *The CCC Offers a Young Man a Chance* (Washington, DC: Government Printing Office, 1938), NACP, RG 35, Records of the Civilian Conservation Corps, entry 102, Division of Planning and Public Relations, Publications 1933–1942, box 2, folder: Pamphlets Misc.

5. Franklin Roosevelt, quoted in "Work Experience That Counts" (Washington, DC: Government Printing Office, 1941), 4, NACP, RG 35, Records of the Civilian Conservation Corps, entry 102, Division of Planning and Public Relations, Publications 1933–1942, box 5, folder: Work Experience That Counts.

6. *The Public Papers and Addresses of Franklin D. Roosevelt* (New York: Random House, 1938), 2:322.

7. "Unemployment Relief," March 23, 1933, Joint Session of the Committee on Education and Labor and the Committee on Labor of the House of Representatives, 1.

8. Neil M. Maher, *Nature's New Deal: The Civilian Conservation Corps and the Roots of the American Environmental Movement* (New York: Oxford University Press, 2008).

9. "Unemployment Relief," March 23, 1933, Joint Session of the Committee on Education and Labor and the Committee on Labor of the House of Representatives, 21–26.

10. Hugh Ford, December 7, 1935, NACP, RG 35, Records of the Civilian Conservation Corps, entry 99, Division of Planning and Public Relations Benefit Letters, 1934–1942, box 2, folder: Letters from CCC Enrollees RE benefits received while in the corps.

11. Dr. Rice (?), MSS, "Training Division: Medical Selection," April 1942 (?), NACP, RG 35, Records of the Civilian Conservation Corps, entry 21, Records Relating to the Proposed Merger of the National Youth Administration and the CCC, box 1, folder: Medical Reports.

12. "Girl Campers Get Fatigue," *Happy Days* (August 12, 1933): 2, NACP, RG 35, Records of the Civilian Conservation Corps, entry 18, Happy Days, box 1; "Camps to Be Opened for 5000 Girls Will Be Similar to CCC," *Happy Days* (December 5, 1936): 20; Blanche Wiesen Cook, *Eleanor Roosevelt*, vol. 2, *1933–1938* (New York: Viking Press, 1999), 88–91; Alfred Emile Cornebise, *The CCC Chronicles: Camp Newspapers of the Civilian Conservation Corps, 1933–1942* (Jefferson, NC: McFarland, 2004), 247n6; Maher, *Nature's New Deal*.

13. John A. Salmond, *Civilian Conservation Corps, 1933–1942: A New Deal Case Study* (Durham, NC: Duke University Press, 1967), 48.

14. Olen Cole, Jr., *The African American Experience in the Civilian Conservation Corps* (Gainesville: University of Florida Press, 1999), 14.

15. Ira Katznelson, *Fear Itself: The New Deal and the Origins of Our Time* (New York: Norton, 2013).

16. Quoted in Salmond, *Civilian Conservation Corps*, 90.

17. Cole, *African American Experience in the Civilian Conservation Corps*, 14.

18. Cole, *African American Experience in the Civilian Conservation Corps*, 56.

19. Beth Linker, *War's Waste: Rehabilitation in World War I America* (Chicago: University of Chicago Press, 2014).

20. Nancy Fraser and Linda Gordon, "A Genealogy of Dependency: Tracing a Key Word of the U.S. Welfare State," *Signs* 19, no. 2 (Winter 1994): 309–336.

21. Alan Brinkley, *The End of Reform: New Deal Liberalism in Recession and War* (New York: Vintage, 1996).

22. Salmond, *Civilian Conservation Corps*, 3–4.

23. John E. Moser, *The Global Great Depression and the Coming of World War II* (New York: Routledge, 2015); Dietmar Rothermund, *The Global Impact of the Great Depression, 1929–1939* (New York: Routledge, 1996); Alessio Ponzio, *Shaping the New Man: Youth Training Regimes in Fascist Italy and Nazi Germany* (Madison: University of Wisconsin Press, 2015).

24. Rep. Frank W. Fries, "To Make the Civilian Conservation Corps a Permanent Agency," *Hearings Before the Committee on Labor, House of Representatives*, 76th Cong., 1st Sess., on H.R. 2990, February 9, 1939, 15.

25. Anna R. Igra, *Wives Without Husbands: Marriage, Desertion and Welfare in New York, 1930–35* (Chapel Hill: University of North Carolina Press, 2007); Ruth Milkman, "Women's Work and Economic Crisis: Some Lessons of the Great Depression," *Review of Radical Political Economics* 8, no. 1 (April 1976): 71–97; Laura Hapke, *Daughters of the Great Depression: Women, Work, and Fiction in the American 1930s* (Athens: University of Georgia Press, 1995); Elaine S. Abelson, "Women Who Have No Men to Work for Them: Gender and Homelessness in the Great Depression, 1930–1934," *Feminist Studies* 29, no. 1 (Spring 2003): 104–127.

26. Margot Canaday, *The Straight State: Sexuality and Citizenship in Twentieth-Century America* (Princeton, NJ: Princeton University Press, 2009), 91–96; Nancy F. Cott, *Public Vows: A History of Marriage and the Nation* (Cambridge, MA: Harvard University Press, 2000), 172–173.

27. Richard R. Brown, "What Is Happening to Youth," in *This New America: The Spirit of the Civilian Conservation Corps*, ed. Alfred C. Oliver, Jr., and Harold M. Dudley (London: Longmans, Green, 1937), 16.

28. Brown, "What Is Happening to Youth," 16.

29. Colin R. Johnson, *Just Queer Folks: Gender and Sexuality in Rural America* (Philadelphia: Temple University Press, 2013), 156–157; Colin R. Johnson, "Camp Life: The Queer History of 'Manhood' in the Civilian Conservation Corps, 1933–1937," *American Studies* 48, no. 2 (Summer 2007): 19–36, 26.

30. Canaday, *Straight State*, 103.

31. Caroline Hunt to Charles Langworthy, November 27, 1923, NACP, RG 176, Records of the Bureau of Human Nutrition and Home Economics, entry 20, Correspondence 1923–30, box 725, folder: Charles F. Langworthy.

32. *Annual Report of the Director of the Civilian Conservation Corps, Fiscal Year ended June 30 1938* (Washington, DC: Government Printing Office, 1938), 92–93; *Department of Labor Appropriation Bill for 1938*, H.R. 5779, *Congressional Record*, 75th Cong., 1st Sess., 169, 188.

33. "Work Experience That Counts" (Washington, DC: Government Printing Office, 1941), 15, NACP, RG 35, entry 102, Division of Planning and Public Relations, Publications, 1933–1942, box 5, folder: Work Experience That Counts.

34. Clifford Putney, *Muscular Christianity: Manhood and Sports in Protestant America, 1880–1920* (Cambridge, MA: Harvard University Press, 2001); Harvey Green, *Fit for America: Health, Fitness, Sport and American Society* (Baltimore: Johns Hopkins University Press, 1988).

35. Gail Bederman, *Manliness and Civilization: A Cultural History of Gender and Race in the United States, 1880–1917* (Chicago: University of Chicago Press, 1995).

36. Jonathan Black, *Making the American Body: The Remarkable Saga of the Men and Women Whose Feats, Feuds, and Passions Shaped Fitness History* (Lincoln: University of Nebraska Press, 2013); John D. Fair, *Mr. America: The Tragic History of a Body Building Icon* (Austin: University of Texas Press, 2015).

37. Harvey A. Levenstein, *Paradox of Plenty: A Social History of Eating in Modern America*, rev. ed. (Berkeley: University of California Press, 2003), 9–10.

38. Janet Poppendieck, *Breadlines Knee-Deep in Wheat: Food Assistance in the Great Depression* (New Brunswick, NJ: Rutgers University Press, 1986), 20.

39. Susan Levine, *School Lunch Politics: The Surprising History of America's Favorite Welfare Program* (Princeton, NJ: Princeton University Press, 2008), 40–41.

40. Poppendieck, *Breadlines Knee-Deep in Wheat*, 24.

41. Rachel Louise Moran, "Consuming Relief: Food Stamps and the New Welfare of the New Deal," *Journal of American History* 97, no. 4 (March 2011): 1001–1022.

42. Michael S. Kimmel, "Masculinity as Homophobia: Fear, Shame, and Silence in the Construction of Gender Identity," in *Theorizing Masculinities*, ed. Harry Brod and Michael Kaufman (Thousand Oaks, CA: Sage, 1994), 119–140.

43. Louis J. Sampel, December 14, 1935, NACP, RG 35, entry 99, Division of Planning and Public Relations Benefit Letters.

44. Cox, "Morale of Good Health," 43; *The Civilian Conservation Corps: Recommendations of the American Youth Commission of the American Council on Education*, pamphlet, 1940, esp. 2, NACP, RG 107, Records of the Office of the Secretary of War, entry A1 E188, box 187, folder: CCC-General.

45. Cox, "Morale of Good Health," 43.

46. It is unclear how often men were *actually* weighed, but they were supposed to be weighed once a month according to camp health guidelines. Robert Fechner to Colonel Duncan K. Major, Jr., July 6, 1933, NACP, RG 35, Records of the Civilian Conservation Corps, entry

PI-11 2, General Correspondence, 1933–1942, box 695, folder 500: War Department—Surgeon General (Physical Examination Forms).

47. J. J. McEntee to Major General Robert U. Patterson, July 9, 1934, box 695, folder 500: War Department (Report on Salient Benefits); Granville Dickey to Office of the Surgeon General, April 9, 1935, box 695, folder 500: War Department—Surgeon General (Physical Examination Forms); Chris H. Taylor to Surgeon General, April 9, 1935, box 695, folder 500: War Department—Surgeon General (Physical Examination Forms); all in NACP, RG 35, Records of the Civilian Conservation Corps, entry PI-11 2, General Correspondence, 1933–1942.

48. Emergency Conservation Work, Office of the Director, "Notes on C.C.C. Activities," February 19, 1937, NACP, RG 35, Records of the Civilian Conservation Corps, entry 102, Division of Planning and Public Relations, Publications 1933–1942, box 3, folder: Food—releases—gen file.

49. Frank Persons and unnamed other writers, Bulletin No. 41 (Washington, DC: Government Printing Press, May 1940), 12, NACP, RG 35, Records of the Civilian Conservation Corps, entry 102, Division of Planning and Public Relations, Publications 1933–1942, box 4.

50. "Statement of Mr. Robert Fechner, Director of Emergency Conservation Work with Regard to the Proposed Bill for Making the Civilian Conservation Corps Permanent," 14, NACP, RG 35, Records of the Civilian Conservation Corps, entry 102, Division of Planning and Public Relations, Publications 1933–1942, box 5, folder: Statement of Mr. Robert Fechner.

51. James McEntee, *Now They Are Men: The Story of the C.C.C.* (Washington, DC: National Home Library Foundation, 1940), 58, NACP, RG 35, entry 53, Division of Selection, Publications 1933–42, box 1, no folder.

52. *Annual Report of the Director of the Civilian Conservation Corps for the Fiscal Year Ended June 30, 1940* (Washington, DC: Government Printing Office, 1940), 9, NACP, RG 35, Records of the Civilian Conservation Corps, entry 3, Annual, Special, Final Reports, 1933–1943, box 1.

53. Robert Fencher, quoted in *Congressional Record*, 75th Cong., 3rd Sess. (Washington, DC: Government Printing Office, June 3, 1938), Civilian Conservation Corps, statement by Hon. Elbert D. Thomas of Utah on the Record of the Civilian Conservation Corps in Fiscal Year 1938, NACP, RG 35, Records of the Civilian Conservation Corps, entry 56, Division of Selection, box 1, folder: Mr. Snyder's Field Trip January 21–February 10, 1939.

54. *Annual Report of the Director of the Civilian Conservation Corps, for the Fiscal Year ended June 30, 1940* (Washington, DC: Government Printing Office, 1940), 25, NACP, RG 35, Records of the Civilian Conservation Corps, entry 3, Annual, Special, and Final Reports, 1933–1943, box 1.

55. *The Civilian Conservation Corps* (Washington, DC: Government Printing Office 1936), NACP, RG 35, Records of the Civilian Conservation Corps, entry 102, Division of Planning and Public Relations, Publications 1933–1942, box 1, folder: Civilian Conservation Corps.

56. Excerpt from *1938 Annual Report*, June 1, 1937–June 30, 1938, 8–9, NACP, RG 35, Records of the Civilian Conservation Corps, entry 102, Division of Planning and Public Relations, Publications 1933–1942, box 1, folder: Civilian Cons. Corps Activities.

57. Civilian Conservation Corps, "What About the C.C.C.?," draft of booklet (Washington, DC: Government Printing Office, 1937), NACP, RG 35, Records of the Civilian Conservation Corps, entry 102, Division of Planning and Public Relations, Publications 1933–1942, box 5, folder: What About the CCC?

58. Bulletin No. 2, April 20, 1933, United States Department of Labor, Washington, DC, 1, RG 35, Records of the Civilian Conservation Corps, entry 102, Division of Planning and Public Relations, Publications 1933–1942, box 1, folder: Bulletin Nos. 1 and 2 (1933).

59. Civilian Conservation Corps, *The Nation Appraises the CCC, April 1933–September 1939* (Washington, DC: Government Printing Office, 1939), 9, NACP, RG 35, Records of the Civilian Conservation Corps, entry 102, Division of Planning and Public Relations, Publications 1933–1942, box 4, folder: "Nation Appraises the CCC."

60. Civilian Conservation Corps, statement by Hon. Elbert D. Thomas of Utah on the Record of the Civilian Conservation Corps in Fiscal Year 1938, *Congressional Record,* 75th Cong., 3rd Sess. (Washington, DC: Government Printing Office, June 3, 1938), NACP, RG 35, Records of the Civilian Conservation Corps, entry 56, box 1, folder: Mr. Snyder's Field Trip January 21–February 10, 1939.

61. "CCC Boys Will Be CCC Boys," *Boston Traveler* (June 17, 1939), quoted in Civilian Conservation Corps, *The Nation Appraises the CCC,* 20.

62. Alfred C. Oliver, Jr., and Harold M. Dudley, eds., *This New America: The Spirit of the Civilian Conservation Corps* (London: Longmans, Green, 1937), 132.

63. "Smiles," *Happy Days,* vol. 1, no. 2 (May 27, 1933): 9, NACP, RG 35, Records of the Civilian Conservation Corps, entry 18, Happy Days, box 1.

64. "Leavenworth Grub Sure Must Be Good," *Happy Days,* vol. 1, no. 2 (May 27, 1933): 9, NACP, RG 35, Records of the Civilian Conservation Corps, entry 18, Happy Days, box 1.

65. A "peavie" or peavey is a hooked foresting tool used for handling logs, and was a common nickname for CCC enrollees.

66. *Happy Days,* vol. 1, no. 8 (July 8, 1933): 12, NACP, RG 35, Records of the Civilian Conservation Corps, entry 18, Happy Days, box 1.

67. "Peavie Gains 18 Pounds in Camp," *Happy Days,* vol. 1, no. 14 (August 19, 1933): 1, NACP, RG 35, Records of the Civilian Conservation Corps, entry 18, Happy Days, box 1.

68. *Happy Days* 1, no. 18 (September 16, 1933): 6, NACP, RG 35, Records of the Civilian Conservation Corps, entry 18, Happy Days, box 1.

69. Ovid Butler, ed., *Youth Rebuilds: Stories from the C.C.C.* (Washington, DC: American Forestry Association, 1934), 104.

70. Maher discusses CCC benefit letters, and uses the transformations described in these letters as evidence that "many young men felt both emasculated and infantilized before enrolling in the CCC." The letters, though, primarily tell us the thoughts of the CCC leadership *about* enrollees, rather than allowing us access to the thoughts of enrollees themselves.

71. L. J. Reader, letter, December 15, 1935, NACP, RG 35, Records of the Civilian Conservation Corps, entry 99, Division of Planning and Public Relations Benefit Letters, box 2.

72. William Howry, letter, December 11, 1935; John R. Curry, letter, December 3, 1935; both in NACP, RG 35, Records of the Civilian Conservation Corps, entry 99, Division of Planning and Public Relations Benefit Letters, Box 1, Folder: Letters from CCC enrollees re: benefits received from the corps.

73. Paul A. Crouch to H. R. Halsey, 1935, NACP, RG 35, Records of the Civilian Conservation Corps, entry 99, Division of Planning and Public Relations Benefit Letters, Box 1, Folder: Letters from CCC enrollees re: benefits received from the corps.

74. Bebe Pagley, letter, December 17, 1935, NACP, RG 35, Records of the Civilian Conservation Corps, entry 99, Division of Planning and Public Relations Benefit Letters, Box 1, Folder: Letters from CCC enrollees re: benefits received from the corps.

75. James Weister, letter, December 1935?, NACP, RG 35, Records of the Civilian Conservation Corps, entry 99, Division of Planning and Public Relations Benefit Letters, Box 1, Folder: Letters of commendation from CCC boys.

76. Dean Neelens to District Headquarters, December 31, 1935, NACP, RG 35, Records of the Civilian Conservation Corps, entry 99, Division of Planning and Public Relations Benefit Letters, Box 1, Folder: Letters from CCC enrollees re: benefits received from the corps.

77. Paul A. Crouch to H. R. Halsey, 1935, NACP, RG 35, Records of the Civilian Conservation Corps, entry 99, Division of Planning and Public Relations Benefit Letters, Box 1, Folder: Letters from CCC enrollees re: benefits received from the corps.

78. Henry Casanta, letter, 1935?, NACP, RG 35, Records of the Civilian Conservation Corps, entry 99, Division of Planning and Public Relations Benefit Letters, Box 1, Folder: Letters from CCC enrollees re: benefits received from the corps.

79. Robert B. Hawkins to Corps Area Education Adviser, "Physical Benefits to Members at Large," December 7, 1935, NACP, RG 35, Records of the Civilian Conservation Corps, entry 99, Division of Planning and Public Relations Benefit Letters, Box 1, Folder: Letters from CCC enrollees re: benefits received from the corps.

80. Joe Campbell, *Happy Days*, vol. 2, no. 49 (April 21, 1934): 9, NACP, RG 35, Records of the Civilian Conservation Corps, entry 18, Happy Days, box 1.

81. Victor Pesek of Lewiston, Idaho, "An Inventory of Character," in *This New America: The Spirit of the Civilian Conservation Corps*, ed. Alfred C. Oliver, Jr., and Harold M. Dudley (London: Longmans, Green, 1937), 106.

82. John Miller, "Self-Respect and Self-Reliance," in *This New America: The Spirit of the Civilian Conservation Corps*, ed. Alfred C. Oliver, Jr. and Harold M. Dudley (London: Longmans, Green, 1937), 107.

83. F. H. Lawson, Senate hearing, "Termination of the C.C.C. and N.Y.A.," March 1942, 251; Transcript, "Conversation with J. S. Billips, Special Investigator," both in NACP, RG 35, Records of the Civilian Conservation Corps, entry 21, Records Relating to the Proposed Merger of the National Youth Administration and the CCC, box 3, folder: Notes of Conversations or Conferences.

84. Andrea Campbell, *How Policies Make Citizens: Senior Political Activism and the American Welfare State* (Princeton, NJ: Princeton University Press, 2003).

Chapter 3

1. Raymond H. Hackney, "One Man's Story from World War II," *Virginian-Pilot* (Norfolk, VA, July 4, 1995): A14.

2. Sanders Marble, "The U.S. Army and Limited Service Manpower," in *Scraping the Barrel: The Military Use of Substandard Manpower, 1860–1960*, ed. Sanders Marble (New York: Fordham University Press, 2012), 141–142.

3. James T. Sparrow, *Warfare State: World War II Americans and the Age of Big Government* (Oxford: Oxford University Press, 2011), 4–11.

4. Keith E. Eiler, *Mobilizing America: Robert P. Patterson and the War Effort, 1940–1945* (Ithaca, NY: Cornell University Press, 1997).

5. Sparrow, *Warfare State*, 204.

6. Sparrow, *Warfare State*, 204.

7. George Q. Flynn, *Lewis B. Hershey: Mr. Selective Service* (Chapel Hill: University of North Carolina Press, 1985).

8. "We Could Be Worse Off but Should Be Better," *Summer Texan* (University of Texas at Austin, August 7, 1941): 4.

9. "Physically Unfit," *Era* (Bradford, PA, January 1, 1940): 14.

10. Nicholas A. Krehbiel, *General Lewis B. Hershey and Conscientious Objection During World War II* (Columbia: University of Missouri Press, 2011), 49.

11. Leonard D. Heaton, foreword to William B. Foster, Ida Levin Hellman, Douglas Hesford, and Darrell G. McPherson, *Physical Standards in World War II* (Washington, DC: Government Printing Office, 1967), ix.

12. WAVES stands for "Women Accepted for Volunteer Emergency Service," but the full name was seldom used. These were female U.S. Navy reservists allowed to serve in a noncombat capacity for the duration of the war emergency, and no longer. For discussions of women's military and civilian sacrifices in World War II, see Karen Anderson, *Wartime Women: Sex Roles, Family Relations, and the Status of Women During World War II* (Westport, CT: Greenwood, 1981); Ruth Milkman, *The Dynamics of Job Segregation by Sex During World War II* (Urbana-Champaign: University of Illinois Press, 1987); and Leisa D. Meyer, *Creating GI Jane: Sexuality and Power in the Women's Army Corps in World War II* (New York: Columbia University Press, 1996).

13. *United States Army in World War II—Special Studies—The Women's Army Corps*, ed. Kent Roberts Greenfield (Washington, DC: Government Printing Office, 1954), 580–581.

14. Greenfield, *United States Army in World War II*, 658.

15. Greenfield, *United States Army in World War II*, 223.

16. Martha Lampland and Susan Leigh Star, *Standards and Their Stories: How Quantifying, Classifying, and Formalizing Practices Shape Everyday Life* (Ithaca, NY: Cornell University Press, 2009); Geoffrey C. Bowker and Susan Leigh Star, *Sorting Things Out: Classification and Its Consequences* (Ithaca, NY: Cornell University Press, 1999); Theodore M. Porter, *Trust in Numbers: The Pursuit of Objectivity in Science and Public Life* (Princeton, NJ: Princeton University Press, 1995.

17. Penelope Johnston, "Dr. Leonard Rowntree: A Canadian Medical Pioneer," *Medical Post* 36, no. 2 (January 2000): 45.

18. Howard M. Leichter, "'Evil Habits' and 'Personal Choices': Assigning Responsibility for Health in the Twentieth Century," *Milbank Quarterly* 81, no. 4 (December 2003): 603–626.

19. Proceedings of the Planning Conference of the AMA and National Committee on Physical Fitness, July 27–28, 1944, National Archives at College Park, College Park, MD (hereafter cited as NACP), Record Group 147, Records of the Selective Service System, 1940–, entry 45, Periodic Reports of Physical Examinations 1942–1946, box 1329, folder: Physical Education, General, January–August 1944.

20. Natalia Malina, *Fit to Be Citizens? Public Health and Race in Los Angeles, 1879–1939* (Berkeley: University of California Press, 2006), 49.

21. Meyer, *Creating GI Jane*, 7–8.

22. Allan Bérubé, *Coming Out Under Fire: The History of Gay Men and Women in World War II* (New York: Plume, 1990); Paul Jackson, *One of the Boys: Homosexuality in the Military During World War II* (Quebec: McGill-Queen's University Press, 2004).

23. Bérubé, *Coming Out Under Fire*, 14–15.

24. Margot Canaday, *The Straight State: Sexuality and Citizenship in Twentieth-Century America* (Princeton, NJ: Princeton University Press, 2009), 171–172.

25. Bérubé, *Coming Out Under Fire*, 13–14.

26. "Is American Youth Physically Soft?," *U.S. News and World Report* (August 2, 1957): 74–77.

27. Wartime Health and Education, Hearings before a Subcommittee of the Committee on Education and Labor, United States Senate, 78 Cong., 2nd Sess., Pursuant to S. Res. 74, Part 5, Washington, DC, July 10, 11, and 12, 1944, 1642; "High School Boys Disprove 'Softy' Charge of Colonel," *Star* (April 17, 1943), NACP, RG 147, Records of the Selective Service System, entry 1, Selective Service System Central Files, box 881, folder 605: Physical Education.

28. Medical Department, United States Army, *Physical Standards in World War II*, ed. Col. Robert S. Anderson (Washington, DC: Government Printing Office, 1967), 132; U.S. War Department, Mobilization Regulation 1–9, "Standards of Physical Examination During Mobilization," August 31, 1940; U.S. War Department, Army Regulation 40–100, "Standards of Miscellaneous Physical Examination," November 16, 1942.

29. Karl E. Friedl, "Body Composition and Military Performance: Origins of the Army Standards," in *Body Composition and Physical Performance: Applications for the Military Services*, ed. Bernadette M. Marriott and Judith Grumstrup-Scott (Washington, DC: National Academy Press, 1992), 41–42.

30. Medical Department, *Physical Standards in World War II*, 3.

31. Medical Department, *Physical Standards in World War II*, 132.

32. In *Straight State*, 172–173, Canaday argues that the vague language used about sexuality shaped both the limits and opportunities of queer postwar citizenship. Bérubé argues in *Coming Out Under Fire*, 6–7, that while the expanded psychological surveillance of the World War II military made service dangerous for young gay men, it also made space for gay subcultures.

33. NACP, RG 165, Records of the War Department General and Special Staffs, NM entry 43, Reports of the Admin of the Selective Training, box 625, vol. 3, Special Problems of the Selective Service System, 208.

34. NACP, RG 165, Records of the War Department General and Special Staffs, NM entry 43, Reports of the Admin of Selective Training, box, 625, vol. 3, Special Problems of the Selective Service System, 205.

35. Periodic Reports of Physical Examinations, NACP, RG 147, Records of the Selective Service System, entry 45, box 1, vol. 1; Bernard D. Karpinos, "Weight-Height Standards Based on World War II Experience," *Journal of the American Statistical Association* 53, no. 282 (1958): 408–419.

36. Periodic Reports of Physical Examinations, NACP, RG 147, Records of the Selective Service System, entry 45, Periodic Reports of Physical Examinations 1942–1946, box 1, vol. 1.

37. *Analysis of Results of Physical Examination*, 196, NACP, RG 147, Records of the Selective Service System, entry NM-32 50B, box 4, vol. 1; William B. Foster, I. L. Hellman, D. Hesford, and D. G. McPherson, *Physical Standards in World War II* (Washington, DC: Office of the Surgeon General, Department of the Army, 1967).

38. Robert H. Owens to Col. Leonard G. Rowntree, June 8, 1942, NACP, RG 147, Records of the Selective Service System, entry 1, Selective Service System Central Files, box 467, folder: Physical Rehabilitation N.H.–Ore. 1942.

39. "Report of Rehabilitation Cases Now in Operation Which Should Be Completed by May 15, 1942," NACP, RG 147, Records of the Selective Service System, entry 1, Selective Service

System Central Files, subject 1940, box 466, folder 604: Physical Rehabilitation, General, May–December 1942.

40. Lewis Hershey to State Directors of Maryland and Virginia, January 21, 1942, 4, NACP, RG 147, Records of the Selective Service System, entry 1, Selective Service System Central Files, box 466, folder 604: Physical Rehabilitation, General, January–April 1942.

41. Maj. Lawrence W. Long to Gen. Hershey, January 9, 1942, NACP, RG 147, Records of the Selective Service System, entry 1, Selective Service System Central Files, box 466, folder 604: Physical Rehabilitation, Md.–Nevada 1942.

42. Lt. Col. Bennett G. Owens to Col. Eans, November 23, 1942, NACP, RG 147, Records of the Selective Service System, entry 1, Selective Service System Central Files, box 471, folder 616: Misc. Defects, General, 1942.

43. L. G. Rowntree to Col. Clarence E. Fronk, December 12, 1942, NACP, RG 147, Records of the Selective Service System, entry 1, Selective Service System Central Files, box 466, folder 604, Physical Rehabilitation, Ala.–Maine 1942.

44. Major James L. Glymph to the Adjutant General, December 10, 1948, NACP, RG 337, Records of Headquarters Army Ground Forces, entry 56, Army Field Forces, box 39, folder 201.5/1. Glymph is specifically discussing the problem of civilians conducting examinations for postwar ROTC recruits, which is, of course, a different issue, but the parallels are striking enough that his description of the problem still applies.

45. Heaton, foreword to *Physical Standards in World War II*, ix.

46. Peggy Pascoe, *What Comes Naturally: Miscegenation Law and the Making of Race in America* (Oxford: Oxford University Press, 2009), 133–134; Nancy Cott, *Public Vows: A History of Marriage and the Nation* (Cambridge, MA: Harvard University Press, 2000); Hendrik Hartog, *Man and Wife in America: A History* (Cambridge, MA: Harvard University Press, 2000); Edward G. Goetz, *New Deal Ruins: Race, Economic Justice, and Public Housing Policy* (Ithaca, NY: Cornell University Press, 2013); Ira Katznelson, *Fear Itself: The New Deal and the Origins of Our Time* (New York: Oxford University Press, 2013).

47. National Headquarters, Selective Service System, *Causes of Rejection and Incidence of Defects: Local Board Examinations of Selective Service Registrants in Peacetime*, Medical Statistic Bulletin No. 2, 1943, 38–39, NACP, RG 147, Records of the Selective Service System, entry 1, Selective Service System Central Files, box 880, folder: Medical Circulars, General 1943.

48. National Headquarters, Selective Service System, *Causes of Rejection and Incidence of Defects: Local Board Examinations of Selective Service Registrants in Peacetime*, Medical Statistic Bulletin No. 2, 1943, 15n2, NACP, RG 147, Records of the Selective Service System, entry 1, Selective Service System Central Files, box 880, folder: Medical Circulars, General 1943.

49. Harry F. Besoda to Col. Carlton S. Dargusch, July 14, 1944, box 1306, folder 346.2: Physically Unfit, Neb.–Wyo. 1944; Carlton S. Dargusch to Hayy F. Besoda, July 27, 1944, box 1306, folder 346.2: Physically Unfit, Neb.–Wyo. 1944; both in NACP, RG 147, Records of the Selective Service System, entry 1, Selective Service System Central Files.

50. Edward A. Beckwith to Robert A. Bier, December 18, 1940, NACP, RG 147, Records of the Selective Service System, entry 1, Selective Service System Central Files, box 37, folder 330: Physical Standards, Ala to Wyo.

51. Robert A. Bier to Edward A. Beckwith, December 26, 1940, NACP, RG 147, Records of the Selective Service System, entry 1, Selective Service System Central Files, box 37, folder 330: Physical Standards, Ala to Wyo.

52. NACP, RG 165, Records of the War Department General and Special Staffs, NM entry 43, Reports of the Admin of the Selective Training, box 625, vol. 3, Special Problems of the Selective Service System, 207.

53. Untitled, bound statistics, NACP, RG 147, Records of the Selective Service System, entry 45, Periodic Reports of Physical Examinations 1942–1946, box 1, vol. 1.

54. *Selective Service as the Tide of War Turns—Third Report of the Director of Selective Service, 1943–1944* (Washington, DC: Government Printing Office, 1945), 191–194, NACP, RG 165, Records of the War Department General and Special Staffs, NM, entry 43, Reports of the Admin of the Selective Training, box 625, vol. 3.

55. L. G. Rowntree to Colonel Dargusch, October 30, 1941; J. J. McEntee to L. G. Rowntree, October 15, 1941; L. B. Hershey to president, October 27, 1941; all in NACP, RG 147, Records of the Selective Service System, entry 45, Periodic Reports of Physical Examinations 1942–1946, box 167, folder 604: Physical Rehabilitation, General, Oct.–Dec. 1941.

56. Hon. Samuel A. Weiss, transcript of speech delivered February 19, 1945, "America's Physical Fitness Failure," *Congressional Record*, 79th Cong., 1st Sess., 1, NACP, RG 147, Records of the Selective Service System, entry 1, Selective Service System Central Files, box 1733, folder 605.

57. William A. Taylor, *Every Citizen a Soldier: The Campaign for Universal Military Training After World War II* (College Station: Texas A&M University Press, 2014).

58. New York State Physical Fitness Standards for Boys and Young Men: A Manual for Instructors, NYS War Council, State Education Dept., 1944 (draft), 1, NACP, RG 147 Records of the Selective Service System, 1940–, entry 45, Periodic Reports of Physical Examinations 1942–1946, box 1330, folder 605: Physical Education Ala.–Wyo 1944.

59. Laura McEnaney, *Civil Defense Begins at Home: Militarization Meets Everyday Life in the Fifties* (Princeton, NJ: Princeton University Press, 2000), 17.

60. *Universal Military Training*, material prepared to supplement War Department testimony before Congress, NACP, RG 319, Records of the Army Staff, Assistant Chief of Staff, entry G2, Intelligence Admin. Division, Publication Files, box 3671, folder: Universal Military Training.

61. Michael S. Sherry, *Preparing for the Next War: American Plans for Postwar Defense, 1941–1945* (New Haven, CT: Yale University Press, 1977), 36–37.

62. John Sager, "Universal Military Training and the Struggle to Define American Identity During the Cold War," *Federal History* no. 5 (2013): 63.

63. Hon. Samuel A. Weiss, transcript of speech delivered February 19, 1945, "America's Physical Fitness Failure," *Congressional Record*, 79th Cong., 1st Sess., 2, NACP, RG 147, Records of the Selective Service System, entry 1, Selective Service System Central Files, box 1733, folder 605; Samuel J. Kopetzky, Medical Bulletin No. 5, June 30, 1941, 2, NACP, RG 147, Records of the Selective Service System, entry 45, Periodic Reports of Physical Examinations 1942–1946, box 167, folder 604: Physical Rehabilitation, General, January–September, 1941.

64. H.R. 2045, 79th Cong., 1st Sess., February 7, 1945, 2.

65. Hon. Samuel A. Weiss, transcript of speech delivered February 19, 1945, "America's Physical Fitness Failure," *Congressional Record*, 79th Cong., 1st Sess., 2, NACP, RG 147, Records of the Selective Service System, entry 1, Selective Service System Central Files, box 1733, folder 605.

Chapter 4

1. George Orwell, *1984* (New York: Signet Classics, 1961), first published 1949.

2. Suzanne Mettler, *Soldiers to Citizens: The GI Bill and the Making of the Greatest Generation* (Oxford: Oxford University Press, 2005), 144.

3. Amy Rutenberg, "Drafting for Domesticity: American Deferment Policy During the Cold War, 1948–1965," *Cold War History* 13, no. 1 (2013): 1–20; Michael Sherry, *In the Shadow of War: The United States Since the 1930s* (New Haven, CT: Yale University Press, 1995).

4. Elaine Tyler May, *Homeward Bound: American Families in the Cold War Era*, Twentieth Anniversary Edition (New York: Basic Books, 2008), is the classic on family in the Cold War.

5. Joanne Meyerowitz, *Not June Cleaver: Women and Gender in Postwar America, 1945–1960* (Philadelphia: Temple University Press, 1994); Daniel Horowitz, *Betty Friedan and the Making of "The Feminine Mystique": The American Left, the Cold War, and Modern Feminism* (Amherst: University of Massachusetts Press, 2000); Dorothy Sue Cobble, *The Other Women's Movement: Workplace Justice and Social Rights in Modern America* (Princeton, NJ: Princeton University Press, 2004).

6. Katherine Turk, *Equality on Trial: Gender and Rights in the Modern American Workplace* (Philadelphia: University of Pennsylvania Press, 2016); Allison Elias, "Learning to Lead: Women and Success in Corporate America," *Business and Economic History On-Line* 13 (2015), http://www.thebhc.org/sites/default/files/Elias_BEHO_Final%20Draft_0.pdf; Allison Elias, "Standardizing Sex Discrimination: Clerical Workers, Labor Organizing, and Feminism" (PhD diss., University of Virginia, 2013); Kathleen M. Barry, *Femininity in Flight: A History of Flight Attendants* (Durham, NC: Duke University Press, 2007).

7. Bud Wilkinson, "Youth Fitness," *Parade* (September 3, 1961): 4, Eisenhower Library, Abilene, KS (hereafter cited as Eisenhower Library), Republican National Committee, News Clippings, box 640, folder: [Youth] National Youth Fitness.

8. "Information Guide: The Committee on Physical Fitness," March 1945, National Archives at College Park, College Park, MD (hereafter cited as NACP), Record Group 208, Records of the Office of War Information, entry NC-148 84, Records of Natalie Davisen, box 3, folder: Physical Fitness.

9. Gen. Lewis B. Hershey, "Need for a Campaign for Physical Fitness," June 17, 1956, 1, John F. Kennedy Library, Boston, MA (hereafter cited as Kennedy Library), President's Office, Departments and Agencies, box 94, folder: 2/61–11/62.

10. H.R. 2045, 79th Cong., 1st Sess., February 7, 1945, 2; Lt. Col. Francois D'Eliscu, *How to Prepare for Military Fitness* (New York: W. W. Norton, 1943).

11. Tom Englehardt, *The End of Victory Culture: Cold War America and the Disillusioning of a Nation* (Amherst: University of Massachusetts Press, 1995); Robert J. Corber, *Homosexuality in Cold War America: Resistance and the Crisis of Masculinity* (Durham, NC: Duke University Press, 1997); William W. Savage, Jr., *Commies, Cowboys, and Jungle Queens: Comic Books and America, 1945–1954* (Hanover, NH: Wesleyan University Press, 1990).

12. Jeffrey Montez de Oca, "'As Our Muscles Get Softer, Our Missile Race Becomes Harder': Cultural Citizenship and the 'Muscle Gap,'" *Journal of Historical Sociology* 18, no. 3 (September 2005): 150.

13. Arthur M. Schlesinger, Jr., *The Vital Center: The Politics of Freedom*, rev. ed. (New Brunswick, NJ: Transaction, 1998), 38.

14. K. A. Cuordileone, *Manhood and American Political Culture in the Cold War* (New York: Routledge, 2005); quotations from K. A. Cuordileone, "Politics in an Age of Anxiety: Cold War Political Culture and the Crisis in American Masculinity, 1949–1960," *Journal of American History* 87, no. 2 (September 2000): 521–522.

15. David K. Johnson, *The Lavender Scare: The Cold War Persecution of Gays and Lesbians in the Federal Government* (Chicago: University of Chicago Press, 2004).

16. The Council has gone through a number of name changes over the years. It began as the President's Council on Youth Fitness, and then became the President's Council on Physical Fitness under Kennedy. President Lyndon B. Johnson renamed the agency the President's Council on Fitness and Sports, a name that stuck for forty years. In 2010, however, President Barack Obama renamed it the President's Council on Fitness, Sports, and Nutrition. I refer to it simply as "the council" throughout, except for places where the specific name matters.

17. On the expansion of the state, see Shane Hamilton, *Trucking Country: The Road to America's Wal-Mart Economy* (Princeton, NJ: Princeton University Press, 2008), 100–111; William D. Hartung, *Prophets of War: Lockheed Martin and the Making of the Military-Industrial Complex* (New York: Nation Books, 2011), 51–68; Helen Bury, *Eisenhower and the Cold War Arms Race: 'Open Skies' and the Military-Industrial Complex* (London: I. B. Tauris, 2014), 12–42. On the growing anxiety over state expansion in the postwar era, see especially Lisa McGirr, *Suburban Warriors: The Origins of the New American Right* (Princeton, NJ: Princeton University Press, 2001), 54–110; and Kim Phillips-Fein, *Invisible Hands: The Making of the Conservative Movement from the New Deal to Reagan* (New York: Norton, 2009), 58–67.

18. John Kelly, quoted in Shelly McKenzie, *Getting Physical: The Rise of Fitness Culture in America* (Lawrence: University Press of Kansas, 2013), 24.

19. Robert H. Boyle, "The Report That Shocked the President," *Sports Illustrated* (August 15, 1955): 30–33, 72–75.

20. Jean Mayer, "Muscular State of the Union," *New York Times Magazine* (November 6, 1955), 17.

21. Boyle, "Report That Shocked the President," 72.

22. Hans Kraus and Ruth Hirschland [a.k.a. Bonnie Prudden], "Minimum Muscular Fitness Tests in School Children," *Research Quarterly* (American Association for Health, Physical Education, and Recreation) 25, no. 2 (1954): 178–188; Boyle, "Report That Shocked the President," 30–33, 72–75.

23. Boyle, "Report That Shocked the President, 30–33, 72–75; "Answering Some Questions on Kraus Weber Test," NACP, RG 235, Records of the Office of Health, Education, and Welfare, entry 35, Office of the Secretary, box 23, folder: Kraus, Hans, 56–61.

24. James R. Morrow, Jr., Weimo Zhu, B. Don Franks, Marilu D. Meredith, and Christine Spain, "1958–2008: 50 Years of Youth Fitness Tests in the United States," *Research Quarterly for Exercise and Sport* 80, no. 1 (2009): 1–11; Dale P. Mood, Allen W. Jackson, and James R. Morrow, Jr., "Measurement of Physical Fitness and Physical Activity: Fifty Years of Change," *Measurement in Physical Education and Exercise* 11, no. 4 (2007): 217–227. For a critique of this model, see Vern Seefeldt and Paul Vogel, "Physical Fitness Testing of Children: A 30-Year History of Misguided Efforts?," *Pediatric Exercise Science* 1 (1989): 295–302, especially 295–296.

25. Marjorie Phillips, "The Health and Fitness of 'American' School Children" (speech, Denver, CO, August 8, 1955), 3, Eisenhower Library, Staff Files, Admin Assistant and Deputy Assistant for Intergovernmental Relations (Pyle), box 38, folder: Packet Materials for Luncheon Meeting with Vice-President Nixon.

26. Marjorie Phillips, "The Health and Fitness of 'American' School Children" (speech, Denver, CO, August 8, 1955), 4, Eisenhower Library, Staff Files, Admin Assistant and Deputy Assistant for Intergovernmental Relations (Pyle), box 38, folder: Packet Materials for Luncheon Meeting with Vice-President Nixon.

27. Boyle, "Report That Shocked the President," 30–33, 72–75.

28. For just a few examples, see Bob Brooks, "Toughen Up: Are You Fit?," *Boys Life* (January 1956): 59; Ken Metzler, "A College Lab Tells How to Measure Physical Fitness," *Popular Mechanics* (December 1957): 145–148; Marjorie Phillips, "How Fit Are Our American School Children," *Journal of Health, Physical Education, Recreation* 26, no. 6 (1955): 14 + ; Gertrude Krauss Shaffer, "Why the American Children Are Physically Unfit," *Physical Educator* 17, no. 2 (May 1, 1960): 60–62; W. Kenneth Lane, "Role of Pediatrician in Physical Fitness of Youth," *Journal of the American Medical Association* 169, no. 5 (January 31, 1959): 421–427.

29. Notes, Meeting of the Committee on Physical Fitness, Federal Security Agency, June 17, 1943, NACP, RG 147, Records of the Selective Service System, entry 45, Periodic Reports of Physical Examinations 1942–1946, box 880, folder 605: Physical Education; Hon. Frank Thompson, Jr., "Are We a Nation of Softies?," extension of remarks made in the House of Representatives, May 2, 1956, NACP, RG 235, Records of the Department of Health, Education, and Welfare, entry 35, Office of the Secretary, box 2, folder: T; Russ Crawford, *The Use of Sports to Promote the American Way of Life During the Cold War: Cultural Propaganda, 1945–1963* (Lewiston, NY: Edwin Mellen Press, 2008).

30. 4-H, "Health and Safety" (flyer), 1953; MetLife, "Why Weight Control," 1953; both in Cornell University Library, Division of Rare and Manuscript Collections, Ithaca, NY, box 115, Guide to the New York State College of Agricultural Extension Service, 4-H Club Records, 1918–2002, folder: Leader's Guide for Health, Chairmen.

31. Dwight Eisenhower to George Allen and Aksel Nielsen, April 27, 1956, box 14, folder: Apr '56 Misc. (1); Dwight Eisenhower to George Allen, April 5, 1956, box 14, folder: Misc. (5); Dwight Eisenhower to George Allen, April 4, 1956, box 14, folder: Misc. (5); all in Eisenhower Library, Papers as President of the United States, 1953–1961, DDE Diary Series.

32. "Ike Discusses Delinquency with Athletes," *Chicago Daily Tribune* (July 12, 1955): B5.

33. This was a perceived problem, not necessarily a real one, as the corrections to the Kraus tests suggest. Some educators and American youth were upset with being categorized as unfit, leading some boys even to protest by doing hundreds of squats. Representatives from the Federal Security Agency, as well as General Rowntree of the Selective Service System, told the protesting boys that their fitness was an exception to the rule. "High School Boys Disprove 'Softy' Charge of Colonel," *Star* (Washington, DC) (April 17, 1943); L. G. Rowntree to William D. Boutwell, April 24, 1943; both in NACP, RG 147, Records of the Selective Service System, entry 45, Periodic Reports of Physical Examinations 1942–1946, box 881, folder 605: Physical Education.

34. Packet Materials for Luncheon Meeting with Vice-President Nixon, August 8, 1955, 3, Denver Meeting on Physical Fitness, Eisenhower Library, Staff Files, Admin Assistant and Deputy Assistant for Intergovernmental Relations (Pyle), box 38.

35. Rick Perlstein, *Nixonland: The Rise of a President and the Fracturing of America* (New York: Scribner, 2008), 42–43; Laura A. Belmonte, *Selling the American Way: U.S. Propaganda and the Cold War* (Philadelphia: University of Pennsylvania Press, 2008), 87–90; Susan Marks, *Finding Betty Crocker: The Secret Life of America's First Lady of Food* (New York: Simon and Schuster, 2005), 198.

36. Matthew T. Bowers and Thomas M. Hunt, "The President's Council on Physical Fitness and the Systemization of Children's Play in America," *International Journal of the History of Sport* 28, no. 11 (August 2011): 1497.

37. Packet Materials for Luncheon Meeting with Vice-President Nixon, August 8, 1955, Denver Meeting on Physical Fitness, Eisenhower Library, Staff Files, Admin Assistant and Deputy Assistant for Intergovernmental Relations (Pyle), box 38.

38. Tracy L. Steffes, *School, Society, and State: A New Education to Govern Modern America, 1890–1940* (Chicago: University of Chicago Press, 2012), 9–11.

39. Martha H. Verbrugge, *Active Bodies: A History of Women's Physical Education in Twentieth-Century America* (Oxford: Oxford University Press, 2012), 201.

40. Press Release, September 18, 1955, Message for Program of Lowry Air Force Base (Denver), President's Conference on Fitness of American Youth (September 27–28), Eisenhower Library, Frederic E. Fox, Records, 1953–61, box 13, folder: Youth, Fitness of American (President's Conference On).

41. Goodpaster to Governor Adams, Memo, August 15, 1955, "Proposed Denver Meeting on Physical Fitness Program," Eisenhower Library, Packet Materials for Luncheon Meeting with Vice-President Nixon, August 8, 1955, Denver Meeting on Physical Fitness, Eisenhower Library, Staff Files, Admin Assistant and Deputy Assistant for Intergovernmental Relations (Pyle), box 38.

42. Bob King to R.N., memo, August 20, 1955, Packet Materials for Luncheon Meeting with Vice-President Nixon, August 8, 1955, Denver Meeting on Physical Fitness, Eisenhower Library, Staff Files, Admin Assistant and Deputy Assistant for Intergovernmental Relations (Pyle), box 38.

43. Elaine Tyler May, *Homeward Bound: American Families in the Cold War Era* (New York: Basic Books, 1998); Lynn Spigel, *Make Room for TV: Television and the Family Ideal in Postwar America* (Chicago: University of Chicago Press, 1992); Thomas Patrick Doherty, *Cold War, Cool Medium: Television, McCarthyism, and American Culture* (New York: Columbia University Press, 2003); Tony Shaw, *Hollywood's Cold War* (Amherst: University of Massachusetts Press, 2007).

44. "Biographical Sketch: T. S. Repplier, President, The Advertising Council, Inc.," July 25, 1956, Eisenhower Library, Lambie Records, box 25, folder: Advertising Council, Repplier, 1956; "Business and Advertising Serving the People: The Advertising Council: What It Does, How It Does," brochure, NACP, RG 235, Records of the Office of Health, Education, and Welfare, entry 35, Office of the Secretary, box 9, folder: unlabeled.

45. Ad Council, *Matters of Choice: Advertising in the Public Interest, 1942–2002*, available at http://www.adcouncil.org/timeline.html.

46. Dwight Eisenhower to Theodore Repplier, April 10, 1953, Eisenhower Library, White House Central Files, Official File, 1953–1961, box 526, folder: OF 122-A-1 Advertising Industry, Advertising Council, 1952–3 (6).

47. Dwight Eisenhower to Theodore Repplier, April 10, 1953, Eisenhower Library, White House Central Files, Official File, 1953–1961, box 526, folder: OF 122-A-1 Advertising Industry, Advertising Council, 1952–3 (6).

48. Robert Jackall and Janice M. Hirota, *Image Makers: Advertising, Public Relations, and the Ethos of Advocacy* (Chicago: University of Chicago Press, 2000), 36–65.

49. James C. Hagerty, press secretary of the president, press release, June 19, 1956, 1–2, Eisenhower Library, Frederic E. Fox, Records, 1953–61, box 13, folder: Youth, Fitness of American (President's Conference On).

50. James C. Hagerty, press secretary of the president, press release, June 19, 1956, 1–2, Eisenhower Library, Frederic E. Fox, Records, 1953–61, box 13, folder: Youth, Fitness of American (President's Conference On).

51. Shelly McKenzie, *Getting Physical: The Rise of Fitness Culture in America* (Lawrence: University Press of Kansas, 2013), 23.

52. William D. Carey to Messrs. Fred Dutton and Ted Reardon, memo, January 27, 1961, Kennedy Library, Papers on John F. Kennedy, White House Central Files, Subject File, box 203, folder: FG 725—President's Council on Physical Fitness 1961, Executive; "Shane MacCarthy," *Sports Illustrated* (October 1, 1956): 80; "Shane MacCarthy Heads Council on Youth Fitness," *Journal of Health, Physical Education, Recreation* 27, no. 8 (1956): 24–25.

53. Shane MacCarthy, press release, 1960, box 2, folder: 1960 Press Releases; "Proposal for the Program of the President's Council on Youth Fitness," box 6, folder: Proposal; "President's Council on Youth Fitness: Basic Council Policies," box 6, folder: Basic Policies; all in NACP, RG 235, Records of the Office of Health, Education, and Welfare, entry 35, Office of the Secretary.

54. Shane MacCarthy, "To the Members of the President's Citizens Advisory Committee," *Newsletter from the President's Council on Youth Fitness* (July 26, 1960): 2, NACP, RG 220, Records of Temporary Committees, Commissions, and Boards, Entry A1 34125A, Records of the President's Commission on Physical Fitness, box 1, folder 2: Fitness in Action, August 1960.

55. Report to the President (July 30, 1963), 11, NACP, RG 220, Records of Temporary Committees, Commissions, and Boards, Entry A1 34125A, Records of the President's Commission on Physical Fitness, box 3, folder: Publications 8.

56. Paul J. McCoy, "Sport Rama" Proposal, August 21, 1956, Eisenhower Library, Central Files, Official File, box 844, folder 156-A-6: Fitness of American Youth (2).

57. Paul J. McCoy, "Sport Rama" Proposal, August 21, 1956, Eisenhower Library, Central Files, Official File, box 844, folder 156-A-6: Fitness of American Youth (2).

58. "Third Monthly Report, Nov. 16–Dec. 15 1957," memo for all council members, December 23, 1957, Eisenhower Library, Fred A. Seaton Papers, Ewald Research Files Series, box 22, folder: PCYF; Shane MacCarthy to conferees, September 9, 1958, NACP, RG 235, Records of the Office of Health, Education, and Welfare, entry 35, Office of the Secretary, box 4, folder: Council Members, Department of Commerce; *Transcript of Proceedings: Conference on Physical Fitness Incentives for Youth*, October 11, 1957, NACP, RG 235, Records of the Office of Health, Education, and Welfare, entry 35, Office of the Secretary, box 9, folder: Oct. 11 Meeting.

59. Dr. Ernst Jokl, Memorandum Proposing the Establishment of a Physical Fitness Laboratory in the University of Kentucky, February 15, 1957; Gov. Pyle to Albert Benjamin Chandler, report, April 29, 1957, both in Eisenhower Library, Central Files, Official File, box 844, folder 156-A-6: Fitness of American Youth (3); "Policy Concerning Some Aspects of a Public Relations Program," May 23, 1958, NACP, RG 235, Records of the Office of Health, Education, and Welfare, entry 35, Office of the Secretary, box 6, folder: Proposal for President's Council on Youth Fitness; "Fitness and the Future," 1960, 4, NACP, RG 220, Records of Temporary Committees, Commissions, and Boards, Entry A1 34125A, Records of the President's Commission on Physical Fitness, box 4, folder: Publications Folder 14.

60. Shane MacCarthy, "A Catalytic Agent," press release, 1960(?), NACP, RG 235, Records of the Office of Health, Education, and Welfare, entry 35, Office of the Secretary, box 4, folder: 1960 Press Releases.

61. Dwight Eisenhower, "President's Ideas," memo, December 28, 1956, NACP, RG 235, Records of Health, Education, and Welfare, entry 35, Office of the Secretary, box 9, folder: President's Ideas.

62. Hon. Murray Snyder to Clarence Francis, January 8, 1957, and Clarence Francis to Hon. Murray Snyder, January 10, 1957, both in Eisenhower Library, Central Files, Official File, box 844, folder 156-A-6: Fitness of American Youth (2).

63. Shane MacCarthy to Sec. of Interior, March 18, 1960, Eisenhower Library, Central Files, Official File, box 844, folder 156-A-6: Fitness of American Youth (4).

64. Shane MacCarthy, press release, 1958(?), NACP, RG 235, Records of the Office of Health, Education, and Welfare, entry 35, Office of the Secretary, box 2, folder: 1958 Press Releases.

65. John F. Kennedy, "The Soft American," *Sports Illustrated* (December 26, 1960): 14–17.

66. Montez de Oca, "'As Our Muscles Get Softer, Our Missile Race Becomes Harder,'" 145–171.

67. Cuordilenone, *Manhood and American Political Culture*, 202.

68. Bud Wilkinson to Timothy Reardon, March 9, 1961, Kennedy Library, Personal Papers of Timothy J. Reardon, Jr., Subjects, box 11, folder: "Youth Fitness 1961, Folder 2."

69. "50 P.C. Failures Reported in Pilot Youth Fitness Test," *New York Times Herald Tribune* (December 3, 1961), Eisenhower Library, Republican National Committee, News Clippings, box 640, folder: [Youth] National Youth Fitness.

70. Anne Christmas, "Physically Unfit Americans Held a Grave Problem," *Washington Star* (August 15, 1961), Eisenhower Library, Republican National Committee, News Clippings, box 640, folder: [Youth] National Youth Fitness.

71. "President Appeals to Schools to Help Youth Gain Fitness," *New York Times* (September 5, 1961), Eisenhower Library, Republican National Committee, News Clippings, box 640, folder: [Youth] National Youth Fitness.

72. Edward T. Folliard, "Physical Fitness Levels Deplored by President," *Baltimore Sun* (July 8, 1962), Eisenhower Library, Republican National Committee, News Clippings, box 640, folder: [Youth] National Youth Fitness.

73. Sarah E. Igo, *The Averaged American: Surveys, Citizens, and the Making of a Mass Public* (Cambridge, MA: Harvard University Press, 2007), 236.

74. John F. Kennedy, "The Vigor We Need," *Sports Illustrated* (July 16, 1962): 12–14.

75. Samantha King, *Pink Ribbons, Inc.: Breast Cancer and the Politics of Philanthropy* (Minneapolis: University of Minnesota Press, 2006), 6–7; Kirsten E. Gardner, *Early Detection: Women, Cancer, and Awareness Campaigns in the Twentieth-Century United States* (Chapel Hill: University of North Carolina Press, 2006).

76. Report to the President, December 10, 1962, 8, NACP, RG 220, Records of Temporary Committees, Commissions, and Boards, Entry A1 34125A, Records of the President's Commission on Physical Fitness, box 3, folder: Publications 8.

77. C. B. Wilkinson to John F. Kennedy, July 29, 1963, Kennedy Library, President's Office Files, Departments and Agencies, box 93, folder: Committee on Physical Fitness 1963.

78. "7 Astronauts to Plug Fitness of US Youths," *Washington Star* (July 23, 1961); Bud Wilkinson, "Youth Fitness," *Parade* (September 3, 1961): 4; both in Eisenhower Library, Republican National Committee, News Clippings, box 640, folder: [Youth] National Youth Fitness.

79. Robert M. Hoffman, "Telling and Selling the Fitness Story," in President's Council on Youth Fitness, "Recreation Planning for Fitness: Workshop Report No. 8, 1960," 8, NACP, RG 220, Records of Temporary Committees, Commissions, and Boards, Entry A1 34125A, Records of the President's Commission on Physical Fitness, box 4, folder: Pub. 14.

80. Robert M. Hoffman, "Telling and Selling the Fitness Story," in President's Council on Youth Fitness, "Recreation Planning for Fitness: Workshop Report No. 8, 1960," Report to the President (July 30, 1963), 4, NACP, RG 220, Records of Temporary Committees, Commissions, and Boards, Entry A1 34125A, Records of the President's Commission on Physical Fitness, box 4, folder: Pub. 14.

81. Ad Council Meeting Minutes, 6, Ad Council Archives, University of Illinois, Urbana, RS:13/2/201, folder: "Meeting Minutes, May–June 1962."

82. Report to the President, July 30, 1964, 9, NACP, RG 220, Records of Temporary Committees, Commissions, and Boards, Entry A1 34125A, Records of the President's Commission on Physical Fitness, box 3, folder: Publications 8.

83. Newsletter from the President's Council on Physical Fitness (November 8, 1963): 2–3, NACP, RG 220, Records of Temporary Committees, Commissions, and Boards, Entry A1 34125A, Records of the President's Commission on Physical Fitness, box 1, folder 2.

84. Report to the President, December 20, 1962, 7, NACP, RG 220, Records of Temporary Committees, Commissions, and Boards, Entry A1 34125A, Records of the President's Commission on Physical Fitness, box 3, folder: Publications 8.

85. Newsletter from the President's Council on Youth Fitness (November 8, 1963): 2, NACP, RG 220, Records of Temporary Committees, Commissions, and Boards, Entry A1 34125A, Records of the President's Commission on Physical Fitness, box 1, folder 2.

86. Jack Gould, "TV Hope and Crosby," New York Times (May 15, 1962).

87. "The Dinah Shore Chevy Show," script, October 6, 1961, NACP, RG 235, Records of the Office of Health, Education, and Welfare, entry 35, Office of the Secretary, box 16, folder: The Dinah Shore Show.

88. JFK Presidential Library and Museum, "About Audio: Chicken Fat," MR2008-63, http://www.jfklibrary.org/Asset-Viewer/9s-yJbLYuUyLS7_xlNTuLw.aspx.

89. Bowers and Hunt, "President's Council on Physical Fitness and the Systemization of Children's Play in America," 1497.

90. Bowers and Hunt, "President's Council on Physical Fitness and the Systemization of Children's Play in America," 1504.

91. "Youth Fitness Head Urges 5-Point Plan," New York Times (August 25, 1961), Eisenhower Library, Republican National Committee, News Clippings, box 640, folder: [Youth] National Youth Fitness.

92. Edward T. Folliard, "Physical Fitness Levels Deplored by President," Baltimore Sun (July 8, 1962), Eisenhower Library, Republican National Committee, News Clippings, box 640, folder: [Youth] National Youth Fitness.

93. President's Council on Physical Fitness, Statements by the President (Washington, DC: Government Printing Office, 1963).

94. 4 Years for Fitness, 1961–1965: A Report to the President (October 1965): 17, NACP, RG 220, Records of Temporary Committees, Commissions, and Boards, Entry A1 34125A, Records of the President's Commission on Physical Fitness, box 3, folder: Publications 8; Bob Broeg, "What Makes Stan Musial the Man," Popular Science (October 1965): 126–128.

95. *Newsletter from the President's Council on Physical Fitness* (July 27, 1964): 2–3, NACP, RG 220, Records of Temporary Committees, Commissions, and Boards, Entry A1 34125A, Records of the President's Commission on Physical Fitness, box 1, folder 2: Fitness in Action, Aug. 1960; Report to the President, July 30, 1963, NACP, RG 220, Records of Temporary Committees, Commissions, and Boards, Entry A1 34125A, Records of the President's Commission on Physical Fitness, box 3, folder: Publications 8.

96. Report to the President, July 30, 1964, 3, NACP, RG 220, Records of Temporary Committees, Commissions, and Boards, Entry A1 34125A, Records of the President's Commission on Physical Fitness, box 3, folder: Publications 8.

97. Report to the President, July 30, 1964, 1–2, NACP, RG 220, Records of Temporary Committees, Commissions, and Boards, Entry A1 34125A, Records of the President's Commission on Physical Fitness, box 3, folder: Publications 8.

98. Transcript for 20-second audio spot, NACP, RG 235, Records of the Office of Health, Education, and Welfare, entry 35, Office of the Secretary, box 46, folder: Gardner Advertising Agency 1964–5.

99. Bud Wilkinson, MSS, "Book of Knowledge," December 26, 1963, 1, NACP, RG 235, Records of the Office of Health, Education, and Welfare, entry 35, Office of the Secretary, box 28, folder: Articles 1963.

100. Form for advertisement, audio transcript: [60 sec spot] (1964 or 1965), NACP, RG 235, Records of the Office of Health, Education, and Welfare, entry 35, Office of the Secretary, box 46, folder: Gardner Advertising Agency 1964–5.

101. President's Council on Physical Fitness, *Official U.S. Physical Fitness Program* (Washington, DC: Government Printing Office, 1963).

102. Bob Steward to Joseph Califano, Jr., December 9, 1965, 6, NACP, RG 235, Records of the Office of Health, Education, and Welfare, entry 35, Office of the Secretary, box 47, folder: Legislation 1965.

103. Johnson, *Lavender Scare*, 146; Margot Canaday, *The Straight State: Sexuality and Citizenship in Twentieth-Century America* (Princeton, NJ: Princeton University Press, 2009), 168.

104. Carolyn Herbst Lewis, *Prescription for Heterosexuality: Sexual Citizenship in the Cold War Era* (Chapel Hill: University of North Carolina Press, 2010), 5–6.

105. Stephanie Coontz, *The Way We Never Were: American Families and the Nostalgia Trap* (New York: Basic Books, 1992).

106. Ruth Milkman, *Gender at Work: The Dynamics of Job Segregation by Sex During World War II* (Urbana: University of Illinois Press, 1987).

107. Alice Kessler-Harris, *In Pursuit of Equity: Women, Men, and the Quest for Economic Citizenship in 20th-Century America* (New York: Oxford University Press, 2001), 18.

108. Bud Wilkinson, *Bud Wilkinson's Guide to Modern Physical Fitness* (New York: Viking Press, 1967), 126.

109. Wilkinson, *Bud Wilkinson's Guide*, 125.

110. Gardner Advertising Agency, television advertisement transcript, n.d., NACP, RG 235, Records of the Office of Health, Education, and Welfare, entry 35, Office of the Secretary, box 46, folder: Gardner Advertising Agency, 1964–5.

111. Wilkinson, *Bud Wilkinson's Guide*, 126.

112. *Newsletter from the President's Council on Youth Fitness* (November 8, 1963): 2; *Newsletter from the President's Council on Youth Fitness* (March 6, 1964): 2; both in NACP, RG 220,

Records of Temporary Committees, Commissions, and Boards, Entry A1 34125A, Records of the President's Commission on Physical Fitness, box 1, folder 2: Fitness in Action, August 1960.

113. Kessler-Harris, *In Pursuit of Equity*.

114. *Years for Fitness, 1961–1965: A Report to the President*, October 1965, 17, NACP, RG 220, Records of Temporary Committees, Commissions, and Boards, Entry A1 34125A, Records of the President's Commission on Physical Fitness, box 3, folder: Publications 8.

115. Report to the President, December 10, 1962, 4, NACP, RG 220, Records of Temporary Committees, Commissions, and Boards, Entry A1 34125A, Records of the President's Commission on Physical Fitness, box 3, folder: Publications 8.

116. "Bud Wilkinson Drumming for Youth Fitness," *Chicago Tribune* (August 4, 1962), Eisenhower Library, Republican National Committee, News Clippings, box 640, folder: [Youth] National Youth Fitness.

117. The council was renamed again in the Obama administration, when it became the President's Council on Fitness, Sports, and Nutrition.

118. Thomas M. Hunt, "American Sport Policy and the Cultural Cold War: The Lyndon B. Johnson Presidential Years," *Journal of Sport History* 33 (Fall 2006): 273–297.

119. John Sayle Watterson, *The Games Presidents Play: Sports and the Presidency* (Baltimore: Johns Hopkins University Press, 2006), 223.

Chapter 5

1. Grace A. Goldsmith, "Clinical Nutritional Problems in the United States Today," *Nutrition Reviews* 23, no. 1 (January 1965): 1.

2. Robert Sherrill, "It Isn't True That Nobody Starves in America," *New York Times* (June 4, 1967): SM12.

3. Lizbeth Cohen, *A Consumer's Republic: The Politics of Mass Consumption in Postwar America* (New York: Alfred Knopf, 2003); William H. Chafe, *The Unfinished Journey: America Since World War II*, 2nd ed. (New York: Oxford University Press, 1991); Andrew Hurley, *Diners, Bowling Alleys, and Trailer Parks: Chasing the American Dream in the Postwar Consumer Culture* (New York: Basic Books, 2001).

4. Fredrick J. Stare, "Malnutrition and Hunger in the U.S.A.," *Nutrition Reviews* 26, no. 8 (August 1968): 228.

5. Marisa Chappell, *The War on Welfare: Family, Poverty, and Politics in Modern America* (Philadelphia: University of Pennsylvania Press, 2010), 4–5.

6. Peter B. Edelman, Oral History Interview—RFK #8, March 13, 1974, interview by Larry Hackman, transcript, 10, John F. Kennedy Library, Robert F. Kennedy Oral History Collection. https://www.jfklibrary.org/Asset-Viewer/Archives/RFKOH-PBE-08.aspx; Marjorie L. DeVault and James P. Pitts, "Surplus and Scarcity: Hunger and the Origins of the Food Stamp Program," *Social Problems* 31, no. 5 (June 1984): 549.

7. Ellen Reese, *Backlash Against Welfare Mothers: Past and Present* (Berkeley: University of California Press, 2005), 76–77.

8. Peter B. Edelman, Oral History Interview—RFK #8, March 13, 1974, interview by Larry Hackman, transcript, 29, John F. Kennedy Library, Robert F. Kennedy Oral History Collection. https://www.jfklibrary.org/Asset-Viewer/Archives/RFKOH-PBE-08.aspx.

9. Michael Harrington, *The Other America: Poverty in the United States* (New York: Macmillan, 1962).

10. Laurie Green, "Saving Babies in Memphis: The Politics of Race, Health and Hunger During the War on Poverty," in *War on Poverty: A New Grassroots History, 1964–1980*, ed. Annelise Orleck (Athens: University of Georgia Press), 133–158.

11. The use of the physical body as evidence of bad citizenship and bad behavior, and the fact that bodies could be read to reveal an assortment of positive or negative qualities, parallels discussions of mothering and reproduction in the United States, especially narratives of sterilization (and defenses against sterilization) in Johanna Schoen, *Choice and Coercion: Birth Control, Sterilization, and Abortion in Public Health and Welfare* (Chapel Hill: University of North Carolina Press, 2005). The use of low-income women's bodies as evidence of their worthiness is not at all unique to my story, but its relationship to the history of nutrition and weight is generally overlooked.

12. Jennifer Jensen Wallach, *How America Eats: A Social History of U.S. Food and Culture* (Lanham, MD: Rowman and Littlefield, 2013), 191.

13. Andrea Elizabeth Shaw, *The Embodiment of Disobedience: Fat Black Women's Unruly Political Bodies* (Oxford: Lexington Books, 2006), 21.

14. Patricia Hill Collins, *Black Feminist Thought: Knowledge, Consciousness, and the Politics of Empowerment*, 2nd ed. (New York: Routledge, 2000), 88.

15. *Hunger, U.S.A.: A Report by the Citizens' Board of Inquiry into Hunger and Malnutrition in the United States* (Boston: Beacon Press, 1968), 3–4.

16. Timothy Hume Behrendt to Orville Freeman, June 12, 1968, National Archives at College Park, College Park, Maryland (hereafter cited as NACP), Record Group 16, Records of the Office of the Secretary of Agriculture, A1, entry 1038, General Correspondence, 1906–1976, box 4664, folder: Farm Program 8-1-1, 2 of 2, June 1, 1968–July 31, 1968.

17. *Hunger, U.S.A.*, 3.

18. Richard A. Cloward and Frances Fox Piven, "Starving by the Rule Book," *Nation* (April 3, 1967): 429.

19. Subcommittee on Employment, Manpower, and Poverty of the Committee on Labor and Public Welfare, *Hunger in America: Chronology and Selected Background Materials*, U.S. Senate, 90th Cong., 2nd Sess. (Washington, DC: Government Printing Office, 1968), 10.

20. Subcommittee on Employment, Manpower, and Poverty of the Committee on Labor and Public Welfare, *Hunger in America: Chronology and Selected Background Materials*, U.S. Senate, 90th Cong., 2nd Sess. (Washington, DC: Government Printing Office, 1968), 13.

21. Sherrill, "It Isn't True That Nobody Starves in America."

22. Marcie Cohen Ferris, *The Edible South: The Power of Food and the Making of a Region* (Chapel Hill: University of North Carolina Press, 2014), 289–290.

23. Subcommittee on Employment, Manpower, and Poverty of the Committee on Labor and Public Welfare, *Hunger in America: Chronology and Selected Background Materials*, U.S. Senate, 90th Cong., 2nd Sess. (Washington, DC: Government Printing Office, 1968), 1.

24. Subcommittee on Employment, Manpower, and Poverty of the Committee on Labor and Public Welfare, *Hunger in America: Chronology and Selected Background Materials*, U.S. Senate, 90th Cong., 2nd Sess. (Washington, DC: Government Printing Office, 1968), 20.

25. Peter B. Edelman, Oral History Interview—RFK #8, March 13, 1974, interview by Larry Hackman, transcript, 48, John F. Kennedy Library, Robert F. Kennedy Oral History Collection. https://www.jfklibrary.org/Asset-Viewer/Archives/RFKOH-PBE-08.aspx; Nick Kotz, *Let Them Eat Promises: The Politics of Hunger in America* (New York: Doubleday, 1971).

26. Lyndon B. Johnson, Speech, "Remarks Upon Signing the Food Stamp Act," August 31, 1964.

27. Citizens' Board of Inquiry into Hunger and Malnutrition in the United States, *Hunger, US* (Boston: Beacon Press, 1968), 11.

28. Subcommittee on Employment, Manpower, and Poverty of the Committee on Labor and Public Welfare, *Hunger in America: Chronology and Selected Background Materials*, U.S. Senate, 90th Cong., 2nd Sess. (Washington, DC: Government Printing Office, 1968), 19; Peter Edelman, *Searching for America's Heart: RFK and the Renewal of Hope* (Washington, DC: Georgetown University Press, 2001), 49–53.

29. Subcommittee on Employment, Manpower, and Poverty of the Committee on Labor and Public Welfare, *Hunger in America: Chronology and Selected Background Materials*, U.S. Senate, 90th Cong., 2nd Sess. (Washington, DC: Government Printing Office, 1968), 15.

30. Subcommittee on Employment, Manpower, and Poverty of the Committee on Labor and Public Welfare, *Hunger in America: Chronology and Selected Background Materials*, U.S. Senate, 90th Cong., 2nd Sess. (Washington, DC: Government Printing Office, 1968), 17.

31. George Mehren to Orville Freeman, April 14, 1967, NACP, RG 16, Records of the Office of the Secretary of Agriculture, A1, entry 1038, General Correspondence, 1906–1976, box 4664, folder: Farm Program 8–1, January 1967–July 1967.

32. Tom Hughes to George Mehren, April 17, 1967, NACP, RG 16, Records of the Office of the Secretary of Agriculture, A1, entry 1038, General Correspondence, 1906–1976, box 4664, folder: Farm Program 8–1, January 1967–July 1967.

33. Rachel Louise Moran, "Consuming Relief: Food Stamps and the New Welfare of the New Deal," *Journal of American History* 76 (March 2011): 1001–1022; Janet Poppendieck, *Breadlines Knee-Deep in Wheat: Food Assistance in the Great Depression* (New Brunswick, NJ: Rutgers University Press, 1986).

34. Tracey A. Deutsch, *Building a Housewife's Paradise: Gender, Government and American Grocery Stores in the Twentieth Century* (Chapel Hill: University of North Carolina Press, 2010), 222–223.

35. Don F. Hadwiger, "The Freeman Administration and the Poor," *Agricultural History* 45, no. 1 (January 1971): 21–32.

36. Sarah T. Phillips, "What Next? The USDA at One Hundred and One Hundred Fifty Years Old," Roundtable on "Reflections on One Hundred and Fifty Years of the United States Department of Agriculture," *Agricultural History* 87, no. 3 (Summer 2013): 315–322.

37. Bill Winders, *The Politics of Food Supply: U.S. Agricultural Policy in the World Economy* (New Haven, CT: Yale University Press, 2009).

38. Jeffrey M. Berry, "Consumers and the Hunger Lobby," *Proceedings of the Academy of Political Science* 34, no. 3 (1982): 72–73.

39. Peter B. Edelman, Oral History Interview—RFK #8, March 13, 1974, interview by Larry Hackman, transcript, 22, John F. Kennedy Library, Robert F. Kennedy Oral History Collection. https://www.jfklibrary.org/Asset-Viewer/Archives/RFKOH-PBE-08.a.

40. Subcommittee on Employment, Manpower, and Poverty of the Committee on Labor and Public Welfare, *Hunger in America: Chronology and Selected Background Materials*, U.S. Senate, 90th Cong., 2nd Sess. (Washington, DC: Government Printing Office, 1968), 37.

41. Robert Cole and Harry Huge, "FBI on the Trail of the Hunger-Mongers," *New Republic* (December 21, 1968): 11–13.

42. Subcommittee on Employment, Manpower, and Poverty of the Committee on Labor and Public Welfare, *Hunger in America: Chronology and Selected Background Materials*, U.S. Senate, 90th Cong., 2nd Sess. (Washington, DC: Government Printing Office, 1968), 40.

43. Peter K. Eisinger, *Toward an End to Hunger in America* (Washington, DC: Brookings Institution Press, 1998), 77–78; Janet Poppendieck, *Sweet Charity? Emergency Food and the End of Entitlement* (New York: Penguin, 1998), 11–12; Janet Poppendieck, "Hunger in America: Typification and Response," in *Eating Agendas: Food and Nutrition as Social Problems*, ed. Jeffrey Sobal and Donna Maurer (New Brunswick, NJ: Transaction, 1995), 19–20.

44. Subcommittee on Employment, Manpower, and Poverty of the Committee on Labor and Public Welfare, *Hunger in America: Chronology and Selected Background Materials*, U.S. Senate, 90th Cong., 2nd Sess. (Washington, DC: Government Printing Office, 1968), 25.

45. Subcommittee on Employment, Manpower, and Poverty of the Committee on Labor and Public Welfare, *Hunger in America: Chronology and Selected Background Materials*, U.S. Senate, 90th Cong., 2nd Sess. (Washington, DC: Government Printing Office, 1968), 23.

46. *Hunger, U.S.A.*, 3.

47. Subcommittee on Employment, Manpower, and Poverty of the Committee on Labor and Public Welfare, *Hunger in America: Chronology and Selected Background Materials*, U.S. Senate, 90th Cong., 2nd Sess. (Washington, DC: Government Printing Office, 1968), 43, 44, 43, 47.

48. Introductory Comment by Robert F. Kennedy, in *Hunger, U.S.A.*, 7–8.

49. Introductory Comment by Robert F. Kennedy, in *Hunger, U.S.A.*, 8.

50. *Hunger, U.S.A.*, 19.

51. "Hungry People and Pampered Pets," *Christian Century: An Ecumenical Weekly* (June 26, 1968): 833.

52. Kotz, *Let Them Eat Promises*, 19.

53. Angela Jill Cooley, "Freedom's Farms: Activism and Sustenance in Rural Mississippi," in *Dethroning the Deceitful Pork Chop: Rethinking African American Foodways from Slavery to Obama*, ed. Jennifer Jensen Wallach and Lindsey R. Swindall (Fayetteville: University of Arkansas Press, 2015), 199–213.

54. Orville Freeman to Walter Reuther, May 10, 1968, NACP, RG 16, Records of the Office of the Secretary of Agriculture, A1, entry 1038, General Correspondence, 1906–1976, box 4812, folder: Farm Program, 2 of 2, March 1, 1968–May 1, 1968.

55. Orville Freeman to Walter Reuther, May 10, 1968, NACP, RG 16, Records of the Office of the Secretary of Agriculture, A1, entry 1038, General Correspondence, 1906–1976, box 4812, folder: Farm Program, 2 of 2, March 1, 1968–May 1, 1968.

56. Aaron M. Altschul to Orville Freeman, May 17, 1968, NACP, RG 16, Records of the Office of the Secretary of Agriculture, A1, entry 1038, General Correspondence, 1906–1976, box 4844, folder: Nutrition, 1 of 2.

57. Subcommittee on Employment, Manpower, and Poverty of the Committee on Labor and Public Welfare, *Hunger in America: Chronology and Selected Background Materials*, U.S. Senate, 90th Cong., 2nd Sess. (Washington, DC: Government Printing Office, 1968), 49.

58. Kotz, *Let Them Eat Promises*, 82.

59. *Hunger in America*, CBS, 1968.

60. *Hunger in America*, CBS, 1968.

61. Laurie B. Green, "'Hunger in America' and the Power of Television: Poor People, Physicians, and the Mass Media in the War Against Poverty," in *Precarious Prescriptions:*

Contested Histories of Race and Health in North America, ed. Laurie B. Green, John Mckiernan-González, and Martin Summers (Minneapolis: University of Minnesota Press, 2014), 211–236.

62. *Hunger in America*, CBS, 1968.

63. Laura S. Sims, "The Ebb and Flow of Nutrition as a Public Policy Issue," *Journal of Nutrition Education* 15, no. 4 (1983): 132.

64. Ernest F. Martin, "The 'Hunger in America' Controversy," *Journal of Broadcasting* 16, no. 2 (Spring 1972): 187.

65. John E. Talbot to Orville Freeman, May 22, 1968, NACP, RG 16, Records of the Office of the Secretary of Agriculture, A1, entry 1038, General Correspondence, 1906–1976, box 4814, folder: Farm Program 8-1-1, 2 of 2, June 1, 1968–July 31, 1968; Jack Gould, "Hunger Is Not for Quibbling," *New York Times* (June 23, 1968): D19.

66. Mr. Hughes to Orville Freeman, May 28, 1968, NACP, RG, 16, Records of the Office of the Secretary of Agriculture, A1, entry 1038, General Correspondence, 1906–1976, box 4814, folder: Farm Program 8-1-1, January 1, 1968–May 31, 1968.

67. "C.B.S. Hunger Show Wins an Emmy," *New York Times* (May 27, 1969): 95.

68. John Steriver to Orville Freeman, May 21, 1968, NACP, RG 16, Records of the Office of the Secretary of Agriculture, A1, entry 1038, General Correspondence, 1906–1976, box 4814, folder: Farm Program 8-1-1, June 1, 1968–July 31, 1968.

69. Marie Dalton to Orville Freeman, May 26, 1968, NACP, RG 16, Records of the Office of the Secretary of Agriculture, A1, entry 1038, General Correspondence, 1906–1976, box 4814, folder: Farm Program 8-1-1, June 1, 1968–July 31, 1968.

70. Hugh Downs, "It Ceases to Be Journalism," *New York Times* (July 21, 1968): D23; Marjorie Hunter, "Hunger Reports Scored in House," *New York Times* (May 24, 1969): 20; "News Slanting Charge Dropped on CBS' 'Hunger' Special," *New York Times* (October 18, 1969): 67.

71. Committee on Agriculture, House of Representatives, *Hunger Study Supplement (Supplement to Hunger Study, June 11, 1968)*, 90th Cong., 2nd Sess. (Washington, DC: Government Printing Office, August 17, 1968), 32.

72. Marie Dalton to Orville Freeman, May 26, 1968, NACP, RG 16, Records of the Office of the Secretary of Agriculture, A1, entry 1038, General Correspondence, 1906–1976, box 4814, folder: Farm Program 8-1-1, June 1, 1968–July 31, 1968.

73. Committee on Agriculture, House of Representatives, *Hunger Study Supplement (Supplement to Hunger Study, June 11, 1968)*, 90th Cong., 2nd Sess. (Washington, DC: Government Printing Office, August 17, 1968), 25.

74. Marie Dalton to Orville Freeman, May 26, 1968, NACP, RG 16, Records of the Office of the Secretary of Agriculture, A1, entry 1038, General Correspondence, 1906–1976, box 4814, folder: Farm Program 8-1-1, June 1, 1968–July 31, 1968.

75. Martin Gilens, *Why Americans Hate Welfare: Race, Media, and the Politics of Antipoverty Policy* (Chicago: University of Chicago Press, 1999), 67.

76. Hortense J. Spillers, "Mama's Baby, Papa's Maybe: An American Grammar Book," *Diacritics* 17, no. 2 (Summer 1987): 65–81; Sander L. Gilman, "Black Bodies, White Bodies: Toward an Iconography of Female Sexuality in Late Nineteenth-Century Art, Music, and Literature," in *Race, Writing, and Difference*, ed. Henry Louis Gates (Chicago: University of Chicago Press, 1987), 223–261.

77. Marie Dalton to Orville Freeman, May 26, 1968, NACP, RG 16, Records of the Office of the Secretary of Agriculture, A1, entry 1038, General Correspondence, 1906–1976, box 4814, folder: Farm Program 8-1-1, June 1, 1968–July 31, 1968.

78. John Dittmer, *Local People: The Struggle for Civil Rights in Mississippi* (Urbana: University of Illinois Press, 1995), 384; Charles M. Payne, *I've Got the Light of Freedom: The Organizing Tradition and the Mississippi* (Berkeley: University of California Press, 1995), 344.

79. Mrs. W. L. Francis Millersville to Orville Freeman, June 16, 1968, NACP, RG 16, Records of the Office of the Secretary of Agriculture, A1, entry 1038, General Correspondence, 1906–1976, box 4814, folder: Farm Program 8-1-1, June 1, 1968–July 31, 1968.

80. Allan Lisle to Mr. Mills, June 19, 1968, NACP, RG 16, Records of the Office of the Secretary of Agriculture, A1, entry 1038, General Correspondence, 1906–1976, box 4814, folder: Farm Program 8-1-1, June 1, 1968–July 31, 1968.

81. John Steriver to Orville Freeman, May 21, 1968, NACP, RG 16, Records of the Office of the Secretary of Agriculture, A1, entry 1038, General Correspondence, 1906–1976, box 4814, folder: Farm Program 8-1-1, June 1, 1968–July 31, 1968.

82. Committee on Agriculture, House of Representatives, *Hunger Study Supplement (Supplement to Hunger Study, June 11, 1968)*, 90th Cong., 2nd Sess. (Washington, DC: Government Printing Office, August 17, 1968), 27.

83. Committee on Agriculture, House of Representatives, *Hunger Study Supplement (Supplement to Hunger Study, June 11, 1968)*, 90th Cong., 2nd Sess. (Washington, DC: Government Printing Office, August 17, 1968), 27.

84. Orville Freeman to Mrs. J. J. Schmidt, July 1, 1968, 1, NACP, RG 16, Records of the Office of the Secretary of Agriculture, A1, entry 1038, General Correspondence, 1906–1976, box 4843, folder: Nutrition, June 1, 1968–September 30, 1968.

85. Orville Freeman to Mrs. J. J. Schmidt, July 1, 1968, 2, NACP, RG 16, Records of the Office of the Secretary of Agriculture, A1, entry 1038, General Correspondence, 1906–1976, box 4843, folder: Nutrition, June 1, 1968–September 30, 1968.

86. Orville Freeman to Frank Stanton, May 27, 1968, 1, NACP, RG 16, Records of the Office of the Secretary of Agriculture, A1, entry 1038, General Correspondence, 1906–1976, box 4814, folder: Farm Program 8-1-1, January 1, 1968–May 31, 1968.

87. Orville Freeman to Henry B. Gonzalez, July 24, 1968, NACP, RG 16, Records of the Office of the Secretary of Agriculture, A1, entry 1038, General Correspondence, 1906–1976, box 4814, folder: Farm Program 8-1-1, June 1, 1968–July 31, 1968.

88. Florence to Orville Freeman, June 10, 1968, NACP, RG 16, Records of the Office of the Secretary of Agriculture, A1, entry 1038, General Correspondence, 1906–1976, box 4814, folder: Farm Program 8-1-1, 2 of 2, June 1, 1968–July 31, 1968.

89. Orville Freeman to Mrs. Harry E. Fredricksen, June 10, 1968, NACP, RG 16, Records of the Office of the Secretary of Agriculture, A1, entry 1038, General Correspondence, 1906–1976, box 4814, folder: Farm Program 8-1-1, 2 of 2, June 1, 1968–July 31, 1968.

90. Committee on Agriculture, House of Representatives, *Hunger Study Supplement (Supplement to Hunger Study, June 11, 1968)*, 90th Cong., 2nd Sess. (Washington, DC: Government Printing Office, August 17, 1968), 6.

91. Press release, House of Representatives, August 18, 1968, 2, NACP, RG 16, Records of the Office of the Secretary of Agriculture, A1, entry 1038, General Correspondence, 1906–1976, box 4843, folder: Nutrition, June 1, 1968–September 30, 1968.

92. Rodney E. Leonard to Orville Freeman, September 4, 1968, NACP, RG 16, Records of the Office of the Secretary of Agriculture, A1, entry 1038, General Correspondence, 1906–1976, box 4843, folder: Nutrition, June 1, 1968–September 30, 1968.

93. Rodney E. Leonard to W., n.d. [September 1968], NACP, RG 16, Records of the Office of the Secretary of Agriculture, A1, entry 1038, General Correspondence, 1906–1976, box 4843, folder: Nutrition, June 1, 1968–September 30, 1968.

94. Committee on Agriculture, House of Representatives, *Hunger Study Supplement (Supplement to Hunger Study, June 11, 1968)*, 90th Cong., 2nd Sess. (Washington, DC: Government Printing Office, August 17, 1968), 1–2.

95. Committee on Agriculture, House of Representatives, *Hunger Study Supplement (Supplement to Hunger Study, June 11, 1968)*, 90th Cong., 2nd Sess. (Washington, DC: Government Printing Office, August 17, 1968), 26.

96. Committee on Agriculture, House of Representatives, *Hunger Study Supplement (Supplement to Hunger Study, June 11, 1968)*, 90th Cong., 2nd Sess. (Washington, DC: Government Printing Office, August 17, 1968), 26, 9, 12.

97. Committee on Agriculture, House of Representatives, *Hunger Study Supplement (Supplement to Hunger Study, June 11, 1968)*, 90th Cong., 2nd Sess. (Washington, DC: Government Printing Office, August 17, 1968), 10–11.

98. Office of Policy Planning and Research, *The Negro Family: The Case for National Action* (Washington, DC: United States Department of Labor, March 1965); James T. Patterson, *Freedom Is Not Enough: The Moynihan Report and America's Struggle over Black Family Life from LBJ to Obama* (New York: Basic Books, 2010); Ruth Feldstein, *Motherhood in Black and White: Race and Sex in American Liberalism, 1930–1965* (Ithaca, NY: Cornell University Press, 2000).

99. Committee on Agriculture, House of Representatives, *Hunger Study Supplement (Supplement to Hunger Study, June 11, 1968)*, 90th Cong., 2nd Sess. (Washington, DC: Government Printing Office, August 17, 1968), 7–8, 4, 10–11.

100. *Hunger in America*, CBS, 1968.

101. Committee on Agriculture, House of Representatives, *Hunger Study Supplement (Supplement to Hunger Study, June 11, 1968)*, 90th Cong., 2nd Sess. (Washington, DC: Government Printing Office, August 17, 1968), 4.

102. Committee on Agriculture, House of Representatives, *Hunger Study Supplement (Supplement to Hunger Study, June 11, 1968)*, 90th Cong., 2nd Sess. (Washington, DC: Government Printing Office, August 17, 1968), 4.

103. Republican Party Platforms: "Republican Party Platform of 1968," August 5, 1968, online by Gerhard Peters and John T. Woolley, The American Presidency Project. http://www.presidency.ucsb.edu/ws/?pid=25841

Chapter 6

1. *Child Nutrition Amendments of 1978, Hearing Before the Subcommittee on Elementary, Secondary, and Vocational Education of the Committee on Education and Labor, House of Representatives*, 95th Cong., 2nd Sess., April 27, 1978, 312.

2. *Child Nutrition Amendments of 1978, Hearing Before the Subcommittee on Elementary, Secondary, and Vocational Education of the Committee on Education and Labor, House of Representatives*, 95th Cong., 2nd Sess., April 27, 1978, 312.

3. Children's Foundation, prepared testimony, in *Child Nutrition Amendments of 1978, Hearing Before the Subcommittee on Elementary, Secondary, and Vocational Education of the Committee on Education and Labor, House of Representatives*, 95th Cong., 2nd Sess., April 27, 1978, 311.

4. Dr. Caro E. Luhrs, White House Fellow, to Aaron M. Altschul, Director, High Protein Foods and Agribusiness Group, IADS, October 7, 1968, National Archives at College Park, College Park, MD (hereafter cited as NACP), Record Group 16, Records of the Office of the Secretary of Agriculture, A1, entry 1038, General Correspondence, 1906–1976, box 4843, folder: Nutrition, October 1, 1968–December 31, 1968.

5. Dr. Caro E. Luhrs, White House Fellow, to Aaron M. Altschul, Director, High Protein Foods and Agribusiness Group, IADS, October 7, 1968, NACP, RG 16, Records of the Office of the Secretary of Agriculture, A1, entry 1038, General Correspondence, 1906–1976, box 4843, folder: Nutrition, October 1, 1968–December 31, 1968.

6. Testimony of the Honorable Clifford H. Hardin, Secretary of Agriculture, Before the Select Committee on Nutrition and Human Needs, May 7, 1969, 7, NACP, RG 16, Records of the Office of the Secretary of Agriculture, A1, entry 1038, General Correspondence, 1906–1976, box 5063, folder: Nutrition, May 1–June 31, 1969.

7. Jean Mayer, "Freeman Criticized on Nutrition," *New York Times* (June 9, 1968), NACP, RG 16, Records of the Office of the Secretary of Agriculture, A1, entry 1038, General Correspondence, 1906–1976, box 4843, folder: Nutrition, June 1, 1968–September 30, 1968; Orville Freeman to Editor of the *New York Times*, June 28, 1968, 2, NACP, RG 16, Records of the Office of the Secretary of Agriculture, A1, entry 1038, General Correspondence, box 4843, folder: Nutrition, June 1, 1968–September 30, 1968; Laura S. Sims, "The Ebb and Flow of Nutrition as a Public Policy Issue," *Journal of Nutrition Education* 15, no. 4 (1983): 132–136, 134.

8. Judith Randal, "White House Nutrition Unit Taps Foundations for Funds," *Washington Evening Star* (November 26, 1969).

9. National Welfare Rights Organization, "White House Conferences Are Part of the Problem," in *White House Conference on Food, Nutrition and Health: Final Report* (Washington, DC: Government Printing Office, 1970), NACP, RG 462, Records of the Food and Consumer Services, Records of the Food and Nutrition Service, A1, entry 69, White House Conference on Nutrition Records, 1969–1971, box 5, folder: Panel Recommendations.

10. Pat Moynihan to Richard Nixon, March 17, 1969, attached to Pat Moynihan to Clifford Hardin, March 17, 1969, 1–2, NACP, RG 16, Records of the Office of the Secretary of Agriculture, A1, entry 1038, General Correspondence, 1906–1976, box 5063, folder: Nutrition, May 1–June 31, 1969.

11. Pat Moynihan to Richard Nixon, March 17, 1969, attached to Pat Moynihan to Clifford Hardin, March 17, 1969, 1–2, NACP, RG 16, Records of the Office of the Secretary of Agriculture, A1, entry 1038, General Correspondence, 1906–1976, box 5063, folder: Nutrition May 1–June 31, 1969.

12. Gregory A. Culley, WIC Family Health Services, Appalachian Regional Hospital, Hazard, KY, in *WIC and Commodity Supplemental Food Programs, Hearing Before the Select Committee on Nutrition and Human Needs, Senate,* 94th Cong., 2nd Sess., March 30, 1976 (Washington, DC: Government Printing Office), 51.

13. *WIC and Commodity Supplemental Food Programs, Hearing Before the Select Committee on Nutrition and Human Needs, Senate,* 94th Cong., 2nd Sess., March 30, 1976 (Washington, DC: Government Printing Office), 77.

14. Robert Dole, in *WIC and Commodity Supplemental Food Programs, Hearing Before the Select Committee on Nutrition and Human Needs, Senate,* 94th Cong., 2nd Sess., March 30, 1976 (Washington, DC: Government Printing Office), 26.

15. George Miller, in *WIC and Commodity Supplemental Food Programs, Hearing Before the Select Committee on Nutrition and Human Needs, Senate,* 94th Cong., 2nd Sess., March 30, 1976 (Washington, DC: Government Printing Office), 28–29.

16. George McGovern, in *WIC and Commodity Supplemental Food Programs, Hearing Before the Select Committee on Nutrition and Human Needs, Senate,* 94th Cong., 2nd Sess., March 30, 1976 (Washington, DC: Government Printing Office), 3.

17. *Child Nutrition Amendments of 1978, Hearings Before the Subcommittee on Nutrition of the Committee on Agriculture, Nutrition, and Forestry,* 95th Cong., 2nd Sess., on S. 2630 A Bill to Extend and Modify the WIC Program, Part I, April 6, 1978 (Washington, DC: Government Printing Office), 195.

18. George McGovern, introduction to *Implementation and Status of the Special Supplemental Food Program for Women, Infants, and Children,* Department of Agriculture, Food and Nutrition Service, submitted to Select Committee on Nutrition and Human Needs, U.S. Senate (Washington, DC: Government Printing Office, October 1974), v.

19. "The Plague of Overweight: Despite Claims, Willpower Is the Only Cure," *Life* 36, no. 10 (March 8, 1954): 120–124; "Nobel Winners Discover How Metabolism Works and What Can Go Wrong," *Life* 54, no. 13 (March 29, 1963): 63–65; Carl C. Seltzer and Jean Mayer, "Body Build and Obesity: Who Are the Obese," *Journal of the American Medical Association* 189, no. 9 (August 31, 1964): 677–684; "New Weight Standards for Men and Women," *Statistical Bulletin of the Metropolitan Life Insurance Company* 40, no. 2–3 (November–December 1959).

20. Jonathan M. Metzl, "Why Against Health?," in *Against Health: How Health Became the New Morality,* ed. Jonathan Metzl and Anna Kirkland (New York: New York University Press, 2010), 2.

21. Ange-Marie Hancock, *The Politics of Disgust: The Public Identity of the Welfare Queen* (New York: New York University Press, 2004).

22. Hancock, *Politics of Disgust,* 50; Regina G. Lawrence, "Framing Obesity: The Evolution of News Discourse on a Public Health Issue," *International Journal of Press/Politics* 9, no. 3 (Summer 2004): 56–75.

23. Victor Olivera, Elizabeth Racine, Jennifer Olmsted, and Linda Ghelfi, *The WIC Program: Background, Trends, and Issues,* USDA, Economic Research Service, Food Assistance and Research Report 27, October 2002, 7.

24. Karen Kruse Thomas, *Health and Humanity: A History of the Johns Hopkins Bloomberg School of Public Health, 1935–1985* (Baltimore: Johns Hopkins University Press, 2016).

25. "Preliminary Report on the Implementation and Status of the Special Supplemental Program for Women, Infants, and Children," *Implementation and Status of the Special Supplemental Food Program for Women, Infants, and Children,* Department of Agriculture, Food and Nutrition Service, submitted to Select Committee on Nutrition and Human Needs, U.S. Senate (Washington, DC: Government Printing Office, October 1974), 7–8.

26. "Preliminary Report on the Implementation and Status of the Special Supplemental Program for Women, Infants, and Children," *Implementation and Status of the Special Supplemental Food Program for Women, Infants, and Children,* Department of Agriculture, Food and Nutrition Service, submitted to Select Committee on Nutrition and Human Needs, U.S. Senate (Washington, DC: Government Printing Office, October 1974), 8.

27. "Preliminary Report on the Implementation and Status of the Special Supplemental Program for Women, Infants, and Children," *Implementation and Status of the Special Supplemental Food Program for Women, Infants, and Children,* Department of Agriculture, Food and

Nutrition Service, submitted to Select Committee on Nutrition and Human Needs, U.S. Senate (Washington, DC: Government Printing Office, October 1974), 8.

28. Marc Bendick, Jr., "WIC and the Paradox of In-Kind Transfers," *Public Finance Quarterly* 6, no. 3 (July 1978): 361.

29. Bendick, "WIC and the Paradox of In-Kind Transfers," 360.

30. *WIC and Commodity Supplemental Food Programs, Hearing Before the Select Committee on Nutrition and Human Needs, Senate*, 94th Cong., 2nd Sess., March 30, 1976 (Washington, DC: Government Printing Office), 15.

31. Bill Winders, *The Politics of Food Supply: U.S. Agricultural Policy in the World Economy* (New Haven, CT: Yale University Press, 2009), 140.

32. Clayton Yeutter to Victor Riesel, March 1, 1974, NACP, RG 16, Records of the Office of the Secretary of Agriculture, A1, entry 1038, General Correspondence, 1906–1976, box 5844, folder: Farm Programs 9.

33. "Preliminary Report on the Implementation and Status of the Special Supplemental Program for Women, Infants, and Children," *Implementation and Status of the Special Supplemental Food Program for Women, Infants, and Children*, Department of Agriculture, Food and Nutrition Service, submitted to Select Committee on Nutrition and Human Needs, U.S. Senate (Washington, DC: Government Printing Office, October 1974), 2.

34. Clayton Yeutter to Charles Percy, January 11, 1974, NACP, RG 16, Records of the Office of the Secretary of Agriculture, A1, entry 1038, General Correspondence, 1906–1976, box 5844, folder: Farm Programs 9.

35. UPI Release, February 13, 1974, NACP, RG 16, Records of the Office of the Secretary of Agriculture, A1, entry 1038, General Correspondence, 1906–1976, box 5844, folder: Farm Programs 9.

36. Earl L. Butz to Miss Gail M. Corey, March 8, 1974, NACP, RG 16, Records of the Office of the Secretary of Agriculture, A1, entry 1038, General Correspondence, 1906–1976, box 5844, folder: Farm Programs 9.

37. Earl Butz to Brooks McCormick, March 25, 1975, NACP, RG 16, Records of the Office of the Secretary of Agriculture, A1, entry 1038, General Correspondence, 1906–1976, box 5844, folder: Farm Programs 9.

38. Anne Schubert to Earl Butz, February 25, 1974, NACP, RG 16, Records of the Office of the Secretary of Agriculture, A1, entry 1038, General Correspondence, 1906–1976, box 5844, folder: Farm Programs 9.

39. Otto Selig to Earl Butz, January 28, 1974, NACP, RG 16, Records of the Office of the Secretary of Agriculture, A1, entry 1038, General Correspondence, 1906–1976, box 5844, folder: Farm Programs 9.

40. "Preliminary Report on the Implementation and Status of the Special Supplemental Program for Women, Infants, and Children," *Implementation and Status of the Special Supplemental Food Program for Women, Infants, and Children*, Department of Agriculture, Food and Nutrition Service, submitted to Select Committee on Nutrition and Human Needs, U.S. Senate, (Washington, DC: Government Printing Office, October 1974), 1.

41. "Overview—Current Status of WIC Program," *Implementation and Status of the Special Supplemental Food Program for Women, Infants, and Children*, Department of Agriculture, Food and Nutrition Service, submitted to Select Committee on Nutrition and Human Needs, U.S. Senate (Washington, DC: Government Printing Office, October 1974), n.p.

42. "Preliminary Report on the Implementation and Status of the Special Supplemental Program for Women, Infants, and Children," *Implementation and Status of the Special Supplemental Food Program for Women, Infants, and Children*, Department of Agriculture, Food and Nutrition Service, submitted to Select Committee on Nutrition and Human Needs, U.S. Senate (Washington, DC: Government Printing Office, October 1974), 33.

43. George McGovern, in *WIC and Commodity Supplemental Food Programs, Hearing Before the Select Committee on Nutrition and Human Needs, Senate*, 94th Cong., 2nd Sess., March 30, 1976 (Washington, DC: Government Printing Office), 1.

44. George McGovern, in *WIC and Commodity Supplemental Food Programs, Hearing Before the Select Committee on Nutrition and Human Needs, Senate*, 94th Cong., 2nd Sess., March 30, 1976 (Washington, DC: Government Printing Office), 6–7.

45. Prepared Statement, Comments by Richard L. Feltner, September 21, 1976, 2, NACP, RG 462, Food and Nutrition Service, A1, entry 70, Department of Agriculture Advisory Committee Papers, 1976, box 1, folder: Committee—1st Consultants Meeting.

46. Edward J. Hekman, U.S. Department of Agriculture, *Advisory Committee on Nutrition to Meet September 21–23*, 1, NACP, RG 462, Food and Nutrition Service, A1, entry 70, Department of Agriculture Advisory Committee Papers, 1976, box 1, folder: Committee—1st Consultants Meeting.

47. "Available Data Which May Be Useful in Assessment of the WIC Program Within the Time Limit of 16 Months," 2, NACP, RG 462, Food and Nutrition Service, A1, entry 70, Department of Agriculture Advisory Committee Papers, 1976, box 1, folder: Committee—2nd Meeting.

48. "Available Data Which May Be Useful in Assessment of the WIC Program Within the Time Limit of 16 Months," 1, NACP, RG 462, Food and Nutrition Service, A1, entry 70, Department of Agriculture Advisory Committee Papers, 1976, box 1, folder: Committee—2nd Meeting.

49. "Available Data Which May Be Useful in Assessment of the WIC Program Within the Time Limit of 16 Months," 1, NACP, RG 462, Food and Nutrition Service, A1, entry 70, Department of Agriculture Advisory Committee Papers, 1976, box 1, folder: Committee—2nd Meeting.

50. "Working Minutes for Consultant Group, October 12–13, 1976," 1, Seattle, WA, NACP, RG 462, Food and Nutrition Service, A1, entry 70, Department of Agriculture, Advisory Committee Papers, 1976, box 1, folder: Committee—1st Consultants Meeting; "Untitled Advisory Committee Report from the 2nd Meeting," 6–7, NACP, RG 462, Food and Nutrition Service, A1, entry 70, Department of Agriculture Advisory Committee Papers, 1976, box 1, folder: Committee—2nd Meeting.

51. Working Minutes for Consultant Group, October 12–13, 1976, 1, Seattle, WA, NACP, RG 462, Food and Nutrition Service, A1, entry 70, Department of Agriculture, Advisory Committee Papers, 1976, box 1, folder: Committee—1st Consultants Meeting.

52. *Medical Evaluation of the Special Supplemental Food Program for Women, Infants and Children*, 5, 94th Cong., 2nd Sess., committee print, Senate Committee on Nutrition and Human Needs, August 1976 (Washington, DC: Government Printing Office).

53. *Medical Evaluation of the Special Supplemental Food Program for Women, Infants and Children*, 38, 94th Cong., 2nd Sess., committee print, Senate Committee on Nutrition and Human Needs, August 1976 (Washington, DC: Government Printing Office).

54. Jennifer Mittelstadt, "'Dependency as a Problem to Be Solved': Rehabilitation and the American Liberal Consensus on Welfare in the 1950s," *Social Politics* 8 (Summer 2001): 228–257; and Jennifer Mittelstadt, *From Welfare to Workfare: The Unintended Consequences of Liberal Reform, 1945–1965* (Chapel Hill: University of North Carolina Press, 2005).

55. Hancock, *Politics of Disgust,* 50; "Dethroning the Welfare Queen: The Rhetoric of Reform," *Harvard Law Review* 107, no. 8 (June 1994): 2021.

56. Annelise Orleck, *Storming Caesar's Palace: How Black Mothers Fought Their Own War on Poverty* (Boston: Beacon Press, 2005), 157.

57. Eileen Boris, "On Cowboys and Welfare Queens: Independence, Dependence, and Interdependence at Home and Abroad," *Journal of American Studies* 41, no. 3 (2007): 601; Martin Gilens, *Why Americans Hate Welfare: Race, Media, and the Politics of Anti-Poverty Policy* (Chicago: University of Chicago Press, 1999).

58. Johnnie Tillmon, "Welfare Is a Women's Issue," *Ms. Magazine* (Spring 1972): 111–116; Teresa L. Amott, "Black Women and AFDC: Making Entitlement out of Necessity," in *Women, the State, and Welfare,* ed. Linda Gordon (Madison: University of Wisconsin Press, 1990), 289.

59. *Child Nutrition Amendments of 1978, Hearings Before the Subcommittee on Nutrition of the Committee on Agriculture, Nutrition, and Forestry, Senate,* 58, 95th Cong., 2nd Sess., on S. 2630 A Bill to Extend and Modify the WIC Program, Part II, April 22, 1978 (Washington, DC: Government Printing Office).

60. *Child Nutrition Amendments of 1978, Hearings Before the Subcommittee on Nutrition of the Committee on Agriculture, Nutrition, and Forestry, Senate,* 55–56, 95th Cong., 2nd Sess., on S. 2630 A Bill to Extend and Modify the WIC Program, Part II, April 22, 1978 (Washington, DC: Government Printing Office).

61. Bendick, "WIC and the Paradox of In-Kind Transfers," 363.

62. Janet Berkenfield, in *WIC and Commodity Supplemental Food Programs, Hearing Before the Select Committee on Nutrition and Human Needs, Senate,* 94th Cong., 2nd Sess., March 30, 1976 (Washington, DC: Government Printing Office), 34.

63. Jenny Vollmar in *WIC and Commodity Supplemental Food Programs, Hearing Before the Select Committee on Nutrition and Human Needs, Senate,* 94th Cong., 2nd Sess., March 30, 1976 (Washington, DC: Government Printing Office), 97.

64. "An Act to Extend the Special Supplemental Food Program and the Child Care Food Program, and for Other Purposes," Public Law 95–627, *U.S. Statutes at Large* 92, 1978, 3611.

65. *Child Nutrition Amendments of 1978, Hearings Before the Subcommittee on Nutrition of the Committee on Agriculture, Nutrition, and Forestry, Senate,* 174, 95th Cong., 2nd Sess., on S. 2630 A Bill to Extend and Modify the WIC Program, Part I, April 6, 1978 (Washington, DC: Government Printing Office).

66. Statement of Carol Tucker Foreman, Assistant Secretary for Food and Consumer Services, April 27, 1978, in *Child Nutrition Amendments of 1978, Hearing Before the Subcommittee on Elementary, Secondary, and Vocational Education of the Committee on Education and Labor, House of Representatives,* 95th Cong., 2nd Sess., 186.

67. Carol Tucker Foreman to Celia Hudson, May 17, 1978, NACP, RG 16, Secretary of Agriculture, UD-WW, entry 10, External Relations 1978, FRC 9, folder: Farm Program 7 (WIC), April 11, 1978–July 17, 1978.

68. Carol Tucker Foreman to Wanda G. Pryor, November 21, 1978, NACP, RG 16, Secretary of Agriculture, UD-WW, entry 10, External Relations 1978, FRC 9, folder: Farm Program 7 (WIC), July 18, 1978–October 31, 1978.

69. *Child Nutrition Amendments of 1978, Hearings Before the Subcommittee on Nutrition of the Committee on Agriculture, Nutrition, and Forestry, Senate,* 95th Cong., 2nd Sess., on S. 2630 A Bill to Extend and Modify the WIC Program, Part I, April 6, 1978 (Washington, DC: Government Printing Office), 154.

70. Bendick, "WIC and the Paradox of In-Kind Transfers," 370.

71. Bendick, "WIC and the Paradox of In-Kind Transfers," 370.

72. United States Department of Agriculture, Food and Nutrition Service, *The Idea Book: Sharing Nutrition Education Experiences,* FNS-234, September 1981, 21.

73. United States Department of Agriculture, Food and Nutrition Service, *The Idea Book: Sharing Nutrition Education Experiences,* FNS-234, September 1981, 36.

74. United States Department of Agriculture, Food and Nutrition Service, *The Idea Book: Sharing Nutrition Education Experiences,* FNS-234, September 1981, 34.

75. United States Department of Agriculture, Food and Nutrition Service, *The Idea Book: Sharing Nutrition Education Experiences,* FNS-234, September 1981, 36.

76. United States Department of Agriculture, Food and Nutrition Service, *The Idea Book: Sharing Nutrition Education Experiences,* FNS-234, September 1981, 1.

77. May Friedman, "Mother Blame, Fat Shame, and Moral Panic: 'Obesity' and Child Welfare," *Fat Studies: An Interdisciplinary Journal of Body Weight and Society* 4, no. 1 (2015): 14–27.

78. Katherine Mason, "Responsible Bodies: Self-Care and State Power in the Women, Infants, and Children Program," *Social Politics* 23, no. 1 (2016): 70–93.

79. *Child Nutrition Amendments of 1978, Hearings Before the Subcommittee on Nutrition of the Committee on Agriculture, Nutrition, and Forestry, Senate,* 95th Cong., 2nd Sess., on S. 2630 A Bill to Extend and Modify the WIC Program, Part I, April 6, 1978 (Washington, DC: Government Printing Office), 216.

80. *Child Nutrition Amendments of 1978, Hearings Before the Subcommittee on Nutrition of the Committee on Agriculture, Nutrition, and Forestry, Senate,* 95th Cong., 2nd Sess., on S. 2630 A Bill to Extend and Modify the WIC Program, Part I, April 6, 1978 (Washington, DC: Government Printing Office), 216.

81. Wanda G. Pryor to Carol Tucker Foreman, July 28, 1978, NACP, RG 16, Secretary of Agriculture, UD-WW, entry 10, External Relations 1978, FRC 9, folder: Farm Program 7 (WIC), July 18, 1978–October 31, 1978.

82. *Nutrition Education, Hearings Before the Subcommittee on Domestic Marketing, Consumer Relations, and Nutrition of the Committee on Agriculture, House of Representatives,* 95th Cong., 2nd Sess., September 27, 1977, Part I, 111–112.

83. Bendick, "WIC and the Paradox of In-Kind Transfers," 371.

84. George G. Graham, "WIC: A Food Program That Fails," *Public Interest,* no. 103 (Spring 1991): 71.

85. Dr. B. C. Richards to Carol T. Foreman, July 6, 1978, 2, NACP, RG 16, Secretary of Agriculture, UD-WW, entry 10, External Relations 1978, FRC 9, folder: Farm Program 7 (WIC), July 18, 1978–October 31, 1978.

86. *Child Nutrition Amendments of 1978, Hearings Before the Subcommittee on Nutrition of the Committee on Agriculture, Nutrition, and Forestry, Senate,* 95th Cong., 2nd Sess., on S. 2630 A Bill to Extend and Modify the WIC Program, Part I, April 6, 1978 (Washington, DC: Government Printing Office), 190–191.

87. *Child Nutrition Amendments of 1978, Hearings Before the Subcommittee on Nutrition of the Committee on Agriculture, Nutrition, and Forestry, Senate*, 95th Cong., 2nd Sess., on S. 2630 A Bill to Extend and Modify the WIC Program, Part I, April 6, 1978 (Washington, DC: Government Printing Office), 190–191.

88. Graham, "WIC: A Food Program That Fails," 71.

89. *Child Nutrition Amendments of 1978, Hearings Before the Subcommittee on Nutrition of the Committee on Agriculture, Nutrition, and Forestry, Senate*, 95th Cong., 2nd Sess., on S. 2630 A Bill to Extend and Modify the WIC Program, Part I, April 6, 1978 (Washington, DC: Government Printing Office), 220.

90. *Child Nutrition Amendments of 1978, Hearings Before the Subcommittee on Nutrition of the Committee on Agriculture, Nutrition, and Forestry, Senate*, 95th Cong., 2nd Sess., on S. 2630 A Bill to Extend and Modify the WIC Program, Part I, April 6, 1978 (Washington, DC: Government Printing Office), 229.

91. Statement of Carol Tucker Foreman, Assistant Secretary for Food and Consumer Services, April 27, 1978, in *Child Nutrition Amendments of 1978, Hearing Before the Subcommittee on Elementary, Secondary, and Vocational Education of the Committee on Education and Labor, House of Representatives*, 95th Cong., 2nd Sess., 184.

92. Celia Hudson (with other public health nurses) to Carol Tucker Foreman, March 27, 1978, RG 16, Secretary of Agriculture, UD-WW, entry 10, External Relations 1978, FRC 9, folder: Farm Program 7 (WIC), April 11, 1978–July 17, 1978.

93. Celia Hudson (with other public health nurses) to Carol Tucker Foreman, March 27, 1978, RG 16, Secretary of Agriculture, UD-WW, entry 10, External Relations 1978, FRC 9, folder: Farm Program 7 (WIC), April 11, 1978–July 17, 1978.

94. Julilly Kohler-Hausmann, "Welfare Crises, Penal Solutions, and the Origins of the 'Welfare Queen,'" *Journal of Urban History* 41, no. 5 (2015): 759–760.

95. Nikolas Rose, *The Politics of Life Itself: Biomedicine, Power, and Subjectivity in the Twenty-First Century* (Princeton, NJ: Princeton University Press, 2007).

96. *Dietary Goals for the United States. Select Committee on Nutrition and Human Needs, United States Senate*, 95th Cong., 2nd Sess., December 1977.

97. Marion Nestle, *Food Politics: How the Food Industry Influences Nutrition and Health* (Berkeley: University of California Press, 2002), 40–41.

98. Letter from William E. Dickinson, President, Salt Institute, to the Committee, printed in *Dietary Goals for the United States—Supplemental Views. Select Committee on Nutrition and Human Needs, United States Senate*, 95th Cong., 2nd Sess., November 1977.

99. "Panel Stands by Its Dietary Goals but Eases a View on Eating Meat," *New York Times* (January 24, 1978): 22.

100. *Child Nutrition Amendments of 1978, Hearings Before the Subcommittee on Nutrition of the Committee on Agriculture, Nutrition, and Forestry*, 95th Cong., 2nd Sess., on S. 2630 A Bill to Extend and Modify the WIC Program, Part I, April 6, 1978 (Washington, DC: Government Printing Office), 243.

101. *Child Nutrition Amendments of 1978, Hearings Before the Subcommittee on Nutrition of the Committee on Agriculture, Nutrition, and Forestry*, 95th Cong., 2nd Sess., on S. 2630 A Bill to Extend and Modify the WIC Program, Part I, April 6, 1978 (Washington, DC: Government Printing Office), 243.

Conclusion

1. I am sometimes asked if the advisory state and advisory techniques actually *work* as a mode of governance. Really, it depends on what you expect it to do. If the advisory state is supposed to make Americans heavier, lighter, more muscular, or fitter—well, then, I have seen limited evidence it works. As I stated up front, however, I have not really been looking for evidence that it works or does not work. My question, rather, is about whether the state attempts to shape Americans, and the ways in which it reaches beyond the boundaries of the private. In permeating those boundaries, the advisory state functions quite well.

2. Marion Nestle, *Food Politics: How the Food Industry Influences Nutrition and Health*, 2nd ed., (Berkeley: University of California Press, 2007); Deirdre Barrett, *Waistland: The Re/evolutionary Science Behind Our Health and Fitness Crisis* (New York: W. W. Norton, 2007); Michael Pollan, *The Omnivore's Dilemma: A Natural History of Four Meals* (New York: Penguin, 2007); Wenonah Hauter, *Foodopoly: The Battle over the Future of Food and Farming in America* (New York: New Press, 2012).

3. Joshua Greenman, "Embrace the Nanny State—But Reject the Soda Ban," *New York Daily News* (June 6, 2012), Opinion; Aaron Sankin, "New California Soda-Tax Bill Under Consideration," *Huffington Post* (April 26, 2013), http://www.huffingtonpost.com/2013/04/26/california-soda-tax_n_3165417.html; Patrick McGreevy, "Oil and Soda Taxes Advance in California Legislature," *Los Angeles Times* (May 1, 2013); Jon Terbush, "Will New York Really Ban Fat Riders from Its Bike Share Program," *Week* (May 3, 2013); "Worry About Food Stamp Growth, Not Junk Food," Editorial, *Chicago Tribune* (May 20, 2013); Karen Harned, "The Michael Bloomberg Nanny State: A Cautionary Tale," *Forbes* (May 10, 2013); Sandra Pedicini, "As Grocers, Restaurants Bicker, Many Menus Still Lack Calorie Count," *Orlando Sentinel* (May 19, 2013); Margaret Hartmann, "City-Funded Study Finds City's Ban on Trans Fats Was a Huge Success," *New York* (July 16, 2012).

4. David Harsanyi, "The Trans Fat Ban Is Worse than You Think," *Reason*, June 19, 2015, http://reason.com/archives/2015/06/19/the-trans-fat-ban-is-worse-than-you-thin; Helena Bottemiller Evich, "Food Industry Braces for Obama Trans Fat Ban," *Politico*, May 16, 2015, http://www.politico.com/story/2015/05/fda-trans-fat-ban-118003.html.

INDEX

ACKNOWLEDGMENTS

Many hands helped make *Governing Bodies* clearer, bolder, and smarter. I owe a major debt to Jennifer Mittelstadt, who helped me understand this project and its significance, and helped me become a better scholar in the process. Lori Ginzberg read countless versions of the project with her typical brilliance. She did her best to kill the adverbs, passive voice, and superfluous adjectives contained within, and bears no responsibility for those that remain. I cannot thank either of them enough.

I was also fortunate to have Margot Canaday's guidance and support. She had a clear vision of the book before I did, as did my editor at the University of Pennsylvania Press, Bob Lockhart. I can hardly count the number of times people told me how lucky I was to work with Bob, and those people were right.

The book required extensive archival research, and as a result I owe debts to archivists at many institutions: Gene Morris has assisted me year after year at the National Archives II. At Cornell, Eileen Keating knew every record group inside and out. Emma Brock at the Advertising Council archives and Janice Goldblum at the National Academies of Science archives both went above and beyond. I am indebted to too many other wonderful archivists to list here, but suffice it to say the broad research of this project would not have been possible without their help at the National Archives in College Park and in D.C., the National Agricultural Library, the National Library of Medicine, and the Eisenhower and Kennedy Presidential Libraries. I have also had great help from librarians at the University of North Texas and at Penn State, with special thanks to Eric Novotny.

That archival research was only made possible through great financial support. I am grateful for the support of a National Science Foundation Grant, a Charlotte Newcombe Fellowship from the Woodrow Wilson Foundation, a Dean's Fellowship in the History of Home Economics from Cornell University, and a short-term fellowship from the German Historical Institute. I also received research funding from the Eisenhower Library and the Cornell School of Human Ecology. At Penn State, I received support from the Departments of History and Women's Studies, the George and Ann Richards Civil War Era Center, the College of Liberal Arts, the Rock Ethics Center, the Institute for Arts and Humanities, and the Crawford Family Fellowship in Ethical Inquiry. I am especially thankful for my time at the Miller Center for Public Affairs and to Brian Balogh, who consistently supported my work while also challenging me to stay committed to the nuances of American political history. I am also grateful for the fellows with whom I shared time and ideas: Emily Charnock, Jack Epstein, Robert Henderson, Kyle Lascurettes, and Mason Williams.

Many people have read and commented on the manuscript, and I appreciate all their insights. In particular, Greg Eghigian and Chloe Silverman pushed me to think about the project's contemporary implications and about the intersections of health and politics. The book also benefited at different points from the wisdom of Lee Ann Banaszak, Eileen Boris, Beate Brunow, Brent Cebul, Arye Chakravartty, Allison Elias, John Hoenig, Matt Isham, Katie Johnson, Beth Linker, Laura McEnaney, Cecilia Márquez, Loren Moulds, Robyn Muncy, Clark Pomerleau, Gabe Rosenberg, Amy Rutenberg, Atia Sattar, Katina Sawyer, Emily Seitz, Michael Sherry, Susan Squier, Sean Trainor, Stephanie Troutman, Jennifer Wallach, Mike Wise, and Steve Wolpern. Additional thanks to the manuscript readers with the University of Pennsylvania Press, who pushed me to sharpen my argument and to better engage with the literatures of sexuality and disability.

I also owe an extraordinary debt to my family, including my brother, Michael, and my mother and father, Marilyn and Tom Moran. Beyond normal support, my dad also put on an editorial hat and read through and corrected the manuscript. My husband, Mark, has been an amazing partner as I navigated this project, and I cannot imagine doing it without him by my side. I am deeply lucky that he came with Brendon and made us a family. Finally, Oskar entered the world as I wrapped this project up, and everything is better for that.